German Churches
and the Holocaust

Edited by
Robert P. Ericksen & Susannah Heschel

Fortress Press • Minneapolis

dedicated to

Beatrix Jessberger and Judith Meyers

BETRAYAL: GERMAN CHURCHES AND THE HOLOCAUST

Copyright © 1999 Augsburg Fortress Publishers. All rights reserved. Except for brief quotations in critical articles or reviews, no part of this book may be reproduced in any manner without prior written permission from the publisher. Write to: Permissions, Augsburg Fortress, Box 1209, Minneapolis, MN 55440.

Chapter 7, "Pius XII, the Jews, and the German Catholic Church" by Guenter Lewy is reprinted from *Commentary*, February 1964, by permission; all rights reserved.

Cover design: Joseph Bonyata
Interior design: Julie Odland Smith
Index: Eileen Quam
Photo credits:
   Cover: Newly elected Reich Bishop Ludwig Müller, surrounded by SA men, raises his
      arm in the Hitler salute. Courtesy of Evangelische Kirche in Deutschland/Archiv,
      Berlin
   Robert P. Ericksen: Expressly Portraits
   Susannah Heschel: Dan Milner
   1: Evangelium im Dritten Reich, 5 November 1933.
   7: Archiv Röhm, Leonberg
   8 and 12: Süddeutscher Verlag/Bilderdienst, Munich
   9 and 10: Ullstein Bilderdienst, Berlin
   11: Bundesarchiv, Koblenz
   17: Sarah B. Amshewitz, *The Paintings of J.H. Amshewitz* (London: Batsford, 1951), plate 25

Library of Congress Cataloging in Publication Data

Betrayal : German Churches and the Holocaust / edited by Robert P.
   Ericksen and Susannah Heschel.
      p.   cm.
   Includes bibliographical references and index.
   ISBN 0-8006-2931-0 (alk. paper)
      1. Antisemitism—Germany—History—20th century. 2. Germany—
   Religion—1933–1945. 3. Christianity and antisemitism. 4. Church
   and state—Germany—History—1933–1945. 5. National socialism and
   religion. 6. Holocaust, Jewish (1939–1945)—Causes. 7. Judaism
   (Christian theology) I. Ericksen, Robert P. II. Heschel,
   Susannah.
   DS146.G4B49 1999
   261.2'6'094309043—dc21   99–11275
                                                                    CIP

The paper used in this publication meets the minimum requirements of American National Standard for Information Sciences—Permanence of Paper for Printed Library Materials, ANSI Z329.48-1984.   ∞™

Manufactured in the U.S.A.   AF 1-2931

03   02   01   00   2   3   4   5   6   7   8   9   10

their wives, girlfriends, or other family members to visit and observe the shootings firsthand. Secrecy about the carnage was not maintained by those in charge, and no sense of shame or guilt seems to have hindered the murderers. Götz Aly, Ernst Klee, Goldhagen, and others have gathered personal letters and diaries written by the perpetrators in which they describe the killing as if it were ordinary work.[4] Given the many photographs taken of Jews just before they were shot, one also wonders about the photographers—what they thought and felt and how they could so calmly take pictures of people being murdered.

The willingness of Germans to be executioners applied not only to Jewish victims. Europe's Sinti and Roma, derogatorily termed *Gypsies,* were also targeted by the Nazis. Even if they were not regarded in terms quite as unredeemably negative as those applied to Jews, they were often shipped to Jewish ghettos in eastern Europe and killed in the same gas chambers in the death camps. Thousands of the Polish intellectual and political elite were also murdered. So were over three million Soviet soldiers, held by the Germans as prisoners of war and either killed outright or forced to die through starvation. Germans were willing to kill fellow "Aryans"[5] as well. Nearly half the mental patients in Germany were among the one hundred and twenty thousand German Aryans put to death during the Third Reich in the Euthanasia Program. While most were selected for death by their doctors, some were turned over to authorities by family members. All were killed against their will. Also against their will, approximately three hundred thousand Germans were sterilized. Carrying out such large-scale atrocities was no simple matter. Hundreds of thousands became involved, directly or indirectly, as perpetrators.[6]

Yet some refused to participate in the murders. Within Reserve Police Battalion 101, Browning estimates, 10 percent or more requested and were granted reassignment, some of them even being allowed to go home to their civilian jobs and families. We can find other examples of refusal to participate in the murder of the Jews: an SS officer in the French town of Le Chambon who looked the other way when the townspeople hid large numbers of Jews;[7] Kurt Gerstein, the SS officer responsible for supplying Zyklon B, the gas used to murder Jews in the death chambers of Auschwitz, who informed Catholic church officials about the death camps in the vain hope of arousing protests.[8] Such examples of actual resistance to the murder program, unfortunately, remain only a handful, and we may well ask why.

Some of those who resisted tell us that they did so for religious reasons. The very low incidence of resistance, however, prompts questions about how religious beliefs and attitudes related to the program of death. What religious convictions sparked resistance in some and compliance in others, and why did so many people simply fail to react? While Franz Stangl encountered a nun and a priest who supported the murder of children, not all clergy were outspokenly supportive of government atrocities. Very few, however, were outspokenly opposed, particularly to the Nazi policies of disenfranchisement, deportation, and murder of the Jews. The question posed by this book is Why? What can we identify in the history, institutional structure, and teachings of the Protestant and Catholic churches in Germany that hindered their active protest against the persecution of the Jews? What led them, instead, to a general support of Adolf Hitler and his policies? How did the churches' attitudes change during the course of the Third Reich, particularly during the war? What could the churches have done, had they wished to protest the treatment of the Jews?

The contention of this book is that the German churches played a far more important role in Nazi atrocities than has hitherto been supposed. Most important, their role involved moral suasion: Through the support for Nazi policies articulated by many religious leaders, ordinary Germans were reassured that those policies did not violate the tenets of Christian faith and morality. This role was actively encouraged by the Third Reich, which viewed propaganda as central to meeting its goals and at first courted the churches as powerful shapers of public opinion. A minister wearing long black robes, preaching from the church pulpit on Sundays, could be far more effective than a politician, especially for believers. A minister claims to be God's voice on earth, while politicians are notorious as nearly universal symbols of duplicity.

In addition, we will present evidence that large and powerful segments of the Catholic and Protestant churches supported Nazism with enthusiasm, under circumstances in which silence would have been morally preferable and politically more judicious. Indeed, the passion for National Socialism witnessed among some theologians and pastors indicates their fervent belief that Nazism was beneficial for church as well as state. Such evidence forces a reevaluation of the churches' role and a new judgment of their behavior during the Third Reich.

The Nature of the Nazi State

During the years immediately following the war, National Socialism was viewed as an iron cage, a totalitarian state that locked its citizens in a grip of terror. In that view, the end of the war in the spring of 1945 came as a liberation to the German people, freed from Adolf Hitler's tyranny. That image is no longer viable. The Nazi government was not absolute, but a maze of intrigue, as various factions within the government, the SS, and the National Socialist

Party fought for power and influence. This was no well-oiled machine, methodically crushing all in its path, but a lurching mechanism, striking more haphazardly. Karl Schleunes has shown, for example, how different officials struggled for control of Jewish policy, with some advocating radical measures to appropriate Jewish property, while others cautioned that such measures would backfire against German efforts at economic reconstruction.[9]

The totalitarian image implies oppression as well as efficiency. While personal liberties were curtailed shortly after Hitler came to power, it would be wrong to view most German citizens as prisoners of the Nazi state. Rather, there was widespread support for Hitler and satisfaction with most of his policies, at least until the later war years began to undermine public confidence. Some of the most frightening aspects of the Nazi regime were not imposed from above but functioned with the cooperation and active support of average citizens. Take, for example, the Gestapo, the very image of the Nazi police state. Robert Gellately has shown that the number of official personnel employed by the Gestapo was shockingly small, given the large German population it kept under surveillance. In Nuremberg in September 1941, there were 150 Gestapo officials responsible for keeping watch over 2,771,720 people spread out over 14,000 square kilometers.[10] Yet the Gestapo managed to write thorough and frequent reports about citizens' actions and beliefs, carry out investigations, and arrest, torture, and try their suspects. Such activities were made possible, Gellately reveals, only by relying upon normal citizens to observe and disclose the activities of their neighbors, co-workers, friends, and family members. This cooperation came readily: The vast majority of investigations undertaken by the Gestapo were initiated by civilian denunciations. Thus, to inspire terror among some Germans, the Gestapo depended upon the enthusiastic teamwork of their ordinary fellow citizens.

If the Nazi state, even in its most frightening manifestations, was a cooperative venture of its citizens, what does this suggest about the German people's relationship to the "Jewish question"? What did they know about the persecution and murder of the Jews? How did they react to the information they received? What guidance did they receive from churches in shaping their responses?

David Bankier provides helpful answers to these questions. According to his examination of Gestapo reports, which attempted to measure the attitude of German citizens in response to Nazi policies, most Germans were pleased in the early years of the regime to see Jews expelled from their jobs in the civil service. The Jews, it seemed to them, were receiving what they deserved— they had become too "uppity" and were now being put in their place. The random and occasional physical attacks against Jews in Germany proved distasteful to many—not, it seems, because of a lack of antisemitic attitudes but because of discomfort over street violence and the breakdown of orderliness. When the German Jews lost their citizenship on the basis of the Nuremberg Laws of 1935, there was general indifference. Some Jews actually responded to these laws with a sense of relief; having any kind of legal status seemed a protection against the hooliganism of SA thugs. Moreover, in preparation for the Berlin Olympic Games in early 1936, street violence and visible signs of antisemitic agitation were suppressed by the regime.

This period of relative calm, which continued through 1937, would prove deceptive, but at the time many Jews hoped that it marked the end of anti-Jewish measures by the Nazi state. By 1938, as Germany began accentuating militarism and war talk, the number and severity of antisemitic incidents increased. A program of "Aryanization" led to the expropriation of Jewish property and its transfer into suitably Aryan hands. Schools and universities expelled Jewish students. Jewish families became subject to house searches and individuals subject to arrest, Jewish stores were defaced, and Jews were required to take the name "Sarah" or "Israel" and have the letter J stamped on their identity card. In late October thousands of Polish Jews living in Germany were sent back to Poland. The young son of one such family, Herschel Grynspan, responded to his parents' plight by shooting an official in the German embassy in Paris, whereupon the Nazi leadership made this minor act the pretext for a nationwide pogrom. On November 9 and 10—the so-called *Kristallnacht*—Nazi thugs smashed windows in Jewish shops and homes throughout Germany, burned and destroyed almost all synagogues, humiliated and beat countless individual Jews, and arrested ten thousand Jewish men, who were then sent to concentration camps.

No one in Germany could be unaware of these events, which transpired in cities, towns, and villages across the nation and received widespread press coverage. How did people react? According to Gestapo reports, most Germans were shocked by the violence, even though, Bankier argues, they remained antisemitic. They had expected a government of law and order and found instead shattered glass in the streets, Nazi thugs beating Jews, massive destruction of property, and a disturbing economic question: Who would pay for the damage? Yet there were neither protests nor demonstrations against *Kristallnacht*. The following Sunday, most pastors and priests in their pulpits did not mention it, not even the widespread destruction of houses of worship that had occurred in their communities. As Bankier notes, aversion to unseemly violence did not equate with moral outrage: "We rarely find rejection of Nazi anti-Semitism on ethical principles, or indignation based on humanitarian values."[11]

As anti-Jewish measures continued to grow in number in the aftermath of *Kristallnacht*, the Ministry of Propaganda poured out antisemitic messages to explain and justify harsh actions. Jews were portrayed as a danger to Germany, a threat to all Germans. They were compared to parasites and bacilli that could infect and destroy innocent Aryans. When war broke out, it was portrayed as a Jewish assault on Germany, especially after 1941, when the participation of both the capitalist Americans and the communist Soviets was attributed to Jewish influence. Thus, it was suggested, German attacks on the Jews were not hostile and aggressive, but defensive efforts to protect the Aryan race.

By this time there were few Jews left in Germany, of course, since Nazi terror had produced massive emigration. By the fall of 1941, only one hundred and fifty thousand Jews remained from a pre-Nazi population of five hundred thousand. These remaining Jews became suddenly more visible, however, when a new decree required them to wear a yellow badge. They produced a mixed reaction among their Christian neighbors. Most of the Jews still in Germany were elderly and poor, and their miserable condition evoked sympathy in some, but contempt in others. Churches were not immune to the latter response—when Christians of Jewish descent, who were considered Jewish under Nazi law, appeared with their yellow badges, some Aryan Christians complained that they did not want to pray or take communion next to Jews.[12] Yet Bankier argues that many Germans exhibited compassion in response to this visible evidence of Jewish hardship. Joseph Goebbels himself is said to have complained about "idiotic sentimentality" among Germans, and the government issued a decree: From 24 October 1941, anyone who showed public sympathy for the Jews would be sent to a concentration camp for three months.[13]

It is important to gauge the response of Germans not only to Jews in their proximity—whether suffering during *Kristallnacht* or donning the yellow star—but also to the millions of Jews in eastern Europe. Bankier tries to measure German attitudes and the effectiveness of Nazi propaganda while rumors of brutality and murder began to spread. Throughout the Nazi period, propaganda had been ubiquitous. Bankier argues, however, that during the war years, especially when rumors of mass murder proliferated, Germans increasingly distanced themselves from the antisemitic propaganda of the state.

Assessing Bankier's claim requires knowing what Germans knew about the murder of Jews and when they knew it, as well as how they reacted to this news. According to Heinz Boberach, already in 1939 in the aftermath of the German invasion of Poland, rumors circulated in some German cities about atrocities and even murders committed against Polish Jews. In the summer of 1941, when the real murder campaign began with the invasion of the Soviet Union, rumors increased, and during 1942 it became difficult to avoid hearing rumors or even gaining direct knowledge of murders and atrocities.

Goebbels intensified antisemitic propaganda during those years, equating Bolsheviks with Jews in the "crusade" against Russia. Ian Kershaw notes that the general public refused to respond to this propaganda barrage, and he suggests that antisemitism was simply a low priority in the face of more important hardships and concerns. Bankier prefers the argument of Martin Broszat, who suggests that Germans tried to distance themselves from the anti-Jewish propaganda of the Nazis because they knew of crimes being committed and wanted to evade complicity.[14] Bankier makes no concession regarding the antisemitic attitudes of the German people, suggesting that popular opinion often pushed harder against the Jewish population than did Nazi edicts. However, Gestapo reports and other evidence suggest a public aversion to antisemitic propaganda by late 1941.

Bankier explains this paradox as based upon self-interest. Aryan Germans, broadly antisemitic in their attitudes, accepted any anti-Jewish policies that hurt Jews, especially when they opened opportunities for Aryan Germans, *unless* the policies might seem counterproductive. For example, hooliganism against Jews bred anxiety about law and order, implicitly suggesting that other Germans might be targeted next. Hooliganism might also hurt Germany's prestige abroad or inspire countermeasures. According to this theory, rumors of genocide prompted not moral outrage but the worry that Germany might suffer revenge, especially if the war should turn in the Allies' favor.[15]

Until the fall of 1941, German troops prevailed wherever they turned. That fall, however, their failure to win a victory over Russia presaged a series of frustrations and defeats. By late 1942 and early 1943, Germany suffered major military losses in North Africa and at Stalingrad, while at the same time Allied bombing of German cities grew in intensity. Some Germans viewed this change of circumstances as punishment for what they had done to Jews, perceiving the bombing of Cologne Cathedral in 1942, for example, as retribution for the destruction of synagogues during *Kristallnacht*.[16] Others believed that Jews themselves dominated American and British policy and picked out targets for bombing specifically in terms of punishment and revenge. Finally, Jews and their allies could be expected to take a particularly harsh revenge should Germany actually lose the war. Under these circumstances, Bankier believes, average Germans refused to accept Nazi antisemitic propaganda, refused to associate themselves with the policies of murder, and tried to avoid knowing or at least to pretend they did not know about what was happening. "People chose to turn a deaf ear to anti-Semitic preaching in order to bury their unpleasant awareness of the extermination. They made a conscious decision to withdraw from it, suppress it and make it taboo, in the belief, whether conscious or not, that they could absolve themselves of collec-

The story is gruesome, as was the entire murder program, and it must have made a significant impression on Stangl, who remembered the details of his hospital visit quite vividly even many years after the war. It also makes an impression today, this claim that his moral qualms about the murder of sick children were laid to rest by a nun and a priest who fervently supported the program. If these representatives of the church found it morally acceptable to put handicapped children to death, how could he, as a Catholic, disagree? Not political ideology or government propaganda, but the moral stamp of approval by clergy played the crucial role in alleviating the pangs of his conscience. By 1942 he was running Treblinka, one of the six major death camps in Poland, where he became responsible for the murder of nine hundred thousand people. What did he think of his role? He later told the journalist Gitta Sereny that he had viewed the Jews who were gassed as so many cattle being slaughtered.

Stangl was certainly not the only German who suffered qualms of conscience when confronting euthanasia, or the murder of Jews, or the slave-labor program. Whereas Stangl was reassured by a nun and a priest that the murder of handicapped children was morally acceptable, others found alternative sources of reassurance. A study by historian Christopher Browning, *Ordinary Men*, examines a troop of reserve police officers from Hamburg who were taken to Poland to murder Jews. Browning reveals that even though the process of mass murder by inexperienced killers involved the most unimaginable horror, including blood and brain matter splashed upon the perpetrators, most of the men willingly participated in the murders. In fact, their commanding officer gave them the chance to opt out, but most carried on with their grisly task.[2] The recent best-seller by Daniel Goldhagen, *Hitler's Willing Executioners*, claims that these murderers were eager and enthusiastic because of long-standing antisemitic traditions in Germany that advocated the elimination of Jews from German society, even at the price of extermination.[3]

Despite differences in interpretation, both Browning and Goldhagen make it clear that the widespread belief that Germans were forced to follow orders on pain of death is nothing more than fantasy. In reality, we have no reports of any German being court-martialed, shot, or seriously punished for refusing to carry out an order to kill civilians. A few, of course, did refuse such orders, but it now seems clear that fear of punishment was not the primary motivation of those who complied. Browning finds peer pressure at work within the battalion of police officers he studied, while Goldhagen, who studied the same battalion, argues that the murderers killed Jews out of conviction—because they wanted to kill Jews. There may have been additional motives at work as well, some of which we may never fully understand. What is striking is that at least some of the murderers felt no qualms about inviting

Introduction

Robert P. Ericksen and Susannah Heschel

Franz Stangl, the future commandant at the death camp Treblinka, worked during the early war years in the so-called Euthanasia Program of the German Reich. Far from "mercy killing," this program permitted the murder of patients (children as well as adults) who were deemed mental, physical, or social burdens on society—"life unworthy of life," as they were designated. "No law compelled the killings"; rather, a bureaucratic structure was established that permitted medical personnel to transfer certain patients to designated killing centers. Physicians, nurses, and orderlies participated voluntarily in the program, while the patients themselves often pleaded for their lives or tried to flee the hospital. Patients' families were told that the patients had died of natural causes. Stangl himself apparently had some moral doubts about the murders. In November 1940, he took the time to visit a hospital, run by a Catholic order of nuns, in order to locate a keepsake belonging to a child patient who had been put to death. The child's mother had received notice of the supposedly natural death and had also been sent the child's toys and other effects, but a candle she had given her daughter was missing and she wanted it back.

> That's why I had to go there: to find the candle. When I arrived, the Mother Superior, who I had to see, was up in a ward with the priest and they took me up to see her. We talked for a moment and then she pointed to a child—well, it looked like a small child—lying in a basket. "Do you know how old he is?" she asked me. I said no, how old was he? "Sixteen," she said. "He looks like five, doesn't he? He'll never change, ever. But they rejected him." [The nun was referring to the medical commission.] "How could they not accept him?" she said. And the priest who stood next to her nodded fervently. "Just look at him," she went on. "No good to himself or anyone else. How could they refuse to deliver him from this miserable life?" This really shook me . . . Here was a Catholic nun, a Mother Superior, and a priest. And they thought it was right. Who was I then, to doubt what was being done?[1]

support of this project. As all scholars in our field know, we have been lucky to have him as our editor. We also want to thank Michael West, who became our very able editor after Marshall's retirement; Patricia Heinicke, for her superb editing of the manuscript; and Julie Odland Smith for producing the book.

We would like to express our thanks to the many archivists who have helped us gather material, at the Berlin Document Center, the Hauptstaats-archiv Niedersachsen, the Universitätsarchiv Giessen, the Universitätsarchiv Göttingen, the Universitätsarchiv Jena, the Bundesarchiv in Koblenz and in Potsdam, the Landeskirchlichesarchiv in Hanover, the Landeskirchenarchiv of Thüringen, the Zentralarchiv der Kirche in Berlin, the YIVO Institute archives in New York City, and the Wiener Library of Tel Aviv University. In particular, Susannah would like to thank Rev. Heinz Koch, director of the Landeskirchenarchiv of Thüringen and himself an expert on church activities during the Third Reich, and Rev. Beatrix Jessberger of Berlin, whose friend-ship made possible the many arduous trips to archives throughout Germany.

Many colleagues have contributed suggestions and advice, including Hans-Joachim Dahms, Louis Graham, Jörg Ohlemacher, Philip Schaeffer, David Toren, Donald Niewyk, Michael A. Meyer, Richard Cogley, David Bankier, Dieter Georgi, Irmtraud Fischer, Peter von der Osten-Sacken, Chris-tian Wiese, Siegfried Virgils, Joseph Tyson, and Christoph Raisig.

Both of us have been allowed research time through the generosity of several fellowships. Bob would like to thank the Alexander von Humboldt Foundation and the National Endowment for the Humanities. Susannah would like to thank the Cleveland Foundation, the Samuel Rosenthal Center for Judaic Studies at Case Western Reserve University, and the National Humanities Center, which granted her a fellowship during the academic year 1997–98, supported by the Rockefeller Foundation and the Lucius Littauer Foundation.

Most important, we thank our partners, Judith Meyers and Jacob Aron-son, for their constant support and encouragement. As academic colleagues as well as spouses, they have given thoughtful consideration to our research and have raised important and critical insights. They are the two finest human beings we know.

ACKNOWLEDGMENTS

The role of the German churches during the Third Reich is a topic that emerges out of our deepest concerns. Both of us were raised in religious households, Bob as a Lutheran, Susannah as an Orthodox Jew. As students we strove to integrate our studies, our religious roots, and the ethical issues of our day. As a child, Susannah was deeply influenced by the role of religious leaders in the Civil Rights Movement and the effort to end the war in Vietnam. Bob, growing up in the Pacific Northwest, came of age as the Civil Rights Movement gradually undermined comfortable assumptions about the moral quality of American life, assumptions further called into question by the escalation of America's role in Vietnam. For both of us, political engagement has been an essential component of religious commitment and a test of the moral integrity of religious leaders.

We first met in December 1992, at a conference where we each presented our research on pro-Nazi Protestant theologians. During the summer and fall of 1993 we collaborated on an article reviewing the historiography on German churches during the Third Reich. By 1994 we had become good friends as well as colleagues and began to plan an edited volume of essays, which eventually became this book.

We are very grateful to our contributors to this volume. Shelley Baranowski, Kenneth Barnes, Doris Bergen, Micha Brumlik, and Michael Lukens each produced valuable contributions. Victoria Barnett, a close friend and colleague who also works in this field, was kind enough to translate Brumlik's article from German into English. Guenter Lewy graciously gave us permission to reprint an article he published some years ago on the German Catholic church; we also thank *Commentary* magazine for granting us permission to reprint that article. The contributors to this volume constitute a core group of scholars concerned with the history of the German churches, paying particular attention to the churches' attitudes toward Jews and Judaism. We appreciate their willingness to synthesize the findings of their archival research for a broader audience.

We are also indebted to Marshall Johnson, recently retired editor in chief of Fortress Press and himself a scholar of theologians in the Nazi era, for his

Contents

CONTENTS

procedure. As a result, few pastors or church leaders lost their positions because of their Nazi past. Even those whose Nazi involvement had been most outrageous found they could leave this past behind. For example, Siegfried Leffler, a leader of the pro-Nazi German Christian movement who joined the Nazi Party in 1929, achieved rehabilitation by 1949 and subsequently served as a leading personality and spokesperson for the Protestant church in Bavaria.[20] The fact that the churches had not taken an active role in protesting the persecution, deportation, and murder of Jews was explained as a result of a lack of knowledge about the fate of the Jews or the fear of retaliation by Hitler against Christian leaders. Such were the common explanations given by church leaders and laypeople in the years following the war.

A second approach to the involvement of the churches has been to deny the significance of churches in modern life, either directly or by inattention. Secular historians tend to ignore churches, as well as Christian teachings, in their attempts to explain the relation between the German people and the Nazi regime. This book assumes, by contrast, that the Christian component in Nazi Germany is worthy of careful consideration. A few figures help clarify the picture. The German census of May 1939 indicates that 54 percent of Germans considered themselves Protestant and 40 percent considered themselves Catholic, with only 3.5 percent claiming to be neo-pagan "believers in God," and 1.5 percent unbelievers.[21] This census came more than six years into the Hitler era. Both Catholic and Protestant churches remained official state churches throughout the Nazi regime, which meant that the state collected a church tax and funded church expenses. Religious education remained a part of the state education system, chaplains served the military, and theological faculties remained funded and active within the state universities. Article 24 in the Nazi Party Program always professed "positive Christianity" as the foundation of the German state.

Clearly, the Nazi regime had no *real* sympathy for Christianity and little use for theologians, but we may still ask how the churches themselves experienced the regime. Certainly, Hitler's effort to separate church from state was perceived correctly by many church leaders as an effort to reduce their power and influence, yet the separation of church from state is hardly an act of persecution. In 1936, when the Nazi Party demanded that the swastika be removed from church newspapers and from church altars, there were loud protests from church leaders.[22] Pastors who had placed the swastika on the altar, next to the cross, claimed the swastika was a key element in the religious life of their congregants. Church officials who placed the swastika on the masthead of their church newspapers meant thereby to proclaim their support for the regime. At the time, the Nazi policy prohibiting church use of the swastika was most likely experienced as an act of persecution, denying

tive guilt by dissociating themselves from the social consensus that had sanctioned so horrible a crime."[17]

By 1943 both police reports and the Nazi press shed light on the predicament facing Goebbels' propaganda machinery. It encouraged Germans to ever greater intensity of effort, with the threat of Jewish and Allied revenge should the German war measures now fail. This was meant to promote a commitment to fight to the finish, a sense that all Germans were in the struggle together. Having embarked upon a solution to the Jewish question, they must prevail in that effort too or suffer retribution. Stressing the danger, however, included the risk that Germans would be tempted more toward defeatism than toward greater effort. Bankier believes that defeatism prevailed. Instead of greater commitment, Germans rejected and distanced themselves from the propaganda, not out of indifference toward antisemitism, but because Nazi policies now seemed to endanger average Germans. As Bankier concludes, "During the war the public sensed collective guilt, since its awareness of killing-operations exceeded mere suspicion. Outward passivity and apathy were the way the public chose to minimize discomfort."[18]

During the years immediately following the war, the common response of Germans to the Holocaust was to deny any knowledge of the murder of the Jews. The collective response was to claim the crimes had been committed far away, that they had been undertaken in great secrecy and without the consent of the general population. *It Wasn't Us, Hitler Did It* is the title of a satirical play written by Hermann von Harten and produced in Berlin during the 1980s. The satire of the title reflects a significant truth: Nearly everyone, even the most prominent figures arrested and tried at Nuremberg, denied personal responsibility for Nazi crimes. Army officers blamed the SS, and the SS blamed commanding officers, who in turn claimed they had to follow orders or they would have been shot. The denial of responsibility was a continuation of the wartime effort to avoid complicity. Knowledge of the murder of Jews was dangerous; to know about the atrocities would demand a response, a protest, yet none had ever been expressed. It was better not to know and to hope that charges of complicity could be avoided.

The Response of the Churches

Christian churches have often been placed outside the framework of Nazi Germany and the Holocaust. In some segments of the German churches, this distancing was accomplished with a myth, which quickly developed after the war, of Christian resistance to Hitler and of Nazi persecution of the churches.[19] Even the Allies proved susceptible to this myth, allowing churches an independent self-examination, rather than a rigorous, external denazification churches full participation in the life of the Third Reich. Yet this is hardly the persecution that church leaders complained of in the postwar years. For historians seeking to evaluate the churches' intentions, the important point is that the church itself did not forbid the swastika.

Did the churches only pretend to be enthusiastic supporters of National Socialism in order to protect themselves? If the churches had truly been persecuted victims, we might expect to have heard a cry of relief when the war ended and Hitler came to his bad end. By the summer of 1945, we would expect to have seen church proclamations vehemently denouncing Nazism and condemning the murder of the Jews. But we do not. This silence is one strong indicator of the attitudes held during previous years.

As subsequent chapters indicate, there were many enthusiastic supporters of National Socialism in both the Catholic and Protestant churches. Conversely, there were few church figures who exhibited a stance, by word or deed, in opposition to the regime. Carl Amery, a Catholic reflecting back upon what he labels the "capitulation" of the Catholic church to the Nazi regime, describes a "milieu Catholicism" that made this capitulation possible.[23] Milieu Catholics believed in discipline, punctuality, cleanliness, and respect for authority; and the Nazi Party advocated all of these traditional virtues. The Catholic and Protestant churches both fervently opposed godless communism, and Hitler professed himself the most powerful anticommunist in Germany. Christians tended to be stridently antimodern, rejecting the modern tendencies toward urban, secular culture that had begun to permeate Germany in the 1920s. They did not like the fast lifestyle of the roaring twenties or the open, democratic practices of Weimar Germany, which advocated freedom of speech and belief and practiced tolerance toward the culturally diverse.

Hitler attracted Christians by criticizing the liberalism of democratic government and by advocating a tougher, law-and-order approach to German society. He opposed pornography, prostitution, abortion, homosexuality, and the "obscenity" of modern art, and he awarded bronze, silver, and gold medals to women who produced four, six, and eight children, thus encouraging them to remain in their traditional role in the home. This appeal to traditional values, coupled with the militaristic nationalism that Hitler offered in response to the national humiliation of the Versailles Treaty, made National Socialism an attractive option to many, even most Christians in Germany.

By way of contrast, one tiny Christian group proved very resistant to the charms of National Socialism, largely *because* of the militaristic nationalism espoused by Hitler. Jehovah's Witnesses,[24] adherents of a religious movement founded in Pennsylvania in the 1870s, refused to participate in violence or the use of military force. National Socialism would not tolerate such a refusal, and this placed male members in harm's way. Furthermore, Jehovah's Witnesses believed in political neutrality, which meant they would not vote for Hitler nor give the Hitler salute, again provoking anger. Finally, Jehovah's Witnesses used Hebraic language and customs, which associated them with Jews, and they did so without apology or a willingness to change. This religious movement had already suffered discrimination in Germany prior to 1933, but it increased under Nazi rule. Adherents continued to distribute pamphlets and otherwise maintain their faith, in opposition to government regulations, which left them open to imprisonment and/or placement in concentration camps. They were never singled out for death, and they were always given an option to renounce their faith and avoid further persecution; thus they cannot be compared to Jews or other racial victims of the regime. However, Jehovah's Witnesses largely held to their faith in the face of trouble, and thus they represent a religious group that refused to endorse or collaborate with the regime.[25]

Catholics and Protestants in general showed more hostility than sympathy for Jehovah's Witnesses, and they shared Hitler's harsh values more than the Witnesses' pacifist ones. We should acknowledge, however, a distinction between Hitler's successful appeal to traditional values and his policies of murder: the Holocaust did not occur because he gave medals to women who stayed home and bore children. Actual genocide requires direct implementation of a policy of death. In the German case, the chief implementers included the SS, the Gestapo, the police, the military, arms and gas manufacturers, transportation experts, maintenance workers for the crematoria, plumbers, electricians, and other technicians who maintained the mobile killing units and the death camps. Banks financed construction of the camps, architects designed them, railroad engineers brought the victims to their deaths. Physicians, nurses, and orderlies carried out the Euthanasia Program, and many SS doctors played crucial roles in the death camps, both in the process of "selection" and in medical experiments on human subjects. Is it appropriate to speak of church leaders, pastors, or priests in the same breath? Did they contribute to genocide?

The most important relation of the German churches to the Holocaust lies in the production of a powerful kind of propaganda, a propaganda underscored by the moral authority of the church. While the German government established a Ministry of Propaganda under the notorious Joseph Goebbels, the evidence presented by Bankier and others suggests that Goebbels could not entirely control people's minds. There will always be some people who are suspicious of governments and politicians. For many, religious leaders are a higher and more reliable source of moral authority. A pastor standing in the pulpit and preaching in the name of God carries a weight of authority and respect hard to find in any other segment of society.

The Nazi regime was not unaware of the churches' authority in the eyes of the civilian population, nor were the Nazis unconcerned about the churches' potential for contradicting or undermining the policies of the regime. Hitler himself evidenced this concern, and police reports regularly highlighted the churches as possible sources of trouble. In 1938 the Gestapo warned that two sources of potential resistance to the regime existed: the political enemies of National Socialism and the churches. Whereas the former had been decimated in the early years of the Reich through the imprisonment, forced exile, and murder of communists, socialists, and trade unionists, the churches had remained relatively intact as institutions.

In some ways the churches had seemed to strengthen their position in the early years of National Socialism. The Protestant church had developed a new national organization accompanied by a transfer of power in most regional churches to those pastors and bishops who supported Hitler. In the first months of the regime, the Roman Catholic Church achieved a long-standing goal, a Concordat with the German government by which both sides agreed to work cooperatively and with respect for their individual spheres. In neither case did these acts of support by the churches achieve what they had hoped for: Hitler's support and respect for them. The Concordat of 1933 never created the safe place for Catholic belief and practice that Catholics had expected from the agreement, but rather led to months and years of political interference and quarrelsome negotiation. On the Protestant side, Hitler had initially spoken out on behalf of the "German Christian" Movement (*Deutsche Christen*), the group of Protestants who called for an overhaul of Christian teachings in line with National Socialist principles. But after 1934 his recognition of intractable quarrels within the Protestant church led him to ignore church affairs. Such neglect left his supporters within the church feeling frustrated. What could the German Christians do to win the attention of Hitler and earn more important places for themselves within the regime? In 1938 they hit upon a plan—a concerted effort to produce antisemitic propaganda from a Christian perspective.

Not all church leaders actively supported the Nazi regime, and some vehemently opposed specific policies. Nonetheless, support of the regime was common among Christians, and the vast majority failed to raise any objection to Jewish persecution. Silence, in this case, speaks loudly. The violation of moral norms that is inherent in the Holocaust requires us to pose questions regarding Germany as a Christian nation. Churches had a high profile in Germany. They exerted formative influence on German culture and German individuals. We know that church leaders expressed praise and enthusiastic support for the "rebirth" of Germany under Hitler's authority. Did they also countenance the Holocaust? Did the moral reassurance experienced by Franz

Stangl during his unease over the Euthanasia Program find its counterpart in Germans killing Jews? Such questions require close attention to the specific subject of Jewish-Christian relations.

Christian Attitudes toward Judaism

The connection between Christian theology and antisemitism is complex, with a massive historiography debating the issues. To begin with, the relationship between Jesus and Judaism is fraught with problems, with some New Testament scholars arguing that Jesus himself acted fully in accord with the Jewish religious beliefs and practices of his day, while the majority present Jesus as rejecting one or another central aspect of Judaism. Paul's writings are similarly debated. The vast majority of New Testament scholars present Paul as a sharp critic of Judaism, while others understand him as a proponent of Jewish theology seeking to include pagans within the community of Jews.

Early Christianity, in its struggle to establish itself as a religion and community independent of Judaism, often engaged in harsh polemics against Jewish religious practices and beliefs, even when some of those Christian polemicists were themselves Jewish. As Christianity rose to dominance, however, its attacks on Judaism became ominous, since they too often transmuted from verbal to physical assaults. Christian attacks against Jews were motivated in part by social and economic factors, to be sure, yet they were all too frequently spurred by Christian theological claims, such as the contention that all Jews were to blame for the death of Jesus. During the Middle Ages, Jews in Christian lands were increasingly demonized—accused, for example, of killing Christian children in order to use their blood to bake matzo, or of desecrating the eucharistic wafer in an effort to wound the body of Christ. Jews were accused of poisoning wells, of mocking Christianity, of performing sexual abominations, of being in league with the devil. It is not surprising that such charges often led to riots against Jews, resulting in the destruction of their property and in beatings, torture, rape, and murder.

At the same time, there were also periods of harmony, in which Jews and Christians cooperated in business ventures and intellectual exchange. Jews, for their part, held an ambivalent attitude to Christianity. Most viewed Jesus and the claims about his virgin birth, the incarnation, and the resurrection as absurd, yet some were also fascinated by the image of the Virgin Mary, the Trinity, and the union of divine and human. Some Jewish religious writing, particularly mystical literature, displays the distinct influence of those Christian concepts.

The Protestant Reformation brought new developments to Christian-Jewish relations. In Germany, Martin Luther had hoped for the conversion of

Jews to his movement, now that he had clarified "true" Christianity, and he became enraged when he realized that the vast majority of Jews repudiated his mission. Late in life he wrote an attack on Jews virtually unsurpassed in its brutality.[26] Theologically, Luther introduced a sharp distinction between law and gospel, identifying the former with the Old Testament and Judaism, the latter with Jesus and Christianity. The affirmation of Christian gospel entailed a denigration of Jewish law, a theological view that Luther claimed to find in Paul. Lutheran theology, as it developed in Germany, became increasingly sharp in its depiction of the misery of the Jews' "life under the law." Judaism, particularly the Talmud, was held up as the quintessence of the kind of religion Christians rejected.

As German Protestant theology developed in the nineteenth century, Jewish theology in Germany also flourished, with Jewish theologians attempting to refute the negative depictions of Judaism in Christian literature. Indeed, one of the central preoccupations of modern Jewish thought has been the attempt to overcome negative images of Judaism in Christian teachings. That effort began in Germany during the second half of the nineteenth century, as Jewish theologians began to examine Christian claims about Jesus and his relationship to first-century Jewish life. The most prominent among them was Abraham Geiger, a scholar and rabbi who carefully monitored Christian depictions of Judaism.[27] Geiger noted that Christian theologians' unjustified description of the Pharisees as hypocrites had led to all sorts of twisted readings of ancient texts, just as the failure of New Testament scholars to read rabbinic literature left them unable to place Gospel passages within what he saw as their proper context. He noted numerous errors in Christian interpretations of the New Testament and related texts that arose because the commentators assumed the legalism of early Judaism and the hypocrisy of Pharisaic religion.

Based on his own reading of rabbinic literature, Geiger concluded that the Pharisees and Sadducees, the major groups within first-century Palestinian Judaism, were liberals and conservatives, respectively. According to Geiger, Jesus was a Pharisee who preached the typical religious and moral teachings of the Pharisaic movement. If anything, Jesus' approach was somewhat conservative, colored most likely by his background in the Galilee—a region characterized, according to Geiger, by its simple, lower-class, nationalistic, uneducated people. In a phrase that made Geiger notorious among Christian theologians, he wrote that Jesus "did not utter a new thought, nor did he break down the barriers of nationality. . . . He did not abolish any part of Judaism; he was a Pharisee who walked in the way of Hillel."[28]

The idea that Jesus might be identified with the Pharisees, those exemplars of hypocrisy, legalism, and religious degeneracy, proved an outrage to

Christian theologians, who minced no words in condemning Geiger. The difficulty, however, lay in refuting Geiger's evidence. The parallels he demonstrated between Jesus' words and those of the rabbis were striking and conclusive. Yet if Jesus said nothing new, what sort of Christian theological claims could be based on his ministry? Further, if liberal Protestants were true to their nineteenth-century goal of looking for the faith *of* Jesus, rather than the faith *about* Jesus, what would it mean to discover that Jesus' faith was Pharisaic Judaism? From Geiger's perspective, Pharisaic Judaism was the liberal, progressive tradition that democratized the aristocratic tendencies of the priestly prerogatives. Only later, with the rise of Christian persecutions of Judaism, Geiger argued, did Pharisaic liberalism deteriorate into the rigid halakhic religion of the Talmud. The Reform Judaism that he helped to establish in the nineteenth century was, for Geiger, a revival and restoration of Pharisaic liberalism. Thus, if a Christian of the nineteenth century truly wanted to find the faith of Jesus, namely, Pharisaic Judaism, the best place to find it would be not within the Christian dogma constructed about Jesus, but among modern Reform Jews of Germany.

Geiger was not alone in claiming Jesus as Jew, rabbi, and even Pharisee. Indeed, most modern Jewish theologians and rabbis have sought to emphasize Jesus' Jewishness as a way to smooth Jewish entry into Christian society; this was, after all, the era of Jewish emancipation and secularization. Yet the more Jewish their depictions of Jesus, the more annoyed their Christian colleagues became. Yes, Jesus was a Jew, Christians acknowledged, but he was an exceptional Jew. Ernest Renan, author of the most widely read book on the life of Jesus published during the nineteenth century, cited Geiger's work on the Pharisees positively, agreeing that Jesus' life had to be placed within the context of his historical setting. Renan, however, then proceeded to describe the Pharisees negatively and to define Jesus in contrast to them: "Jesus recognized only the religion of the heart, whilst that of the Pharisees consisted almost exclusively in observances."[29] Moreover, Renan argued, "One of the most prominent faults of the Jewish race is its bitterness in controversy, and the abusive tone which it always throws into it. . . . Jesus, who was almost exempt from all the defects of his race, was led against his will into making use of the style used by all the polemics."[30] Although Jesus began by trying to reform Judaism, he eventually gave up, Renan argued, and after visiting Jerusalem, "he appears no more as a Jewish reformer, but as a destroyer of Judaism. . . . Jesus was no longer a Jew."[31]

Geiger criticized Renan in an "Open Letter," which he published as an appendix to one of his most popular books, a survey of Jewish history. Geiger wrote that Judaism functioned in Renan's work as a negative background to "let the picture of a rising Christianity stand out in more dazzling brilliancy," and as the brunt of the blame for "whatever in Christianity did not please [him]."[32] Geiger identified that same technique in the work of most of the Christian New Testament scholars writing during the 1860s and 1870s, a period that inaugurated a revival of interest in the historical background of the New Testament.[33] Although New Testament scholars cited the research of Geiger and other Jewish historians, they consistently elevated Jesus as a superior religious figure whose message constituted not a reform within Judaism, but an utter rejection of it.

By the early twentieth century, Protestant theologians and scholars conceded that Jesus' moral message was derived historically from Judaism. Adolf von Harnack made such a concession, but he immediately insisted that it was precisely a sign of Jesus' extraordinary religious genius that he had been able to extract moral teachings from the sterile legalism of his day. Harnack enshrined this idea in 1900, in his classic statement of liberal Protestantism, *Das Wesen des Christentums*, in which he wrote that although the religious message Jesus proclaimed had already been stated by the Pharisees, nonetheless the Pharisees "were in possession of much else besides. With them [religion] was weighted, darkened, distorted, rendered ineffective and deprived of its force by a thousand things which they also held to be religious and every whit as important as mercy and judgment. . . . [T]he spring of holiness . . . was choked with sand and dirt, and its water was polluted." With Jesus, "the spring burst forth afresh, and broke a new way for itself through the rubbish."[34] For Harnack, then, the significant fact was not that Jesus' teaching was unoriginal but that it was pristine.

Harnack's portrayal of a legalistic Judaism was countered by the Berlin rabbi Leo Baeck, who distinguished between Jesus' criticism of Pharisaic Judaism and Paul's rejection of rabbinic law. Christianity, by following Paul, violated Jesus' own adherence to the law and created, in Baeck's words, a "romantic religion" of mysticism in which human beings remain trapped by their sinful nature, passively awaiting salvation through grace: "In this ecstatic abandonment, which wants so much to be seized and embraced and would like to pass away in the roaring ocean of the world, the distinctive character of romantic religion stands revealed—the feminine trait that marks it. There is something passive about its piety; it feels so touchingly helpless and weary, it wants to be seized and inspired from above, embraced by a flood of grace which should descend upon it to consecrate it and possess it— a will-less instrument of the wondrous ways of God."[35] Feminine Christianity, Baeck argued, fails to foster moral responsibility, in contrast to the masculine "classical religion," Judaism, which places ethical commandments at the forefront and demands no belief in irrational dogma.

The Jewish critique of Christian theological portrayals of Judaism continued vigorously until the Nazi era, but without making a serious impact. In Germany, there were no Jewish studies faculties at universities, and few Christian theologians were interested in studying classical Jewish texts. As a result, the denigrating stereotypes continued unabated. The highly influential and widely respected German theologian Rudolf Bultmann published in 1944 a study of early Christianity that contained the same kinds of distortions that Jewish scholars had been protesting for a hundred years. Bultmann argued that the Jews' observance of the commandments "meant making life an intolerable burden." He went on in this vein: "The motive of ethics was obedience. . . . The ritual commandments having lost their original meaning, man's relation to God was inevitably conceived in legalistic terms"; "For Judaism God has become remote."[36] By contrast, Jesus was "a tremendous protest against contemporary Jewish legalism"; in Jesus' teachings, God is concerned with "inner motive"; Jesus "brought God out of the false transcendence to which he had been relegated by Judaism and made him near at hand again." The uniqueness of Jesus is that he taught that "God is near, and hears the petitions we address to him as a father listens to the requests of his children"—as if no other Jew had experienced closeness to God.[37]

The debates over the relationship between Jesus and Judaism continue to this day. Ernst Käsemann's recent "Protest!" in the journal *Evangelische Theologie* is a case in point, arguing that to call Jesus' teachings Jewish is insulting and renders Christianity meaningless. Käsemann is one of the most highly respected and liberal figures in the field of German Protestant New Testament scholarship. That he would continue to feel so threatened by Jesus' Jewishness indicates the depth and persistence of the theological dilemma.[38]

We need to view German attitudes toward Jews in a larger context in order to realize that they did not develop in a vacuum. On the contrary, the growth of a significant community of Jewish scholars in Germany during the nineteenth century gave rise to a two-sided discussion. Geiger and his colleagues did not write for a Jewish audience alone; their work was also read and studied and discussed by Christians. Yet the fact that the discussion was two-sided makes the question of culpability even stronger: Those Christian theologians who produced damning stereotypes about Judaism cannot claim they knew no better, or had no access to Jewish historical scholarship.

The Postwar Era

Equally troubling is the long delay after 1945 before the churches began to consider their culpability in the Holocaust. The initial response of German church leaders was to claim that Christians had been involved in the resistance against Hitler. The 1945 Stuttgart Declaration, the earliest Protestant postwar response, says nothing about the murder of the Jews, just as the 1934 Barmen Declaration, the strongest anti-Nazi statement issued by the Confessing Church during the Third Reich, had said nothing about Nazi antisemitism. Only in the 1960s and again in the late 1970s did a few Protestant theological voices begin to suggest that Christianity had to revise its attitude toward Judaism and the Jewish people. The Second Vatican Council, convened in the early 1960s, caused some change in Catholic attitudes, as did the enormous controversy over Rolf Hochhuth's play *The Deputy*. An international sensation, the play condemned both the Vatican and the German Catholic church for deliberately turning away from reliable reports about the death camps and failing to exert moral or diplomatic efforts to intervene.

In the first years after the war, German churches were unable to muster even a strong *condemnation* of the murder of the Jews, much less an expression of responsibility for its horrors. This should not surprise us, perhaps, for church leadership remained, with a few exceptions, in the same hands that had guided the churches under Hitler. Furthermore, German theologians writing after 1945, even those who had opposed some aspects of National Socialism, had all been trained in an environment hostile to Judaism. Few were untainted by the antisemitic mentality of Nazi propaganda or the formidably anti-Jewish slant within the universities' theological teachings. Even a generally admired figure such as Theophil Wurm, Bishop of Württemberg, illustrates the problem. In a January 1949 letter to lay church members meeting at Darmstadt to formulate a declaration about the Holocaust, he wrote: "Can anyone in Germany speak about the Jewish question without mentioning how Jewish literature sinned against the German people through its mockery of all that is holy, since the days of Heinrich Heine? Or of the suffering endured in numerous regions by German farmers at the hands of Jewish money-lenders? And if one wants today to speak out against antisemitism, can one remain silent on the misfortune caused by the Occupying Forces, who have given power to emigré Jews, so that they might give expression to their understandable feelings of rage?"[39] Not surprisingly, given the tone of Wurm's advice, the Darmstadt Declaration ultimately blamed the Holocaust on the Jews' refusal to become Christians.

During the 1970s the churches of the Rhineland, Baden, and Brandenburg tried to rid themselves of centuries of anti-Jewish theology and forge a new affirmation of Judaism's continued vitality and legitimacy. It is worth noting that those efforts began among German churches influenced by Calvinist more than by Lutheran traditions. Individual pastors, such as Benjamin Locher of the Rhineland, played crucial roles in formulating a 1960 declaration by the German Protestant Church, or Evangelische Kirche Deutschland (EKD), and an even more influential 1980 declaration by the Church of the Rhineland. Locher insisted that the Holocaust was not one of many Christian concerns, but the central problem of Christian theology. "Something is false in our faith. There must be something false at its heart that we as Christian teachers or practitioners are teaching or representing."[40] One of today's groundbreaking Protestant theologians in Germany, Friedrich Wilhelm Marquardt, has attempted to formulate a Christology that would affirm Jesus as the embodiment of the Jewish faith, not as a teacher who sought Judaism's destruction. Marquardt's efforts begin with the question, "What meaning does it have for us to speak of God after Auschwitz?"[41]

Despite these tendencies, the situation in today's German theological community is mixed. Numerous theologians, pastors, and laypeople continue to promulgate the outdated and denigrating portrayals of Judaism they have inherited. A recent bestseller by journalist Jörg Zink suggests that if Jesus instead of Moses had taught the Ten Commandments, they would have been formulated as loving suggestions, rather than apodictic laws.[42] His argument recapitulates the stereotype of Jewish legalism in contrast to Christian love, as well as the idea that the God of the Old Testament is not the same as the God of the New Testament. A German feminist theologian, Christa Mulack, maintains that Jewish adherence to divine commandments is analogous to Nazi obedience to the criminal orders of their superiors. She describes the Holocaust as the triumph of Jewish patriarchal ethics over the feminist morality taught by Jesus, thus characterizing Jews as victims of their own religion.[43]

Other theologians are more subtle. Jürgen Moltmann, Germany's most famous contemporary Protestant theologian, does not emphasize Christian responsibility for antisemitism but instead places Christians with Jews as victims of persecution: "There is only one people of hope in the world, the one people of God. It is the one people of God, the people of the old and new covenant. Because Jews and Christians have a common hope for 'the one who is to come,' the messiah, they are on the way together to God's kingdom and future. That is why they are persecuted together and suffer together. When Israel is led to the slaughter, the church goes with her—if things are as they should be."[44]

In actuality, Jews and Christians are not "one people of hope in the world." Since the time of Jesus, they have no shared history, but rather two different histories, which often were rent apart by Christian persecution of Jews. The notion that "when Israel is led to the slaughter" the church ought to accompany her is troubling. Most of us would contend that neither Jews nor Christians should ever be slaughtered. Most disturbing, however, is Moltmann's inability to concede that the major reason for the murder of Jews during the course of Western history has been Christian anti-Judaism. His sentimental vision of what should be diverts attention from the appalling image of what has been. Instead of declaring Christian readiness to be killed with Jews, Moltmann could honestly acknowledge the widespread Christian share of responsibility for past slaughter.

At the same time, leading theologians in contemporary Germany are making important efforts to repudiate the kind of anti-Jewish tradition exemplified even by respected figures such as Harnack and Bultmann. Institutes for Jewish studies are found at most of the leading German universities, and increasing numbers of students of Christian theology are writing dissertations to expose and repudiate aspects of Christian anti-Judaism. Few theologians outside Germany have devoted as much energy and passion to creating a Christianity that will affirm Judaism, and few Christian theology students are as engaged in studying Hebrew and Judaism as are German students. Many German theologians today view the Holocaust and the centuries of Christian anti-Judaism that flourished in Germany as the central problems to be addressed if Christianity is to have a future in Germany, and if Germany is to have moral standing in the community of nations.

Assessing the Heritage

German Protestant Theologians, Nazis,
and the "Jewish Question"

Robert P. Ericksen

German Protestant theology stood at the center of Christian thought in the nineteenth century. This was the tradition that sought the "historical Jesus." It was the tradition that tried to bring theology into the modern world, tried to use the rational tools of the Enlightenment, tried to apply a historical, critical analysis to the biblical record. Theologians in Britain and America learned to read German, bought German books, and in many cases traveled to Germany to study this modern theological tradition. Germany had also been the birthplace of Protestantism and, of course, the home of Martin Luther.

This same Germany that nurtured Protestant theology also raised up Adolf Hitler and perpetrated the Holocaust. Is there a connection? Hitler was not born a German, but an Austrian. He was not raised a Protestant, but a Catholic. After sloughing off his early religious training, he was not a Christian, but an advocate of his own worldview of German racial destiny. However, the Germany that Hitler led remained 95 percent Christian and 55 percent Protestant. Most of the Germans who welcomed Hitler's rise to power—who saw Jews increasingly deprived of their rights, who witnessed the burning synagogues and broken glass of *Kristallnacht,* who watched the removal of Jews from German soil, who listened to rumors of the annihilation of Jews in Poland and Russia—were self-professed Christians. Most of the actual perpetrators—members of the SS and of the reserve police battalions, the shooters and the scientists, those who ran the trains and those who ran the camps—received religious training in the Protestant or Catholic tradition.

Did their religious training and beliefs have an impact on their behavior? We know there was a conspicuous absence of voices denouncing Hitler's anti-

Jewish policies and only rarely was there a refusal to participate in them. Except for a few individuals, neither active Christians nor other Germans rose up at any stage to protest the mistreatment of Jews. This failure has often been attributed to fear: Common people had to cooperate or they would be shot. Scholarship has increasingly shown, however, that the Nazi police state was less oppressive, and the willingness of "ordinary men" to commit brutalities much greater, than we had imagined.[1]

This chapter assumes that one piece of the puzzle of German behavior under Hitler lies in an assessment of religious beliefs. What were these people taught in Sunday school or in their religious education? What attitudes prevailed in the Protestant mind? In particular, who were the Protestant theologians who formulated the response of the churches to the political questions of the 1920s and 1930s; who taught the pastors and religious educators of Germany, and what did they teach? The German theological legacy from the nineteenth century has an impressive reputation, but how did it play out in Protestant teachings in the twentieth?

We will consider three men whose childhoods spanned the turn of the century and whose theological education took place in the comfortable years prior to the outbreak of World War I. Paul Althaus (1888–1966), Emanuel Hirsch (1888–1972) and Gerhard Kittel (1888–1948) established themselves among the brightest of their generation. Each rose to prominence in the 1920s, and each became a dominant figure in German theology by the 1930s. These men not only inherited a theological tradition, they consciously reshaped it for the crisis years in which they lived, a crisis beginning with German participation and loss in World War I and culminating in the Hitler years and the Holocaust. The Protestant theology they inherited and shaped allowed them to endorse enthusiastically the rise of Hitler and to accept without complaint the removal of Jews from German life.

Paul Althaus

As professor of systematic theology at Erlangen University from 1925 and as president of the Luther Society from 1926, Paul Althaus occupied a prominent place among Luther scholars until deep into the postwar period. He wrote prolifically, and his books remained standard texts in theological education, both in Germany and America, through the 1950s and 1960s. Althaus practiced a political theology, trying to relate the teachings of Luther and of the Christian tradition to the political circumstances in Germany after World War I. He summarized his reaction to the rise of Hitler with the words, "Our Protestant churches have greeted the turning point of 1933 as a gift and miracle of God."[2]

It is important to note Althaus's language. He does not merely accept Hitler as an adequate leader or as the lesser of two or more evils. Rather, he claims God's intervention in German affairs and proclaims Hitler's rise a "miracle." He also claims to speak for the Protestant churches as a whole, citing several church statements in corroboration, and he adds, "So we take the turning point of this year as grace from God's hand. He has saved us from the abyss and out of hopelessness. He has given us—or so we hope—a new day of life."[3]

It seems safe to conclude that Althaus really did speak for most Protestant Christians in Germany in 1933. It was commonplace for theologians, pastors, and church officials to oppose democracy and the openness of the Weimar Republic, which they associated with national weakness and moral decadence. A very few leaders in the church stood on the left as advocates of religious socialism, but most were conservative nationalists. Although today we decry Hitler's regime as a police state, Althaus appreciated Nazi "law and order," which he contrasted to the "bleeding heart" liberalism of the Weimar Republic: "The dissolution of criminal law into social therapy and pedagogy, which was already far along in development, has reached an end: punishment shall again be taken seriously as retribution. . . . It [the Nazi state] has destroyed the terrible irresponsibility of the parliament and allows us to see what responsibility means. It sweeps away the filth of corruption. It restrains the powers of decomposition in literature and the theater. It calls and educates our Volk to a strong new will for community, to a 'socialism of the deed,' which means the strong carry the burdens of the weak."[4]

Instead of rejecting the totalitarian nature of Hitler's rule, Althaus defended it: "But a state which knows itself as servant to the life of its Volk will not rob the other associations and orders in the Volk . . . of their self-reliant, spontaneous life. It will embody totalitarianism—not as an inflexible system, but it will call forth the free spirit of totality, i.e., the spirit of responsibility for all forms and spheres of life in the presence of the duty to be Volk."[5] Confident that Hitler's totalitarianism would prove a blessing, he went on to prescribe how Christians should respond: "As a Christian church we bestow no political report card. But in knowledge of the mandate of the state, we may express our thanks to God and our joyful preparedness when we see a state which after a time of depletion and paralysis has broken through to a knowledge of sovereign authority, of service to the life of the Volk, of responsibility for the freedom, legitimacy, and justice of *völkisch* existence. . . . We Christians know ourselves bound by God's will to the promotion of National Socialism, so that all members and ranks of the Volk will be ready for service and sacrifice to one another."[6]

Althaus loved his fellow Germans, provided they were members of the mysterious Volk. Did he also love his fellow Germans who happened to be

Jewish? On the positive side, he never denied Christian connections to Judaism, despite the "embarrassment" of this connection under a racially antisemitic regime. He defended the Old Testament, he stated that Jews remained God's chosen people, and he acknowledged the seemingly obvious fact that Jesus was a Jew.[7]

In 1933, as some within the Protestant church advocated the ecclesial implementation of the Aryan Paragraph, which would remove so-called non-Aryan clergy from the church rosters, Althaus responded that such individuals already in office should not be removed unless specific circumstances warranted.[8] However, this defense of non-Aryan Christians proved very limited. When Rudolf Bultmann and the Marburg theological faculty opposed any application of the Aryan Paragraph to church affairs, stating that race was entirely irrelevant to Christian categories, the Erlangen faculty asked Althaus and Werner Elert to draft a reply. They acknowledged the "threat" of emancipated Jewry to the German nation and the right of the German state to defend itself, concluding that "the church must therefore demand of its Jewish Christians that they hold themselves back from official positions."[9]

In fact, Althaus's continued emphasis on the German Volk, a *völkisch* church, and *völkisch* theology carried with it an implicit racism. He sometimes made this explicit: "Among the factors which determine and make up a Volk, the community of blood or race has become decisively important for us Germans. . . . It has to do with a specific, closed, blood relationship. Race is not already Volk, the biological unity is not already historical unity. But the unity of race in a significant sense and its protection is an essential condition for the formation and preservation of the Volk."[10] On those occasions when Althaus avoided racial categories, his *cultural* antisemitism emerged as no less virulent: "It does not have to do with Jewish hatred—one can reach an agreement directly with serious Jews on this point; it does not have to do with blood or with the religious beliefs of Judaism. But it does involve the threat of a quite specific disintegrated and demoralizing urban spirituality, whose representative now is primarily the Jewish Volk."[11]

Between 1933 and 1938, Althaus placed his theological reputation squarely within the National Socialist camp, both in terms of politics in general and in terms of the racist ideal of the German Volk. Then a change seemed to occur. Although he never retracted earlier writings, after 1938 Althaus refrained from further explicit endorsement of the regime. This may well have reflected his aversion to the brutality of *Kristallnacht,* a night of bloodshed and burning synagogues in November 1938. Althaus's son, though only three years old at the time, reports the family story that his father was incensed by *Kristallnacht* and predicted that God's judgment would fall on the German people in due course. Whether or not this is true, Althaus never meaningfully protested the mistreatment of Jews, and he proved unable to rise above the cultural antisemitism of his milieu. When his perplexed son questioned him on the subject in the mid-1950s, he merely said, "You have not experienced the Jews."[12]

Emanuel Hirsch

Emanuel Hirsch—who taught church history, New Testament, and systematic theology at Göttingen University—shared a friendship and much else with Paul Althaus. They had been friendly rivals as young theologians. They shared an intense love for Germany and the German Volk and a conservative, antimodern critique of Germany's problems.[13] In the first years of the Nazi regime, they may have been the two most important theologians to parlay these attitudes into unequivocal support for Hitler. Hirsch did so in an open letter of April 1932, advocating Hitler's election.[14] He also published his views soon after Hitler's rise, echoing Althaus's "gift and miracle of God" statement: "All of us who stand in the present moment of our Volk experience it as a sunrise of divine goodness after endless dark years of wrath and misery."[15]

The main difference between these two friends is that Hirsch shared all of Althaus's pro-Nazi positions, but with less restraint. For example, Hirsch chose to join the Nazi Party and to become a "supporting member" of the SS.[16] As dean of his theological faculty, he worked to promote National Socialism in hiring and curriculum policies, and he did not hesitate to denounce colleagues and students whose support for the regime might be suspect.[17] Hirsch's support for the regime, unlike Althaus's, never seemed to waver— not after 1938, possibly not even after 1945.[18] In all of these ways, Hirsch's attachment to the Nazi regime was more intense and less restrained. He also had a more important reputation as a theologian.

In 1945 Hirsch departed the official faculty at Göttingen, using a medical retirement to slip past the threat of removal by "denazification." He then remained one of the few faculty members never allowed to return to the university, partly due to the technicalities of his medical retirement and partly to the unwillingness of the postwar theological faculty to forgive his open and unrestrained support for the Hitler regime.[19] Although Hirsch published prolifically in the postwar years, including a definitive, multivolume treatment of Søren Kierkegaard, he received no invitations to university events, and students could come to him only by invitation to his private sessions. In Germany today the "Hirsch Circle"—a core of loyal followers who sat at his feet in those private seminars in the 1950s and 1960s, many of whom are now professors of theology—believe their mentor has been unjustly pilloried and ignored. They hope to restore his reputation and significance, some going so far as to call him the greatest theologian of this century. Implicit in the argument of the Hirsch Circle is the belief that his brilliance as a theologian has been unfairly clouded by a mistaken political stance.[20]

Because of his significance as a theologian, Hirsch represents an important bridge between the heritage of nineteenth-century German theology and the horrors of the National Socialist regime that earned his support. Both as church historian and systematic theologian, Hirsch was extremely conversant with the Protestant theological tradition. He grew up in the so-called Luther Renaissance led by Karl Holl, proclaiming himself a part of the "young, national Lutheranism." He described the political stance of this group as follows: "In the inner German struggle, it [young, national Lutheranism] placed itself with passionate determination on the side of those who could not inwardly accept the condition brought about by the defeat and revolution of 1918. In struggle against the ideas of 1918, against the dream of an international world culture of democratic or Marxist orientation and pacifist ideology, the dream of a leveling of peoples, they wanted to protect the will of the German Volk to itself, to a German rebuilding."[21]

Hirsch knew the ideas of the nineteenth century very well. He knew Hegel and analyzed Marx in light of Hegelian metaphysics. He knew the attractions of Tolstoy and his pacifist idealism. He knew the challenge of Nietzsche to Christian, middle-class moral values. He became Germany's leading expert on Kierkegaard, the father of twentieth-century existentialism. As Hirsch worked his way through this intellectual heritage, he fell back not only upon Luther but upon the Germanness of Luther and the German romantic nationalism prolific in the previous century: "Everything that a Fichte, a Kleist, a Heinrich von Treitschke expresses concretely about the relationship of Volk to fatherland is as if it were burned into my heart. I know along with them that God meets me through Volk and fatherland. God encloses me with a binding and consecrating and exciting reality, sustaining my life from the primordial depths and shattering my self-sufficiency."[22]

Hirsch, Althaus, and like-minded colleagues, drawing upon their pride in Luther and the heritage of the nineteenth century, created a theology enthusiastically committed to German nationalism and to the mysterious idea of the Volk. This theology assumed that each separate Volk organically creates its own norms, its own law, and that this becomes a part of God's law for that Volk.[23] Given the significance of nation in this understanding, Hirsch felt no need to apologize for his patriotism and its overlap with his understanding of politics and Christianity. He believed in a "God of history," in a God who speaks anew to each generation through history; and he believed that his nation's history had been blighted by the humiliation of World War I and the Versailles Treaty: "We were a world Volk, a noble Volk, perhaps the most flourishing and best of all. We now stand in danger of being humiliated or even destroyed as a Volk, so that only a formless mass of workers in the service of foreign interests remains."[24] When Hitler emerged as the self-proclaimed savior of the German Volk, it was difficult or impossible for theologians such as Hirsch and Althaus to stand aside.

Once they merged their *völkisch* ideas with Hitler's, however, the implicit racism of a theology of the Volk became increasingly clear. When they spoke of God's special concern for the German Volk, when they claimed God's endorsement of those committed to "save" Germany, they fully accepted the antisemitic Nazi idea that there existed an underlying "Jewish question." Jews could not be a part of the rebuilding process. The true German Volk was an Aryan, Christian community. Jews were the problem, or at least a big part of the problem, and not a part of the solution. Hirsch readily accepted the idea that Christians of Jewish descent should be denied a role in the Christian ministry. They were "foreign" by race and history, and it was perfectly suitable for a Volk church to apply racial criteria to its clergy roster, that is, to insist that only members of the Volk should serve.[25]

In 1939 Hirsch carried the racist implications of his *völkisch* theology much further. In attempting to describe the "essence" of Christian teachings, Hirsch picked up and argued the crude antisemitic case that Jesus himself was not Jewish but really Aryan. How could this intelligent theologian, this prolific scholar, this Kierkegaard expert for the German-speaking world sink to the level of a charlatan? It is interesting to note that the evidence that Hirsch gathered, stretched, and bent to his purpose has at least some shred of plausibility. He credited German theological scholarship with the discovery that Galilee had been "heathen" from the fall of the Northern Kingdom until it was reconquered about 100 B.C.E. He suggested that implausible and inconsistent New Testament stories about Jesus' birth represent an early Christian attempt to cover up this fact. Matthew 2, for example, invents the story of Herod's wrath to explain Jesus' departure from Bethlehem to Egypt and his eventual home in Nazareth in Galilee. Hirsch also noted that the genealogical tables in Matthew and Luke do not match. Finally, he cited a first-century Jewish nickname for Jesus, "Son of Panther," and the derogatory gossip that Mary had an adulterous affair with a Greek of that name. Hirsch concluded that early Christians knew Jesus was not Jewish but that they covered this up in order to maintain the son-of-David messianic claim.[26]

On the surface this might look like a scholarly—if radical—thesis. It is impossible to imagine, however, that Hirsch would ever have posed this question about Jesus' racial background or proposed an "Aryan" answer without heavy antisemitic impetus. That is why it is embarrassing, why this work is never mentioned by the Hirsch Circle today, and why no one since

1945 has pursued this historical topic. In the *extremely* unlikely case that Jesus had non-Jewish ancestry, no one today would care, and no one, then or now, can possibly remove Jesus from the Jewish religious and cultural tradition in which he grew up.[27]

Another work by Hirsch on Judaism has not suffered the same ignominy. In 1936 he wrote a book, *Das Alte Testament und die Predigt des Evangeliums,* which appeared in a fiftieth anniversary edition in 1986, edited by Hans Martin Müller, professor at Tübingen and one of Hirsch's enthusiastic supporters. In this book Hirsch wrestled with the question of how the Old Testament should be understood by Christians. He wrote that as a young man arriving at university, he had already recognized that the Old Testament was "no Christian book."[28] Therefore, when his Old Testament professors expressed the same point of view, it did not shake his belief system but only helped fill out his knowledge of the legendary components and the borrowings from other religious traditions to be found within the Hebrew Bible.

Hirsch then argued that within Christian theology, the "flaws" of the Old Testament are not adequately understood or transmitted to contemporary teaching and preaching. Making frequent use of his two favorite words, "honesty" and "truth," he suggested that the Old Testament is an embarrassment to Christianity unless its proper place is recognized. Then he set it up as the very image of legalistic religiosity against which the gospel of the New Testament can properly be understood as God's real truth.

Hirsch acknowledged that his message might be seen by some as part of the political landscape sown by National Socialism. Some enthusiasts in the antisemitic camp had attacked the Old Testament by calling it a Jewish book, but that was not his impetus.[29] In 1937 he commented, "the Old Testament . . . is no longer a genuine religious point of contact, and not just since 1933."[30] He believed that the contribution of historical-critical analysis on the one hand and law versus gospel theology on the other was to reveal Judaism as only a negative counterpoint to the truth of Christianity.

In 1928, in the midst of controversy over the publication of a revised Luther Bible, Hirsch accepted the idea that Luther had distorted the Old Testament in his German translation in order to make it point more clearly toward the New Testament. In light of these issues, Hirsch eventually concluded: "First, it became necessary to show that the struggle of Jesus against Pharisaism and his crucifixion, pushed forward by the leader of the Jewish church, as well as the Pauline message about Christ as the end of the law . . . [all] understood in the sense of the Lutheran dialectic of law and gospel— these . . . are the essential, the most decisive expression of the historical relationship of the Old Testament-Jewish and the Christian religion."[31] This expressed Hirsch's reiterated thesis that law and gospel stand in dramatic opposition to one other, that the absolute essence of Christianity is gospel, that Jesus showed this in his attack on the Pharisees, that Paul showed this in his development of the Christian message, and that Luther retrieved this message in his reformulation of Christian teachings. According to this view, the Old Testament and Jewish religion can only represent evil reliance upon law and religiosity, against which the pure truth of the gospel must constantly be directed.

Hirsch's goal was to distill this message more fully than Paul or Luther had been able to. "Secondly, it became necessary to place into the correct light the fact that honesty required a giving up of the New Testament use of prophesy as proof. Paul's use of the Abraham legend [claiming Abraham as the father of Christianity] and the entire New Testament treatment of the Old as a Christian book which did not belong to the Jews—all this had to go."[32] Note that this goal seems very close to that of the most radical Deutsche Christen in Germany: "dejudaizing" the New Testament.

Is this goal antisemitic? Hirsch himself denied that he was motivated by the politics of 1933, but rather by a long theological tradition now reaching its logical conclusion in his work. Hans Martin Müller, in the process of bringing Hirsch's work once more before the public, acknowledges the question of antisemitism—just long enough to dismiss it. The crisis of Old Testament interpretation, Müller writes, "is not caused, according to Hirsch, through 'factors of most recent date which are outside theology and church' [i.e., the rise of National Socialism] . . . but [it is] based in the thing itself."[33]

Müller then quotes a passage, circa 1964, in which Hirsch maintained his interpretation of Judaism and Christianity as two antithetical forces: "The relationship of the Old to the New Testament becomes identical with that of law to gospel. One is an earthly religion and the other a living faith in God focused on eternity."[34] Müller notes approvingly, "Hirsch held fast his entire life to this insight achieved so early. It determined his frequently criticized insistence that the Old Testament equals law and the New Testament gospel."[35] Müller adds that the motive is clear, as it was for Hirsch already in the 1930s: "No anti-Jewish effect but the concern that Christian preaching could sink into the proclamation of a spiritualized law and an earthly kingdom of God."[36]

Charlotte Klein would not agree with Müller's confident assertion that there is no "anti-Jewish effect" in Hirsch's theology of the Old Testament. In the mid-1970s, while teaching a course on Judaism in the period between the Old and New Testament, she discovered that her German students could not recognize the richness and diversity of Jewish thought two thousand years ago. Instead, they turned to the stereotypes provided by Old and New Testament Christian scholars who continued—despite Auschwitz—to propound the biased ideas of their predecessors from the nineteenth and early twentieth centuries. Klein writes, "It is notable how little impression the historical events of the last decades have left on university teachers; only in a very few cases have they led to any attempt at a new interpretation of the relationship between the Jewish community and the early Christian Church and to a better understanding of the role of Judaism."[37] She goes on to give her view of the typical attitude of these postwar theologians, who assume they have "the right to pass judgment on Judaism, its destiny, and its task in the world" and who make judgments "without bothering about the Jewish interpretation of the sources or considering how the Jews see themselves."[38] Klein complains that these Christian authors "never use the word 'Torah,' but only its pejorative Greek translation: *nomos*, 'law.' 'Torah,' however, means much more than 'law': it means instruction, path, God's word and call to Israel as his part of the covenant; it is also Israel's grateful response to this covenant. . . . [Among German theologians] the Torah is made to appear in Jewish understanding merely as a collection of legal prescriptions and summed up in terms of works and their reward. This preconceived judgment assumes that unmerited grace and 'justification by works' are irreconcilably opposed to one another."[39]

Another scholar, Willy Schottroff, has concluded that Hirsch corrupted his theology by accepting the theological significance of blood. For example, Hirsch wrote, "If the blood spoils, the spirit will also perish, for the spirit of the peoples [*Völker*] and of humans grows out of the blood."[40] Schottroff argues, "It hardly requires further proof that here, in an underhanded way, the antisemitic clichés of the time flow into and . . . determine the theological discussion."[41]

It is also important to note the *nonresponse* of Emanuel Hirsch to the issue of antisemitism. He *cannot* have been unaware of the brutal antisemitic rhetoric of National Socialism when he gave his enthusiastic support to Hitler. When the Deutsche Christen advocated the Aryan Paragraph and consequently suffered widespread opposition, he took their side. When Jewish colleagues were removed at Göttingen University, he raised no protest. On the contrary, by his fervent endorsement of Nazi politics in the university, he revealed his implicit acceptance of the purge of Jews. At no time before or after 1945 did he indicate convincingly that the antisemitism of the Hitler era violated his wishes. He employed the Nazi language and concept of blood, and his attack on the Old Testament as a non-Christian book went further than most. Can we possibly assume in retrospect that no antisemitic prejudice colored his views?

Hirsch's response to criticism of his book on the Old Testament, written as an "Afterword" in 1937, carries us further. After making sarcastic and dismissive comments toward some of his critics, he suggested that the prominent theologian Johannes Hempel recognized the real issue: the question of the "entire sense" and "entire character" of the Old Testament. Hirsch then explicitly stated his view: "The central point of the Old Testament is belief in the selection of the Israelitic-Jewish people by Yahweh, which takes place in the covenant by which Yahweh becomes God of this Volk and this Volk becomes the Volk of Yahweh. Both in a special sense create a situation in which the entire ordering of the Volk in its service to God and in its morality, law, and justice are placed under the idea of the fulfillment of the law of the group but also under the realization of the will and rule of Yahweh."[42] Hirsch argued that everything in the Old Testament, both law and prophets, fits under this rubric, and that this rubric fits the "Old Testament-Jewish religion" and no other. "We cannot escape the fact that the Old Testament is a document of the Old Testament-Jewish religion, which is another religion and not Christian; and we cannot make of any figures in the Old Testament something other than what they are: they are all believers and servers of a religion which we hold to be untrue."[43]

For his part, Hempel tried to show that the Old and New Testaments stand in closer historical and religious relationship to each other than Hirsch had allowed. Hirsch admitted that truth about the "hidden" God can be found in Judaism, as it can in all religions. He even admitted there are particularly close connections between Judaism and Christianity. But this place of the "similar and shared" is exactly where the battle over what is different must be fought: "And this, exactly this, I have defined as the essence of the historical relationship between Old and New Testament. The similar and shared which show up are to me the similar and shared of all religion, and the special historical contact in expression and form of this similarity can only be understood when it is seen as the other side of the most passionate religious opposition known in all of religious history."[44]

What Hirsch argued in this debate with Hempel is that the "question of absolutes," the absolute claim of Christianity to truth, ultimately undermines any connection between Christianity and Judaism. He brought Hempel to the point where, Hirsch argued, he must agree that the content of Jewish faith is different and *inferior* to the content of Christian faith. Then Hirsch concluded that he and Hempel did not really disagree in substance. He was convinced that his emphasis on the antithesis of law and gospel, Old and New Testament, remained the best way to understand the true message of the Christian faith. It is very clear that Müller agrees.

This, I believe, highlights the connection between Hirsch's theology and mainstream Christian theology, whether in the nineteenth or twentieth century. In fact, Hirsch's analysis of the Old Testament has been compared, by mainstream theologians *outside* the Hirsch Circle, to the work of Bultmann,

Friedrich Baumgärtel, and Karl Barth. That is because each of these men read the Christian Bible in light of the gospel and with an assumption that Christian truth is absolute, just as did Hirsch.[45] Schottroff notes that Wolfgang Trillhaas and A. H. J. Gunneweg are among the theologians who find Hirsch's Old Testament theology fruitful.[46] He also notes that Hirsch borrowed from Kierkegaard. In *Fear and Trembling,* published in 1843, Kierkegaard made the Abraham and Isaac story a paradigm for Christian faith. Later he revised that view, however, asserting that Abraham's faith was still "Jewish," that is, rooted in the kingdom of this world, not the kingdom of God.[47]

Hirsch tied Kierkegaard to his study of the Old Testament by quoting two passages as prologue. One reads as follows: "Christianity could have had no other religion as precursor, for no other but Judaism could establish, by means of negation, so definitely, so decisively what Christianity is."[48] Although it may seem shocking to find that Kierkegaard's words suit Hirsch's purposes so well, they add simply one more connection between the nineteenth-century heritage—in this case Danish—and Hirsch's theology. Hirsch, the same man who could write about an "Aryan Jesus," cited Kierkegaard to help establish his negative view of the Old Testament and earned the respect of Müller, Trillhaas, Gunneweg, and other postwar theologians.

Schottroff is not happy with this result. He emphasizes that a post-Holocaust Christian theology must carefully analyze its own part in the brutal policies of Nazi Germany, rather than ignore and dismiss any connection whatsoever. He also argues that Hirsch's belief in an extreme contrast between Christianity and Judaism does not match the historical evidence. "The Jesus movement and the early church show themselves . . . to be an inner-Jewish messianic grouping, of which there were many. The conflict, which the Jesus tradition documents, was an inner-Jewish, not an anti-Jewish, dispute. And the Bible, by which Jesus and his followers lived and which so decisively formed them, was the Hebrew Bible—a self-evident possession shared by the early church and the synagogue."[49] Schottroff clearly thinks Christian theologians should research this common bond rather than stress difference. Hirsch's emphasis on Jews and Judaism as alien to the German Volk and his stress on the antithesis of law-Judaism and gospel-Christianity allowed him to fit very comfortably within the antisemitic world of his fellow Nazis.

Gerhard Kittel

Unlike Althaus and Hirsch, Gerhard Kittel did not write prolifically about politics. He was not a systematic theologian and could not match their ability to tie Luther and the German theological tradition to the post–World War I needs of the German Volk. He was a very prominent theologian, however, with a famous father, a prestigious chair in the highly reputed theological faculty at Tübingen, and the editorship of a major reference work, *The Theological Dictionary of the New Testament.* Though less inclined to philosophy than Althaus or Hirsch, Kittel fully shared their views on the events of 1933. He quickly joined the National Socialist German Workers Party (NSDAP) and threw his energies and considerable reputation into the Nazi cause.

Kittel's link to the nineteenth-century theological tradition was unusually direct, given his father's career. Rudolf Kittel had established himself as a premier scholar by the turn of the century, producing a new translation of the Old Testament that inspired appreciation even among Jewish readers. Gerhard focused on New Testament studies, but he developed an expertise in the language and culture of Judaism at the time of Jesus so that he could examine early Christianity in that light. Ironically, his early writings on Jews and Judaism give an impression of respect. He notes the great similarity between Talmud and New Testament and thereby affirms Jesus' Jewish roots:

> One need only make these connections clear to know how absurd and historically false it is, without any exception, to attempt to separate Jesus and Christianity from the Old Testament and from the spiritual history of its people. . . . The ethic of Jesus did not arrive unassisted, it did not grow *ex nihilo*. . . . It is nothing less than the most concentrated development of that powerful movement of Israelitic-Jewish religious history which finds its condensation in the literary complex that we call the Old Testament. That means, obviously, that Christianity, which prides itself on being the "majesty and moral cultivation of Christendom" . . . may never forget that the Old Testament is not in its Bible by accident. All Christian culture and all Christian ethics have their roots in the moral consciousness of Old Testament piety. That cannot and may not be wiped away.[50]

Kittel's praise of Judaism and respect for Christian ties to Jews did not last into the Nazi era. On the contrary, he parlayed his expertise into prominence among those academics who tried to create a scholarly foundation for the National Socialist worldview. This began on 1 June 1933, when he gave a public lecture in Tübingen on the Jewish question. In this lecture Kittel argued that Jews in Germany should be considered guests, not citizens. This would allow special legislation to remove them from positions of influence, such as law, medicine, education, or journalism. Kittel acknowledged that many upstanding, innocent Jews would be hurt by this policy, and he realized that Christians in particular might be tempted to feel sorry for them. But, he concluded, God does not ask Christians to be sentimental or soft: "It is hard if officials, teachers, and professors, who have no guilt except that they are Jewish, must move aside. It is hard if Germans, who with their fathers and grandfathers have conditioned themselves for hundreds of years to being equal citizens, must find themselves again in the role of the foreigner. But such considerations must never lead to a sentimental softening and paralysis."[51] Anticipating criticism, Kittel showed that he was not prepared to back down: "We must not allow ourselves to be crippled because the whole world screams at us of barbarism and a reversion to the past. . . . How the German Volk regulates its own cultural affairs does not concern anyone else in the world."[52]

One of Kittel's former admirers, a rabbinical scholar at Cambridge University, wrote to complain: "It is a grievous disillusionment to find that one's idol has feet of clay." But to his suggestion that Kittel had bowed to political pressure, Kittel would only respond, "I can answer you in no other way . . . except that I stand by my former opinion. . . . It is also not true, as you suggest, that I wrote my book under political or any other kind of pressure. What I say today I have said for many years, only I always had hoped that insightful men would understand what was necessary before violence set in."[53]

As if to prove there was no inconsistency in his stance, Kittel spent the next decade trying to show the difference between the Jews of the Old Testament, whom he still accepted, and the Jews of the modern world, whom he saw as the bane of German and Western Christian existence. Much of this work appeared under the auspices of an antisemitic organization established by Walter Frank—the Reich Institute for the History of the New Germany. Kittel was a charter member of this Nazi organization and also of its Research Section on the Jewish Question. From its founding in 1936, Kittel had spoken at its meetings and sat on the dais with Nazi dignitaries and antisemites. His work no longer drew upon biblical sources, nor did he analyze the teachings of Jesus. Rather, he tried to show the racial and moral breakdown of the Israelites of the Old Testament into the "degenerate" Jews of the modern world.

Kittel argued that the Diaspora beginning in about 500 B.C.E. left the Jews without a homeland and caused them to give up their healthy, rural existence for the corrupting lifestyle of the city. Accepting racist stereotypes, he suggested that intermarriage produced a "mongrelization" of Jews. Then, accepting the illogic typical of antisemitism, he argued that these mongrelized, inferior Jews were trying to take over the world and might well succeed. Working together with the racial scientist, Eugen Fischer, Kittel coauthored an entire volume of Frank's journal, *Forschungen zur Judenfrage,* in which they argued that the story of Esther is a prototype of the Jewish drive for world power: "There is always one goal: power over the world. . . . Always, at all times, whether in the first or the twentieth century, the dream of world Jewry is sole domination of the world, now and in the future."[54]

He also analyzed obscene terra cotta figures found near Trier, which were thought to date from the third or fourth century. Since these caricatures depict men and women in "shameless" poses, Kittel was convinced they represent hostility to Jewish men who tried to seduce or rape Aryan women: "Perhaps it is . . . no accident that these judgments show themselves to us—if in veiled form—just where the world of the old [Roman] Empire, which had brought the Jews along with it, came up against a [German] population of unbroken instinct and youthful power."[55]

Kittel also wrote for an antisemitic journal published by Joseph Goebbels, in which he stated that in the Talmud, "a deep-seated hatred against the non-Jew comes to expression, out of which all consequences are drawn, right up to the full freedom to murder; for example, when it can read: You may kill even the best among the gentiles, just as you would smash the brains of even the best snake."[56] Kittel tried to prove his claim by citing passages that suggest a different moral culpability for actions, depending upon whether Jews or non-Jews are affected. He admitted that animosity toward foreigners can be found in many cultural traditions, and he acknowledged other Talmudic passages that endorse love and justice. However, Kittel believed that modern Jews have "seized upon" these milder traditions, while they are weak and vulnerable, only to hide their real intention to take over the world, with murder as a secret weapon.[57] This eccentric interpretation of the Talmudic tradition appeared in 1943, long after Jews had disappeared from German streets and the murder of Jews had become Nazi policy. Furthermore, Kittel admitted after the war that early in 1943 he had learned of the annihilation of Jews from his son who served on the Russian front.[58] It seems hard to avoid the conclusion that Kittel offered Goebbels and his readers a justification for preemptive violence against Jews!

Kittel's last public statement on Hitler, National Socialism, and the Jewish question came in 1944 in a guest lecture at the University of Vienna. Unabashed by his knowledge of horrors committed against Jews, he continued to justify Nazi policies against the "Jewish threat." He blamed the fall of Rome on careless racial practices that led to the racial decomposition of its citizenry. In fact, he said, as the power of Rome faded, Jews had threatened to take over the world and were halted only by the strength and determination of Christianity. Kittel noted that the Enlightenment and liberal democratic ideas opened the floodgates to Jewish emancipation in the eighteenth and nineteenth centuries, but Hitler had now risen up to save the day. National Socialism and Christianity stood together as twin bulwarks protecting western civilization against the Jewish menace.[59]

Gerhard Kittel's behavior and motives are hard to fathom, especially in light of his relatively friendly treatment of Jews and Judaism prior to 1933. It is possible that he practiced sheer opportunism, attempting to advance his career by endorsing the prejudices of the regime. He seems to have recognized quickly that he could claim to be the leading expert on the Jewish question among theologians, and this allowed him to swagger in the hallways of Walter Frank's institute and elsewhere. However, in postwar statements Kittel vigorously defended his academic integrity and Christian commitment. He even compared himself to Moses, called by God against his will.[60] He had felt an obligation to join the NSDAP and to work from within to provide a spiritual corrective (note that Kittel writes of himself in the third person here): "Kittel was in a special, wholly unique situation. . . . A completely unique opportunity was given to him to become accepted in circles outside the church and to build for them a path to the truth. This was an opportunity which in this form was available to Kittel and to no one else. So, if he had kept silent and made no use of this opportunity, an essential and irrecoverable positive element would have been omitted in the struggle over the Bible and Christianity. On this basis Kittel felt himself bound to express himself within the scope of his Christian and scientific convictions wherever he could."[61]

The problem with Kittel's "spiritual corrective" is that it matched so closely the vulgar antisemitism of Nazi ideology. He defended himself in 1945 by claiming that he was no more antisemitic than Paul: "Certainly Kittel has exposed the degeneration in modern as well as ancient Jewry as sharply as any antisemite. . . . In these cases, however, Kittel can point to the fact that the words of Paul on the Jews of his day were often interchangeable with the anti-Judaism of contemporary heathens."[62] He also implicated Jesus: "Never has a more terrible judgment been spoken against the so-called world Jewry as a demand for power than in the 'woe' of Jesus Christ in Matthew 23:15; never a more negative characterization of the Jewish religion as a religion of privilege than that found in John 8:40-44!"[63]

In truth there is in the Christian tradition a long history of abuse of Jews and Judaism. Kittel certainly damaged his postwar reputation by allying himself so closely with the rhetorical justification of Hitler's treatment of the Jews. His stance is now stigmatized, and his actual scholarship, or pseudoscholarship, for the Nazi cause seems hopelessly outside the boundaries of academic inquiry. However, it is also a reflection on the theological tradition he inherited that this bright and successful man could justify "spiritual" antisemitism both before and after 1945.

Conclusion

This study of Althaus, Hirsch, and Kittel implicates three Protestant theologians in terms of their support for the Nazi state and their insensitivity toward Jewish victims. Does it do more than that? Does it have broader implications about German Protestants and the Holocaust? Several questions must be considered.

First, is this study fair, even to Althaus, Hirsch, and Kittel? Does it correctly represent their lives and who they were? Without doubt, the passages quoted and arguments cited illustrate their most positive statements about National Socialism and their most negative statements about Jews. Althaus probably lost his enthusiasm for Hitler by the time of *Kristallnacht,* and all three expressed some restraint on the Jewish question. For example, they were hesitant to endorse purely racial categories or unnecessarily brutal policies toward Jews. But there is simply no doubt that they endorsed Hitler, publicly and enthusiastically, nor is there any doubt that they accepted the basic antisemitic assumptions of the Nazi worldview. They may have preferred cultural explanations to racial or materialistic ones, but they agreed that Jews posed a problem that Germany must solve.

Are Althaus, Hirsch, and Kittel representative figures? Althaus and Hirsch may have been more enthusiastic and outspoken than the average theologian in their political response to Hitler, but there seems no reason to believe their views fell completely outside the norm. Christians during the 1920s tended toward conservative, antidemocratic and anticommunist politics, and most Germans tended to be hypernationalistic in response to the Versailles Treaty. Members of the Protestant clergy and university professors shared these tendencies, and these are the tendencies that led Althaus and Hirsch to endorse Hitler. Kittel may have succumbed to and participated in the anti-Jewish propaganda of the Hitler state more than most theologians, perhaps due to the opportunity provided by his area of expertise. However, he can also be seen as a moderate figure in some respects, as in his refusal to question the place of the Old Testament in the Christian Bible. Despite the outrageous nature of his anti-Jewish writings, he always claimed to be giving the Christian, spiritual critique of Jews. There is no convincing reason to believe he was widely adrift of the typical antisemitism of Christians in Germany.[64]

Do these theologians really represent rather than misuse the widely admired theological heritage of the nineteenth century? We know that their careers prospered, that they were among the brightest and most successful of their generation. They were leading figures in prestigious theological faculties at Erlangen, Göttingen, and Tübingen, and each published prolifically, bending the shelves of many a library and lending their words, their names, and their editorial skills to leading journals. They knew their predecessors and self-consciously built upon the German theological tradition. The nineteenth-century heritage can and should be studied on its own, but it was, at the very least, vulnerable to the interpretations extracted by Althaus, Hirsch, and Kittel.

Some might argue that these men abused Christianity, that they could not have been Christian and taken the stance they did. It is important to note their self-understanding in this regard. Each of these theologians recognized the difference between nominal Christianity and a Christianity based upon personal faith and a personal meeting with and acceptance of Christ, and each professed himself in the latter camp. These men were often asked to preach on Sunday mornings, and they practiced their piety throughout the week, with regular Bible reading and prayer. Their self-definition as believing Christians cannot be doubted.

Did these religious men influence the German people? It is difficult or impossible to trace the words of an Althaus, Hirsch, or Kittel directly to the mobile killing units or the death camps. It is even difficult to trace their words directly to sermons preached in country churches or lessons taught in Sunday school. We know, however, that they taught a generation of pastors and religious educators, and we know their publications brought their ideas far beyond the sound of their own voices. Once we know the content of their lectures and publications, once we know their enthusiasm for the Nazi state and their willingness to bring Christian teachings into line with a *völkisch* Germany, once we recognize their scorn for Jews and Judaism, is there not a prima facie connection with Nazi brutality? We cannot simply assume that Christian teachings opposed Hitler and the Holocaust. "Ordinary men" proved willing to execute brutal orders against Jews, their Christian training providing far less impediment than we might like to think.

Storm Troopers of Christ

The German Christian Movement and the
Ecclesiastical Final Solution

Doris L. Bergen

Introduction: The German Christians and the "Racially Pure" Church

A signboard hanging in Lippe, Westphalia, in 1935 crudely summed up the views of the German Christian Movement (Glaubensbewegung "Deutsche Christen"): "Baptism may be quite useful, but it cannot straighten a nose."[1] The German Christians, as adherents of the movement came to be called, believed National Socialism and Christianity to be mutually reinforcing. Racist antisemitism formed the core of their program. Accordingly, they aimed to purge Christianity of everything they deemed Jewish and to reconstitute the church as an association of *blood* and *race*.

Studies of the churches and the Holocaust often presume a natural opposition between Christianity and Nazism. That assumption reflects important ideals but falls short as a means to understand the role that church people played in the Third Reich. As late as 1940, after years of Nazi propaganda deriding Christian institutions, over 95 percent of Germans remained taxpaying members of a recognized church.[2] The overwhelming majority of those people never resisted Nazism in the name of their Christian faith. What vision of Christianity enabled them to reconcile devotion to a religion that grew out of Judaism and endorsed its principles of justice and love with the imperatives of a regime predicated on brutal antisemitism? In what forms did Christians in Germany and in German-controlled Europe—many of whom supported or at least tolerated Nazi plans to annihilate Jews and eradicate Judaism—continue to practice their religion? An important part of the answers to these questions involves the approximately six hundred thousand members of the German Christian Movement.[3] With their self-conscious attempt to fuse Christianity and National Socialism, the German Christians articulated a task that faced every Christian who accepted Nazism as legitimate. Studying this specific group thus provides insights into attitudes of broader circles within German society as well.

The German Christians were a group of predominantly Protestant laypeople and clergy in Nazi Germany.[4] From the movement's official formation in 1932 throughout the Nazi era and even beyond, its members acted out their vision of a "racially pure" church. Even before Adolf Hitler became chancellor, the self-styled "storm troopers of Christ" began to attack Jewish influences in Christianity. Drawing on a range of precursors that included Martin Luther as well as overseas missionaries, they created an ecclesiology defined by race. For the next twelve years, despite endemic factionalism, vociferous opposition at home and abroad, and an ambivalent reception from the National Socialist state, the German Christians continued to seek a synthesis of Nazi ideology and Protestant tradition and to agitate for a "people's church" based on blood. With their fusion of traditional Christian anti-Judaism and biological racial obsessions, the German Christians represented a blend of what Donald Niewyk has dubbed the "old" and the "new" antisemitisms.[5]

The German Christian Movement spread its views through gatherings and publications of all kinds. Organizers sponsored huge rallies with tens of thousands of the faithful; publicists churned out newspapers, broadsheets, and scholarly monographs. In Sunday-morning sermons all across Germany, pastors preached the movement's call for a church of blood. Lay members propagated antisemitic, chauvinist ideas in the schools, on church councils, and at skat games around the *Stammtisch*. Through all these efforts, the German Christian Movement both reflected and contributed to the religious and social situation that made the Holocaust possible.

The German Christians did not merely echo the Nazi assault on Jews and Judaism. Instead they launched their own crusade from within the Protestant churches of Germany. Throughout the 1930s and into the 1940s, they harassed converts from Judaism to Christianity and their families and fought to bar people defined as non-Aryans from the pulpits and pews of German Protestant congregations. In a process that became more brazen as Nazi plans for genocide unfolded, they rejected the canonicity of the Old Testament, denied the Jewish ancestry of Jesus, and expunged Jewish words like *hosanna* and *hallelujah* from hymns. As pastors, chaplains, and teachers of religion, they gave their blessing to the German war against the Jews. Instead of a fundamental dichotomy between Christianity and Nazism, German Christians found that components of their religious tradition, even those most closely linked to its Jewish origins, could become weapons in the attack.

The German Christian View of Race

The core ideas of the German Christian Movement remained remarkably constant throughout its years of existence. German Christians aimed to create a *Volkskirche*, a "people's church" defined by "blood" that would embrace all "true" Germans and provide a spiritual homeland for the Aryans of the Third Reich. The movement's members considered Jewishness to be a racial category. Baptism, they claimed, could never change the status of a Jew; it only allowed alien elements to enter the Aryan bloodstream. In their efforts to fuse church and nation, the German Christians blurred two contentions: baptism could not make a Jew a German, they argued, and by extension, baptism could not make a Jew a Christian. Just as Jewishness for German Christians was both religious and racial, so German Christianity, its polar opposite, constituted both a religious and a racial category.

For the German Christians race was a divine command that sanctified their cause. Accordingly, they considered establishment of an anti-Jewish church to be a sacred task. In 1934, Guida Diehl, founder of the nationalist New Land League in Eisenach and an early German Christian enthusiast, pledged commitment to a "renewal of faith." That rejuvenation, Diehl announced, would be based on an understanding of race, together with "the family, Volk, and fatherland," as the first revelation of God.[6] In July 1939, a German Christian publication declared recognition of the sacred meaning of race to be Germany's gift to the twentieth century. God, the author rejoiced, had called Germany to be a "pathbreaker" to a new age when every race would recognize that it could only accept Christianity "in a way true to its nature."[7]

German Christian attempts to create a purely Aryan, anti-Jewish church reflected the fundamental illogic of the Nazi definition of Jewishness. Nazi ideology posited Jewishness as a biological fact; German Christians shared that view. But the Nazi concept of Jewishness had religious dimensions, too; by law, the religion of one's grandparents determined one's race.[8] As German Christians discovered, the religious aspect of the Nazi definition of Jewishness had disadvantages for them. Nazi theorists, neopagans, and anti-church agitators sneered at Christianity as nothing but diluted Judaism. That derision egged on the German Christian offensive against Jewish elements in Christianity while putting German Christians on the defensive against the very Nazi worldview they embraced.

But the notion of Jewishness as an intangible spiritual force that had infiltrated Christianity also presented opportunities to German Christians. As antisemitic fervor mounted in Nazi Germany, the German Christian attack on Jewish influence in Christianity became immune from open opposition. They could point to their anti-Jewish activities as evidence of their loyalty to the

Nazi regime; they could silence critics with accusations of treason. And the notion of Jewishness as both racial and religious lent credence to the German Christians' own conviction that Germanness too comprised both categories of identity; only Christianity, they maintained, could provide the spiritual content of true Germanness.

Chronology: From Ascendancy to Postwar Reintegration

The German Christians remained a minority within Germany's Protestant population, but they exerted an influence far out of proportion to their numbers. By 1933, members of the movement occupied key posts all across the country—in national church governing bodies, within theological faculties, as regional bishops, on local church councils. Many remained active in those positions until 1945. After the collapse of the Nazi regime, most of them melted back into the Protestant mainstream. Between 1932 and 1945, the German Christian Movement developed in five identifiable phases: ascendancy, fragmentation, regrouping, ambiguous success, and reintegration. A survey of those stages provides chronological background for this discussion.

Ascendancy characterized the movement's trajectory from its inception in 1932 to the so-called Sports Palace Affair in November 1933. During that time, German Christians enjoyed open support from Nazi party and state organs. In July 1933 Protestant church elections were held across the country to fill a range of positions, from parish representatives to senior consistorial councilors.[9] Hitler himself endorsed the German Christians in a special radio address,[10] and the movement won two-thirds of the votes cast. Affirmed by the biggest voter turnout ever in a Protestant church election, in the summer of 1933 the German Christians seemed unstoppable. They dominated the historic process that unified Germany's twenty-eight regional Protestant churches into the German Protestant Church; they imposed one of their own, Ludwig Müller, as Germany's first and last national Protestant bishop, or *Reichsbishof*.[11] German Christians gained control of ecclesiastical government in all but three regions—Bavaria, Hanover, and Württemberg—and rode the crest of a wave of religious-nationalist fervor that inspired such spectacles as the mass church weddings of German brides and their storm trooper or SS grooms.[12]

The euphoria of ascent proved short-lived. Withdrawal of party support—symbolized in the declaration of neutrality in church affairs by Hitler's deputy, Rudolf Hess, on 13 October 1933—engendered a crisis of identity in the German Christian Movement.[13] Tensions between those who sought only an adjustment of Christianity and others who urged complete overhaul, exploded in the Sports Palace rally on 13 November 1933. To an audience of twenty thousand, the rally's key speaker, Berlin German Christian leader

Reinhold Krause, attacked the foundations of Christianity as having unacceptable marks of Jewish influence. Krause vilified the Old Testament, the Apostle Paul, and the cross as a symbol of atonement.[14] His speech incited a wave of departures from the ranks and precipitated a shake-up in the leadership.[15] The dramatic response to the Sports Palace Affair ushered in the second phase of German Christian development: fragmentation.

Throughout 1934 and 1935, the movement's central organization lay in shambles. Initiative passed to the regional and local levels as personal rivalries, disagreements about tactics, and inertia paralyzed the national leadership. Yet the German Christian Movement was by no means defunct; its pastors went on preaching in pulpits across the country; German Christian parish representatives, synodal officers, and regional bishops elected or appointed in 1933 remained in office and continued to propagate the cause.[16] The frenetic proliferation of splinter groups in this period itself indicates the intense energies bound up in German Christianity.

In July 1935, Hitler created the new Ministry for Church Affairs under Hanns Kerrl.[17] That attempt by Nazi authorities to increase their control of church issues signaled the onset of a new era in German Christianity: regrouping. Initially, Kerrl's personal proclivities and his ministry's efforts favored the German Christians, who exploited the new conditions to expand their activity. Particularly in 1936 and 1937, subgroups of the movement came together, often under Thuringian leadership.[18] By the time German troops invaded Poland in September 1939, almost the entire spectrum of German Christian splinter groups had reestablished ties.[19]

The war triggered the fourth phase of German Christian evolution, a period of ambiguous success.[20] War brought fulfillment of many German Christian aims. The movement had demanded an aggressive Christianity that united the nation against its foes. It claimed to find that spiritual solidarity in the Third Reich under arms. German Christians had insisted on the exclusion of so-called non-Aryans and of Jewish influences from the German religious community. That goal would be realized by default, through the deportation and systematic murder of those defined as Jews. But these successes came at a high price. State and party authorities demonstrated increasingly open hostility to Christianity, even in its pro-Nazi variants. Thus, German Christians discovered that they were both the beneficiaries and targets of National Socialist war aims.

The final phase of the German Christian odyssey—reintegration—began as the Third Reich crumbled in the spring of 1945. Their movement discredited, German Christians faced the task of justifying their involvement over the past years—to occupation authorities, denazification boards, fellow Germans, and even themselves.[21] German Christians used different strategies to try to salvage their positions in the absence of the regime on which they had based their hopes. Many of their efforts focused on their ideal of the people's church in an attempt to prove genuine spiritual motivations. Thus, the ecclesiology that had unified the movement throughout the Nazi years—stripped of its most obvious racist overtones—proved to be an effective tool for reintegrating individual members into the postwar church.

Continuity and Context: The German Christian Movement within German Culture

Not mere opportunists, the German Christians were rooted in the culture around them and built their movement on trends familiar to their fellow German Protestants. Three impulses converged in the establishment of the German Christian Movement. In the summer of 1932, a group of politicians, pastors, and party members met in Berlin to discuss how to win the Protestant churches of Germany for National Socialism. They planned to call their association "Protestant National Socialists" but according to their accounts, Hitler vetoed that label and suggested "German Christians" instead.[22] Meanwhile in Thuringia, Siegfried Leffler and Julius Leutheuser, two outspoken young pastors and war veterans, had been preaching religious renewal along National Socialist lines since the late 1920s.[23] They also called themselves "German Christians." Soon the two groups began to cooperate.

A third initiative came from the Protestant, *völkisch* associations. The 1920s had spawned many such groups, dedicated to the revival of church life through increased emphasis on German culture, antisemitism, and ethnic identity. Some of them merged with the German Christians; others maintained a separate existence but lost members to the new movement or cooperated with it on specific projects.[24] Such interchange was eased by the fact that the German Christians as a whole did not break away from the established church. Instead, adherents tried to take over Protestant church government, from the local to the national levels.

Who Were the German Christians?

Although members of the clergy remained the movement's main spokesmen, German Christians represented a cross-section of society from every region of the country: women and men, old and young, pastors, teachers, dentists, railroad workers, housewives, and farmers, even some Catholics. Wilhelm Kube, Gauleiter of Brandenburg, chairman of the National Socialist group in the Prussian Landtag, and later Generalkommissar in White Ruthenia, was a German Christian. So were Joachim Hossenfelder, a hotheaded young pastor who became the movement's national leader in 1933, and

Dörthe Kisting, a Berlin woman with poetic aspirations who was active in her church community. Respected theologians like Friedrich Gogarten, Gerhard Kittel, and Heinrich Bornkamm spent at least some time in the movement.[25] Laypeople were often more faithful. Eleanor Liebe-Harkort, a Westphalian homemaker and active proponent of women's rights, was an enthusiastic German Christian, even after the end of the war. As leader of the Protestant Women's Service of Westphalia (with twenty-five thousand members) she used her influence to push for exclusion of so-called non-Aryans from the clergy.[26] Despite their diversity, members of the German Christian Movement shared allegiance to a vision of the Christian church as the spiritual homeland of the German Volk. Central to that ecclesiology was the quest for an explicitly anti-Jewish Christianity.

Through their bid to revamp German Protestantism, the German Christians unleashed a fight for control of the church known as the "church struggle" (*Kirchenkampf*).[27] Their main rival was the Confessing Church (Bekennende Kirche), with its slogan, "Church must remain church." Its name notwithstanding, the Confessing Church, like the German Christian Movement, existed within official Protestantism. The vast majority of Protestant clergy and laypeople remained neutral in the conflict.[28] And even the chasm between the two rivals was not always unbridgeable. Some German Christians, like Martin Niemöller's brother Wilhelm, later joined the Confessing Church; other people moved in the opposite direction.[29] Division was bitter, but, as Dietrich Bonhoeffer pointed out in 1934, factions in the church struggle did not correspond neatly to political categories.[30] Nazi party members and antisemites numbered among the neutrals and could be found in the Confessing Church as well as in the German Christian Movement.

Throughout the 1930s and 1940s, German Christians faced antagonism not only from within Protestant circles but also from neopagan groups outside the church.[31] The German Faith Movement, until 1936 under the leadership of Tübingen professor Jakob Wilhelm Hauer, was a special thorn in the German Christians' side.[32] Not only did it maintain the largest and most active membership of the neopagan organizations,[33] but in its beliefs it was closer to Hitler and his inner circle than the German Christians were. Moreover, its name—German Faith Movement (Deutsche Glaubensbewegung)—was so similar to that used by German Christians throughout 1933—German Christian Faith Movement (Glaubensbewegung Deutsche Christen)—that people were forever confusing the two. Such confusion highlights the German Christians' ongoing struggle to differentiate themselves, on the one hand from fellow church people who also showed enthusiasm for Nazism, and on the other hand from racist compatriots who shared their contempt for the Jewish origins of Christianity.

Precursors and Connections

The German Christians, with their anti-Jewish campaign, represented an extreme position among German Protestants. Yet like National Socialism, the German Christian Movement contained little that was new. Its tenets represented a conglomeration of old and not-so-old ideas drawn from sources that included everything from medieval texts to the racial theories of Houston Stewart Chamberlain. Adherents of the movement especially liked to cite Luther as a precursor of their attitudes toward Jews and Judaism. With glee they reprinted his essay "Against the Jews and Their Lies" and presented him as a champion of antisemitism. A 1940 religious instruction book quoted Luther's instructions to "set their synagogues and schools on fire, and whatever will not burn, heap dirt upon and cover so that no human ever again will see a stone or a cinder of it."[34] A German Christian publication from 1943 urged its readers to be hard like Luther in their attitudes toward Jews.[35]

German Christians also found forerunners in more recent German history. Throughout the 1920s and 1930s, *völkisch* enthusiasts agitated within Protestant communities to abolish collections for missions to the Jews, to remove Old Testament sayings and stories from religious instruction and the worship service, and to purge hebraisms such as *Jehovah, hallelujah,* and *hosanna* from the hymnbook. One of the most active of such groups was the German Church League (Bund für deutsche Kirche, or Deutschkirche). Founded in 1921, the league existed in some areas alongside the German Christians until at least 1936.[36] Many of its ideas and more than a few of its adherents resurfaced in the German Christian Movement. For example, German Christians recirculated a German Church League publication of 1927 that described Jesus as "the transfiguration of the Siegfried idea," who could "break the neck of the Jewish-Satanic snake with his iron fist."[37]

Some German Christian ideas about race stemmed from a less obvious source: overseas missions. Since the late nineteenth century, German missions had stressed the need to adapt the Christian message and its presentation to suit each Volk. German Christians took that message as justification for a racially exclusive church. According to one German Christian, missions taught that in "God's order of creation, there is no 'humanity,' rather only German Christians, English Christians, Chinese Christians, and so on."[38] Another German Christian grumbled in 1935 that, "We allow every Negro and every Indian to have a form of Christianity that fits to the life of his soul; only we Germans are supposed to have a Jewish or a Roman style of Christianity."[39]

In addition to legitimizing the racially exclusive church, the overseas mission experience offered an example of racist thinking that could in turn be applied to the Jews. In order to make concrete their view of Jewishness as a racial category, the German Christians compared Jews to the African and

Asian subjects of German missionary efforts. By doing so, they transferred the feelings of superiority, fear, and loathing that they experienced about the foreign "heathens" onto German Jews. In 1932, one German Christian used overseas missions to explain why converts from Judaism could not be part of a German church. Missions, that author intoned, "do not eradicate differences among the races. . . . Just as a baptized Negro becomes a Negro Christian," he contended, "so the Jew will remain racially a Jew; 'only' from the religious point of view will he become a Jewish Christian."[40] Siegfried Knak, a prominent mission leader, summed up his view of proper race relations with the phrase: "What God has put asunder let no man join together."[41]

Eventually most missionaries parted ways with the German Christians as they came to recognize that the movement's inner logic, with its emphasis on racially and nationally specific religion, doomed overseas outreach. Nevertheless, German Protestant missionaries did contribute to the German Christian theory of race, linking it to familiar stereotypes and giving legitimacy to the acceptance and promotion of racial distinctions within the community of faith.

Common ideas about gender also helped German Christians bind their efforts to the Nazi cause. According to German Christian publicists, only a church devoid of feminine qualities like compassion and capable of manly resolve could become a frontline fighter against racial impurity. Reich Bishop Ludwig Müller voiced that view in 1939. By keeping their "German blood pure," he argued, and by banning "the Jewish influence that is foreign to our nature from all areas of German life," Germans demonstrated their "love for the German homeland and the German people." Such love, Müller claimed, had a "hard, warrior-like face. It hates everything soft and weak because it knows that all life can only then remain healthy and fit for life when everything antagonistic, the rotten and the indecent, is cleared out of the way and destroyed."[42]

German Christians used divisions between the sexes to justify the introduction of racial distinctions into the church. Just as Christian faith did not eradicate physical differences between male and female, they maintained, it did not negate the "biological fact" of race. Wilhelm Stapel, a prolific German Christian theologian, spelled out this line of thinking in 1934. "In the earthly congregation," he wrote, "one cannot revoke the difference between the sexes, even though, 'in the resurrection they neither marry nor are given in marriage' (Matthew 22:30)." It was just as impossible, Stapel went on, "to declare invalid physical, mental, and spiritual differences among peoples, simply because, 'by one Spirit are we all baptized into one body, whether we be Jews or Gentiles' (I Corinthians 12:13)." Stapel used the analogy between gender and race to justify exclusion of non-Aryans from pastoral office. Just as Paul, "for very earthly reasons" forbade women to speak in the church, he argued, so German Protestants could "forbid the Jews to speak in our German congregations."[43]

A German Christian circular from 1935 pointed to Galatians 3:28: "In Christ there is neither Jew nor Greek, slave nor free, male nor female." Some people, the publication indicated, tried to use that verse to "deny the validity of the racial idea in the church." But any child, the author scoffed, could see the foolishness of such a claim: "When there is no longer 'man and woman' in the earthly church, then we will also believe that there is no longer any difference between German and Jewish."[44] By stressing the gap between the visible church where race and gender reigned and the invisible, universal church, German Christians attempted to legitimize the exclusion of people defined as non-Aryans from their spiritual community.

"Euthanasia" and the Question of Opportunism

It is perhaps tempting to dismiss German Christian ideas about race as nothing more than efforts to ingratiate themselves with Nazi authorities. And indeed, while German Christians linked their views of race to God's will, they did consider practical benefits on earth, often offering proof of racist antisemitism in exchange for National Socialist favor. Yet a comparison between members' attitudes toward Jews and non-Aryans and their stance regarding measures against the handicapped reveals the limits of the explanatory power of opportunism.

In Nazi theory and practice, racial and eugenic doctrines formed related parts of an ideology of the master Aryan race.[45] If opportunism motivated German Christian engagement in Nazi racial policy, one would expect to find members of the movement among the most vocal supporters of the eugenics and so-called euthanasia programs as well. Instead, German Christians generally showed reticence on those subjects.

The Sterilization Law of 14 July 1933, officially titled the "law for the prevention of hereditarily diseased offspring," provided for the compulsory sterilization of all people afflicted with a wide range of diseases or disabilities, such as deafness, feeblemindedness, alcoholism, and schizophrenia.[46] It sparked considerable discussion among Christians, particularly Catholics, but the German Christians remained silent. Nor did they respond with any volume to the euphemistically named Euthanasia Program, initiated in 1939, as Hitler, top aides, scores of doctors, other medical personnel, institutional administrators, and social workers cooperated to murder some seventy thousand Germans deemed "lives unworthy of living."[47]

German Christians who publicly addressed issues related to eugenics represented the exception rather than the rule. A few spokespersons for the group paid lip service to Nazi attacks on the handicapped or on alleged carriers of genetic defects, but they lacked the engagement that members of the movement showed in the "Jewish question." Some even apologized for their stance. For example, an article in the 1935 German Christian Reich Calendar admitted that the "race question" made difficult demands in its implications for the handicapped. Of course, it continued, "no reasonable representative of the racial idea would dispute the human obligation and the Christian duty toward the sick, the old, and the weak." But those obligations, it suggested, were only one side of the command to love one's neighbor. After all, the author asked, "Is it not a healthy thought that there, where in accordance with God's will a beautiful flower can bloom, no thistle or nettle is standing?"[48]

Only one full-length book sought to justify Nazi eugenics in German Christian terms. Titled *Genetic Cultivation and Christianity (Erbpflege und Christentum)*, this work by the Protestant theologian Wolfgang Stroothenke appeared in 1940. The author posited race consciousness as the core of "positive Christianity," which he defined as "bound to the Volk" and committed to "racial purity."[49] Yet even he acknowledged the complexity of eugenics issues and rejected coercive measures.[50] Instead of embracing Nazi policy about eugenics and euthanasia, German Christians seem to have ignored it as much as possible. Eager to assert an anti-Jewish stance, they were much less enthusiastic about measures against the handicapped. The German Christians may have been willing to use their antisemitism in opportunistic ways, but the limits of their support for Nazi policy toward people deemed handicapped suggests that they were not mere mouthpieces for official Nazi views. Instead their opportunism rested on a firm commitment to their project of an anti-Jewish church.

Dejudaizing the Church:
The Ecclesiastical Final Solution

The German Christian quest for racial purity in the church was not just an ecclesiological whim or a rhetorical convention. Members of the movement acted on their words, and in the context of a brutal antisemitic state, those actions took on terrible significance. In 1933, while Jewish civil servants lost their jobs, German Christian pastors fought to eject non-Aryans from the Protestant clergy. Two years later, as the Nuremberg Laws deprived German Jews of the rights of citizenship, German Christian parishioners rejected use of Old Testament texts in their worship services. In 1938, Germans torched synagogues all over their country, destroyed Jewish homes and property, and incarcerated thousands of Jewish men. Just months later, German Christians formalized their "dejudaization" of Christianity by founding the Institute for Study and Eradication of Jewish Influence in German Church Life. During the war, while German soldiers, SS, and their henchmen murdered Jews on the eastern front, German Christian church council members expelled non-Aryans from their congregations. Through their quest for an anti-Jewish church, the German Christians endorsed, imitated, and profited from the crimes of the Third Reich.

Non-Aryans in the Church

German Christian goals targeted non-Aryan clergy and laypeople for harassment and exclusion. In 1933, the movement's leadership tried to imitate the state's dismissal of Jewish civil servants by introducing the so-called Aryan Paragraph in the Protestant church. That regulation would have forced all converts from Judaism, as well as their children and in some cases grandchildren, out of church offices. But German Christian efforts foundered as a result of international criticism and opposition mounted by the Pastors' Emergency League, led by Martin Niemöller. Niemöller himself sympathized with the German Christian claim that the Aryan Paragraph was a necessary response to congregations' prejudices. That is, he too worried that antisemitic parishioners would be alienated by "Jewish Christian" clergy. But, he argued in 1934, for the sake of the Confession, the church would have to endure the disagreeable racial fact of Jewishness.[51]

Undaunted by the early setbacks, German Christians found less formal ways to attack clergy defined as non-Aryan. In a 1936 case, for example, they mobilized local Nazi Party youth organizations to sabotage a pastor's confirmation ceremony. They circulated fliers denouncing the "Jewish half-breed" to state and church authorities as well as to members of his Berlin congregation. They rallied their followers for a showdown with the pastor's supporters that ended in fisticuffs outside the church.[52]

German Christians continued to agitate for the introduction of an Aryan Paragraph in the church, even when institutionalized antisemitism in Nazi Germany more or less ensured racial exclusion. In the summer of 1939, church offices in Berlin, under the influence of purportedly moderate German Christians, ordered regional churches to collect proof of "ancestry from German blood" for all pastors and their wives.[53] Only wartime exigencies led to relaxation of that demand in August 1944.[54] Nevertheless, German Christians had achieved their goal: effective exclusion of non-Aryans from pastoral office in the Protestant churches of Germany. Yet the movement could hardly take much credit for that outcome. There had never been more than a few non-Aryan pastors; most of those had left on their own.[55] Nazi policies made sure that people defined as Jews were shut out of German society, while organs of church government—and not only those controlled by German Christians—had added their own administrative measures to restrict non-Aryan clergy.

The German Christians found their goals of racial exclusion fulfilled by default with regard to non-Aryan laypeople as well. Nonetheless, the movement's members took their own steps to demonstrate hostility toward Jews and so-called non-Aryans. By the early months of 1939, in the wake of *Kristallnacht,* German Christian-dominated regional churches began passing regulations to exclude non-Aryans from the religious community. In February 1939, the Thuringian Protestant church decreed that people defined as Jews under the law could not become members. Pastors were not obligated to perform services for "Jews" already in the church; church rooms and equipment were not to be used for services or sacraments for non-Aryans. Non-Aryan Christians were to pay no more church taxes.[56] The churches in Mecklenburg, Anhalt, Lübeck, and Saxony produced similar legislation.[57]

German Christian timing followed the Nazi regime's assault on Jews. As of September 1941, police regulations forced all people defined as Jews to wear the identifying star. General deportations of Jews to the east began a month later.[58] In December 1941, representatives of seven regional churches, all dominated by German Christians, issued their own proclamation to ban "racially Jewish Christians" from the church. Leaders of church government in Saxony, Nassau-Hesse, Schleswig-Holstein, Thuringia, Mecklenburg, Anhalt, and Lübeck echoed Nazi charges that Jews had "instigated" the war and placed themselves and their flocks "in the front of this historic defensive struggle." Ever since the crucifixion of Christ, they claimed, Jews had "opposed Christianity." Baptism, they added, changed "nothing about the racial essence of Jews." Therefore, they concluded, "racially Jewish Christians have no room and no rights" in a German church.[59]

Having adopted race as the organizing principle of their project of church renewal, German Christians ended up equating the anti-Jewish people's church with the genocidal German nation. An excerpt from a German Christian publication of April 1944 captures that identity: "There is no other solution to the Jewish problem than this: that one day the whole world will rise up and decide either for or against Judaism, and we will keep on struggling with each other until the world is totally judaized or completely purged of Judaism. We can say with an honest, pure conscience that we did not want this war and did not start this war. But we can proudly profess before all the world—the world of today as well as of tomorrow—that we took up the gauntlet with the firm resolve to solve the Jewish question for ever."[60]

The Old Testament

Much German Christian energy focused on purging Christianity of Jewish influences. The Old Testament provided the most obvious target for that dejudaizing fervor. Throughout the 1920s and 1930s, *völkisch* elements within the

Protestant church had assaulted the Old Testament as "too Jewish." From 1933 on, German Christians took the lead in that offensive. In November 1933, the German Christian-dominated church government in Schleswig-Holstein limited the use of the Old Testament in religious instruction in schools. The binding of Isaac was the first story axed as "un-German."[61]

Although adherents of the movement agreed that the Old Testament belonged out of the scriptural canon, they differed as to whether and how portions of it might be retained. Reinhold Krause's speech at the movement's rally at the Berlin Sports Palace on 13 November 1933 exposed the extremist position. Krause, a schoolteacher and leader of Berlin's German Christians, based his attack on the need for the church to appeal to all National Socialists. "Those people need to feel at home in the church," he thundered. To that end, he demanded "liberation from everything un-German in the worship service and the confessions—liberation from the Old Testament with its cheap Jewish morality of exchange and its stories of cattle traders and pimps." If National Socialists refused even to buy a tie from a Jew, he went on, "how much more should we be ashamed to accept from the Jew anything that speaks to our soul, to our most intimate religious essence."[62] Krause's speech shocked many, but he was no anomaly. To the contrary, his words anticipated the definitive German Christian view of the Old Testament by the late 1930s.

In the fall of 1935, Hitler's state propagated the Nuremberg Laws, denying citizenship to Jews and codifying a definition of "Jew." Those laws unleashed a new phase in the Nazi onslaught, and German Christians responded with a harsher tone against the Old Testament. In September, a German Christian speaker in Bavaria ridiculed the Old Testament as a saga of racial defilement. His remark that "Moses in his old age had married a Negro woman" drew boisterous laughter and enthusiastic applause from his audience.[63] A Rhenish pastor quit the movement in the wake of the Nuremberg Laws, appalled by increasing radicalism. The fight against Judaism had gone so far, he protested, that its champions denounced anyone who did not reject the Old Testament as "already 'devoured by Jews.'"[64]

Public antisemitism encouraged a heightening of German Christian attacks on the Old Testament; in turn, German Christian ideas found resonance in a society that refused membership to those defined as Jews. In late 1936, a Confessing Church pastor described how teenage girls in his confirmation class reacted to a discussion of Jesus' words, "Think not that I am come to destroy the law, or the prophets: I am not come to destroy, but to fulfill" (Matt. 5:17-19). The girls went wild, denouncing "the Old Testament with its filthy stories," the "Jews as a criminal race."[65] It was precisely such attitudes that German Christian pastors and schoolteachers encouraged.

By late 1938, in the wake of *Kristallnacht,* leading German Christians decided they needed a more formal organization to express their full participation in Nazi antisemitism and to develop an effective defense of Christianity. On 4 April 1939, they gained such a structure with the founding of the Institute for Study and Eradication of Jewish Influence on German Church Life. From then on, the institute orchestrated the attack on the Old Testament and its legacy, finding an especially warm reception during the early years of the war. Propaganda that presented the war as mortal combat against "international Jewry" and, after the fall of 1941, deportations of Jews from the Reich, gave new meaning to German Christian efforts to destroy Jewish influence on the religious front.

During the war German Christian rhetoric against the Old Testament merged with the language and practice of genocide. In late 1941, the Thuringian German Christian Julius Leutheuser, writing from the eastern front, declared the Old Testament and the religiosity of the past to be foes of German Christianity and Germanness. For Leutheuser, National Socialist war aims promised a chance to realize German Christian goals. He called on his people "to build a National Church, as this final world struggle breaks out, the struggle against Judaism. We now hold the means to strike the weapons from the hands of Judaism for good."[66] From his vantage point in the east, Leutheuser must have known that those "means" involved extermination of the Jews.

Despite bombardment with anti-Jewish tirades in the 1940s, some German Christians continued to use favorite parts of the Old Testament. In 1942, German Christian pastors in Westphalia circulated a list of Bible readings suitable for wedding ceremonies: one-third came from the Old Testament, all of those from the Psalms.[67] Even a 1943 circular from the National Church group, reputedly the most radical German Christians, cited cherished bits of the Old Testament. But it emphasized that anti-Jewishness would be the guide in deciding the fate of those Old Testament "gems." "As a code of Jewish ethics," the publication explained, the Old Testament was unacceptable. But as a piece of religious literature, it had redeeming qualities. One needed only to select from it the "numerous religious treasures that . . . stem from the best Aryan tradition but have been stolen after the manner of Jewish peddlers." Once freed from that "unworthy context," the German Christians insisted, their "formative power in German popular piety and German, especially Nordic, art and culture" could be celebrated.[68] Such contorted reasoning suggests that German Christians were both eager to add their weight to the Nazi destruction of Judaism and committed to preserving some cultural vestiges of Christianity.

The New Testament

Rejection of the Hebrew Bible formed the basis for German Christian repudiation of scriptural authority in general and provided a criterion for selection
within the New Testament. In the drama of Christianity's redemption from
Jewish influence, as German Christians construed it, the Old Testament
played the role of the scapegoat that bore away all traces of Jewishness, and
the New Testament would provide marching orders for an anti-Jewish faith.

Anti-Jewish revision was simplified by the New Testament's focus on the
theological foundations of Christianity. Antagonistic to considerations of
dogma in any case, the German Christians simply excluded unacceptable portions from their field of vision and concentrated on those features of the
Gospel accounts that informed their cultural identity: Jesus, the manger, the
cross. Instead of progressive radicalization, as in the case of the Old Testament,
they displayed steadfast consistency on two key points, insisting that Jesus was
not a Jew and that the essence of the gospel's message was anti-Jewishness.

The German Christians based negation of Jesus' Jewishness on their own
presumption of his antisemitism. Jesus, they asserted, could not have been a
Jew because he opposed Judaism. This argument formed the core of their
Christology and allowed them to preserve the figure of Jesus in their anti-
Jewish Christianity. In late 1933, one German Christian offered biblical citations that, he claimed, revealed Jesus' attitude toward Judaism: "A 'mur-
derer,' a 'liar,' a 'father of lies.' It is impossible to reject Jehovah and his Old
Testament in sharper terms!" In places, he admitted, the gospels seem to suggest the opposite. But those were not the words of Christ, he contended; they
were "lies," "Jewishness," the "voice of the Old Testament."[69] Another German Christian advised mothers how to respond if children asked whether
Jesus was Jewish. They should point out, the author counseled, that "because
Christ was the 'opponent' of the Jews, it is impossible that he himself could
have been of Jewish blood and spirit."[70]

As National Socialist attacks on Jews intensified after 1938, German
Christians reduced their assessment of what was genuine in the gospels to
those fragments that best served an antisemitic agenda. In March 1939, a German Christian confirmation examination presented the "German Volk" as the
"temple of God," Hitler as Jesus the purifier. As the exchange between pastor
and candidates reveals, German Christians retained the symbol of Jesus only
to use it to sanctify assault on Jews: "[Jesus] is no Jew. . . . He was persecuted
because he said to the people who considered themselves the chosen ones:
God calls pagans, not Jews; God is sick of you chosen people! But why did he
not come to the Germanic peoples, this God-man? Why precisely in Judea?
He appeared where the enemy was strongest: the Jews are children of the
devil and so the offensive had to begin there."[71]

The heart of the Gospels' message, the German Christians insisted, was a racial struggle. German Christians proffered their reinterpretation of the New Testament as a "purification" and "liberation." Reinhold Krause's 1933 speech had demanded removal from the New Testament of an "exaggerated emphasis on the crucified Christ."[72] German Christians took up that challenge, attacking the notion of human sinfulness as a Jewish accretion to the true gospel. In September 1935, a speaker in Kempten, Bavaria, attacked "Jewish-Semitic additions" that "perverted and encrusted" the gospel. The entire "teaching of sin and grace," he insisted, "was a Jewish attitude and only inserted into the New Testament."[73] Concern with sin, a German Christian leader concurred in a 1942 address to assembled women's groups, was a Jewish element to be purged from Christianity.[74]

During the war, the German Christians reduced Jesus to an ally in the campaign against Jews. A 1939 publication used the language of the apocalypse to sound the call to an anti-Jewish crusade: "Christ is the general leading the troops against Jehovah; our age needs him. . . . Jehovah is a force! The world situation shows just how powerful a one. He was triumphant, not only politically and economically in the old Europe, but above all spiritually. . . . He must be defeated spiritually. That is only possible if all those striving unite under one name. That name is Christ."[75] This interpretation continued throughout the war; in 1944, a former Catholic priest and prominent German Christian in the Thuringian group released a brochure titled "The Sermon on the Mount as a Declaration of War against Judaism." [76]

The German Christians accompanied their anti-Jewish reading of the gospels with rewriting. The circle around Bishop Heinz Weidemann of Bremen published the first new, anti-Jewish scripture. Titled "The German Gospel of John" ("Das Evangelium Johannes deutsch"), it appeared in 1936.[77] Weidemann chose to begin "germanization of the New Testament" with the Gospel of John, he explained, because it constituted "the most sharply anti-Jewish document."[78] He claimed that fourteen thousand copies were printed.[79] Weidemann's version presented Jesus' entire mission as an onslaught against Judaism.[80] Some passages remained virtually unaltered, most notably those that depicted Jesus' conflicts with certain scribes and Pharisees. As part of an explicitly anti-Jewish document, however, those accounts took on new meaning. While preserving many details of the Gospel of John, Weidemann produced a document that presented, not a story of salvation, but a manifesto of hatred toward Jews.

A more ambitious attempt toward a dejudaized New Testament emerged from the Institute for Study and Eradication of Jewish Influence on German Church Life. Part one of this work, "The Message of God" ("Die Botschaft Gottes"), was the only portion completed, appearing in December 1939.[81]

According to one account, it sold two hundred thousand copies within six months.[82] The ninety-six-page work took a different tack than had Weidemann's project. It drew heavily on the Gospel of Mark. It avoided the word "Jew," opting instead for a vague depiction of Christianity as a mixture of familiar words and pithy sayings. Rather than narrating the life of Jesus, it limited itself to well-known passages like Matthew 6:28: "Consider the lilies of the field, how they grow; they toil not, neither do they spin." Jesus appeared in a historical and geographic vacuum; the story of his birth contained nothing about Mary and Joseph's roots in "the house and lineage of David," nor did the book mention the resurrection.[83]

German Christians reached no final consensus on a text of the New Testament. While some used the new versions, others continued to rely on their old Bibles. Some kept to the Gospels, others drew from the entire New Testament. In any case, since the new scriptures grew out of a denial of canonicity, they could hardly claim to present the definitive message of Christianity. But German Christians did agree on one thing: They all accepted the criterion of anti-Jewishness to decide what to teach from the New Testament and how to understand it.

Church Music

On the basis of a racial imperative, the German Christians overturned Scripture. They eschewed doctrinal or ethical considerations, and their understanding of Christianity consisted of attachment to a handful of symbols and rituals they associated with Christian tradition. But even in that limited sphere of Christian culture, German Christians encountered evidence of Jewish influence, most notably in church music. On this front, their offensive was less intense than it had been against the Old and New Testaments. Although German Christians tinkered with the language of hymns, they never transformed church music itself into a weapon in the Nazi war against Jews. This reticence did not reflect any misgivings about their racial vision of Christianity. On the contrary, it illustrates that for the German Christians, the only elements of Christianity worth preserving and defending were the cultural trappings familiar to them from their childhoods: the baby Jesus, the church buildings, beloved hymns.

Early German Christian events reflected no particular concern about Jewish influence in church music. In June 1933, for example, German Christians met in Dortmund. The program included congregational singing of two familiar hymns that contained what German Christians later would decry as hebraisms: The second stanza of Luther's "A Mighty Fortress" refers to Jesus as "Lord Sabaoth," an ancient title meaning commander of the hosts of heaven; and "Oh Come, My Soul with Singing" mentions "Zion" as well as the "God of Jacob."[84] The program provided the standard texts of the hymns, complete with those terms.

Throughout 1933 rumblings about Jewish influence in church music suggested potential for a dejudaizing assault. Reinhold Krause, whose Sports Palace proscriptions with regard to the Old and New Testaments proved accurate predictions of subsequent developments, also called for transformation of the worship service, including attention to church music: "We want to worship God in the church, in the congregations, with German words and from a German spirit. We want to sing songs that are free from all Israelite elements. We want to liberate ourselves from the language of Canaan and turn to our German mother tongue. Only in the German mother tongue can humanity express its prayers, praise, and thanks in the most profound way."[85]

But only in late 1935, after propagation of the Nuremberg Laws, did German Christians begin anything approaching a systematic purge of Christian hymns. The impetus originated high in the movement's ranks with a concern for the church's ability to attract an increasingly antisemitic membership. Unlike the purge of the Old Testament, the subjection of traditional hymns to considerations of racial purity brought a sense of loss to German Christians. Nevertheless, the cause demanded self-denial; according to one member, it was "more Christian to make sacrifice in external forms than through them to kill the spirit and life."[86]

In 1935, the German Christian Wilhelm Bauer published a liturgical guide called "German Christian Celebrations." Bauer decried Jewish influence in church music, complaining, for example, about a plodding musical style that, in his view, was "borrowed from the synagogue." He saved his most detailed criticism for the texts of hymns, contending that it would hardly "contravene the spirit of the Bible or injure the Confession" if phrases like the "people of Israel" were replaced with the "people of God," or the "cedars of Lebanon" with the "firs of the German forest."[87] Although Bauer encouraged musical innovation, he did not advocate transforming church music into a weapon against Judaism. His reticence on that score reflected not moral or doctrinal but aesthetic considerations. In the church, he reminded readers, it was "in bad taste" to sing militaristic or folksy music that "clashed" with the solemn tones of the organ and violated the "hallowed stillness" of the house of God.[88]

Shortly before the war began, the Bishop Weidemann in Bremen coordinated the release of a new German Christian songbook, "Songs of the Coming Church" ("Lieder der kommenden Kirche").[89] It allegedly sold ten thousand copies in the first weeks. Weidemann considered his hymnbook "truly German," its songs purged of all "Judaisms," including Jewish and foreign words.[90] Most of the hymns included were traditional, although references to the Old Testament had been expunged. The new additions, while often focused more on Germany than on Christianity, did not express explicitly anti-Jewish sentiments. Even the firebrand Weidemann, who showed no compunction in rewriting the Gospel of John into a tirade of hatred toward Jews, appeared bound by considerations of what was tasteful and appropriate in church music.

The largest collection of dejudaized hymns assembled by German Christians appeared in a 1941 release named after a familiar hymn: "Holy God We Praise Thy Name" ("Großer Gott wir loben Dich!"). Containing 339 hymns in a mixture of old and new German material, the book was a product of the Institute for Study and Eradication of Jewish Influence on German Church Life.[91] Here, too, the result was a self-consciously conventional hymnbook minus Old Testament vocabulary, not a declaration of war on Judaism in general.

It was in the sphere of church music, far from the core of Christian belief, that the German Christians appeared least eager to complete their ecclesiastical final solution. Notions of taste and appropriateness exercised a much more effective brake on the German Christian project of dejudaization than did doctrinal, theological, or ethical considerations.

Postwar Implications

In July 1948, a former leading German Christian wrote to church authorities requesting reemployment in the church. In order to forestall charges of anti-semitism, he described an encounter during the Nazi years with a non-Aryan colleague. He had tried to comfort the man, the erstwhile German Christian reported, given his "difficult situation" as a Jew in the Third Reich. But the non-Aryan had rebuffed his overtures, "on the basis that he was not Jewish." The German Christian had been astonished, and had explained to his fellow pastor that because he had been "baptized into Christianity as a Jewish child," he remained "purely physically, according to race, Jewish."[92] The German Christian had then encouraged his colleague to serve his own Volk through the mission to the Jews. Had he not shown compassion to the Jews, the would-be penitent now asked church authorities?

For the German Protestant church and former German Christians, 1945 brought much that was new. But as that pastor's letter indicates, it was no "zero hour." Neither the German Christians nor the attitudes that had characterized their movement simply disappeared. Continuities and links to the past remained part of the legacy of the postwar church. Beginning in 1945, the German Christian Movement in general served as a useful red herring in the denazification of both individual lay leaders and of the Protestant church as a whole. Most individual German Christians were reintegrated into the Protestant mainstream. And even some of their racist and antisemitic ideas showed remarkable tenacity.

The German Christian Movement and Denazification in the Church

The job of rebuilding the Protestant church after the war fell to neutral and Confessing Church clergy. Preoccupied with efforts to restore normalcy amid postwar confusion, many of them preferred to close the book on old church-political struggles. No one seemed enthusiastic about instituting some test of orthodoxy to determine, as one pastor put it, "who still had a Christian basis of faith at all among those who wanted to come back to the church."[93]

The Protestant church faced external pressures as well. American occupation authorities in particular urged the church to purge its leadership or risk imposed denazification.[94] Prominent churchmen—Martin Niemöller and Bishops Meiser and Wurm in Bavaria and Württemberg—argued that secular powers had no business determining who was or was not fit to serve the church. That decision, they insisted, had to be based on loyalty to Scripture and the confession of faith.[95] Their efforts paid off; by 1946, autonomous church boards won control of denazification of the clergy, but the problem of balancing internal demands for stability and external calls to denazify remained.

For the German Protestant church, the Stuttgart Declaration of Guilt of October 1945 constituted an important step toward regaining international credibility. That statement, signed by church leaders on behalf of German Protestantism, acknowledged a "great solidarity of guilt" between the Protestant church and the German people. It expressed repentance "for not witnessing more courageously, for not praying more faithfully, for not believing more joyously, and for not loving more ardently."[96] Yet while the Stuttgart Declaration bought goodwill abroad, it alienated some of the church's constituency at home. Even though it avoided any reference to specific crimes and noted the church's "long struggle" against Nazi violence, it sparked resentment from Protestants who denounced it as an admission of "war guilt" tantamount to a "second Versailles."[97]

In this context, the German Christians provided an ideal target for ecclesiastical denazification efforts. Thanks to foreign press coverage of the church struggle, the movement had gained considerable notoriety abroad. The American Occupation Forces' questionnaire even listed it separately as a Nazi organization.[98] Censure of German Christian clergy seemed likely to satisfy occupation authorities as an adequate expression of denazifying zeal. At the same time, focus on the movement promised not to disturb most Protestants at home. In the summer of 1945, a former German Christian estimated optimistically that the movement had about fifty thousand adherents in Bavaria and eight thousand in Baden.[99] Clergy made up only a small percentage of those totals. Once labeled the sole Protestant collaborators, a few German Christian pastors could be removed from their positions and the rest of the church could consider its hands clean.

Accordingly, efforts to denazify the Protestant church zeroed in on German Christian pastors. In September 1945, church leaders from Westphalia and the Rhine Province passed a regulation to discipline clergy compromised by Nazism. They set up a committee to hear the cases of those who had shown themselves unworthy of their calling or violated Scripture and the confession of the faith.[100] But no general investigation of orthodoxy throughout the churches followed. Instead the committee summoned only German Christians for hearings. Other regional churches followed similar patterns. Church authorities then pointed to measures taken against the German Christian Movement to prove that further purges were unnecessary. In late 1947, the central office of the Protestant church in Germany declared the German Christian threat eradicated. This statement announced that even in Thuringia, once a stronghold of the movement, the regional church had cleansed its jurisdiction of "German Christian heresies" and removed German Christians from pastoral office. Denazification of the Protestant church, the report implied, was now complete.[101]

Some observers recognized the postwar focus on the German Christian Movement as something of a smoke screen. In October 1945, German Christian pastor Friedrich Buschtöns protested that regulations to cleanse the church were aimed not at denazification but at removal of German Christians. "Why," he wanted to know, "were questionnaires about membership in the party and its organizations not sent to all pastors in Westphalia, for example, with the embarrassing questions: Who had been contact men of the Security Service; who had dedicated party flags, held speeches at party events, and baptized under the flag of war?"[102] The Württemberg theologian Hermann Diem, an outspoken opponent of National Socialism, had occupied a position at the opposite end of the church struggle from Buschtöns. But he, too, saw ways in which exclusive focus on the German Christians made a sham of ecclesiastical denazification.[103] It is not surprising that Buschtöns, a pugnacious German Christian, found little support. But Diem, whose record as an opponent of National Socialism was spotless, stood equally alone.[104]

Rationalization, Silence, Denial

Protestant denazification efforts targeted the German Christian Movement as a whole but showed less stringency in dealing with individual members. Lay adherents encountered few barriers to reintegration. And despite initial disciplinary actions (often complete with pensions for those removed from their posts[105]), by 1950 even the hard-liner Buschtöns had to admit that almost all German Christian clergy had reentered the service of the church or were in the process of doing so.[106] But how did German Christians as individuals deal with their past?

Given the sources available, that question is difficult to answer. The most common public responses to past involvement with the German Christian movement ranged from rationalization to silence and denial. German Christians found that some of the very arguments they had used to defend themselves or to justify their beliefs and behavior during the Nazi years also served as effective postwar rationalizations. In 1953, a former German Christian seeking a church post boasted that the denazification commission of West Berlin had rehabilitated him. He possessed a certificate from the Protestant Consistory testifying that, through his "efforts for positive Christianity and for a just treatment of the Jews," he had been active as an "antifascist," ejected from the Nazi Party, and called to account by the Gestapo.[107] Eleven years earlier that same man had sought to extricate himself from the very party criticism he later presented as evidence of resistance by sending Nazi authorities a copy of an anti-Jewish confirmation sermon he had delivered.[108]

In the Third Reich, German Christians had sought to justify the dejudaization of Christianity by pointing to their desire to build a church that met the needs of the Volk. After the war, they returned to that same line of argumentation. In the 1970s, one sympathizer of the movement described its revised liturgy, hymns, and scriptures as its greatest achievement, with no reference to the antisemitism that had motivated those innovations. Echoing the vocabulary of the 1930s and 1940s, he decried the continued use of the "language of Canaan" in the church. The church has always adapted its preaching, he argued, pointing to the example of "the mission to the Eskimo." Eskimos, he explained, could not understand the term "lamb of God." Missionaries substituted the "seal of God," an ethnic adaptation appropriate to "Greenlander Christianity."[109] German Christianity, he concluded, had been no different.

The German Christian Movement's frenzied activities up until 1945 stand in stark contrast to most members' postwar silence. Many showed particular reticence about the very issues that had been at the heart of their agenda: their stance on Judaism, Jews, and non-Aryan Christians. It was as if they had forgotten their efforts to purge Jewish elements from Christianity, as if they had never read, heard, or uttered the scathing denunciations of Jews and Judaism that had made up the core of their agitation.

Guida Diehl, in memoirs she wrote in the 1950s, dismissed aggression against Jews as an inexplicable quirk of Hitler's. She described the *Kristallnacht* pogrom of 9 November 1938 as "the blackest day in the history of National Socialism" and claimed she did not see "one single face . . . that approved of this cruel corruption."[110] Diehl said nothing about the fact that at least since the 1920s, she herself had been an active proponent of dejudaized and anti-Jewish Christianity. Her silence was rewarded. Arguably the most prominent female German Christian, after the war Diehl was able to reestablish her New Land League, first in Thuringia, and subsequently in Hesse, with the support of none other than Martin Niemöller.[111]

The most effective silence, as Diehl's memoir proved, was selective. Another prominent German Christian provided further evidence of this principle. One of the most explicit postwar recantations from within the movement came from Siegfried Leffler, former leader of Thuringian German Christians and director of the Institute for Study and Elimination of Jewish Influence in German Church Life. In 1947, Leffler, incarcerated in Ludwigsburg, performed public penance in a widely circulated letter. Since soon after the war began, he claimed, he had been "haunted" by guilt that his actions and words had "harmed" the "Christian church and the German as well as the Jewish people." But Leffler refused to take any responsibility for the anti-Jewish teachings of the movement he had headed. It was not the case, he insisted, that he had "personally hated or stirred up hatred!"[112] Protestant publications printed his letter with sympathetic commentary,[113] and by 1949, he too was back in the service of the church.[114]

Silence could represent defiance, shame, remorse, or even a kind of solidarity between former German Christians who did change their ways and their colleagues who did not. In postwar retrospect, the widow of a prominent German Christian recognized that the movement's ideals, pure as they seemed to her at the time, were illusions, branded such by "euthanasia, concentration camps, persecutions of Jews." She had been wrong, she confessed, but she made that admission in private and concluded that for her, nothing remained "but silence."[115]

A minority of German Christians eschewed silence in favor of blatant defiance. In 1947, a clergyman from the Rhineland told a denazification tribunal that he had been a committed antisemite before National Socialism and remained so after its collapse. To defend his stance he pointed to Luther's hostility toward Jews. The board then produced an antisemitic poem he had written in 1937 for the birth announcement of his daughter. When asked if, with such sentiments, he had not entered the ranks of those guilty of murdering millions of Jews, the pastor dismissed the poem as a "harmless private joke."[116] In 1948, a church member in Ludwigsburg complained about a pastor who had once "preached the ideas of Rosenberg and the party with fiery zeal and rejected Christ as a Jew." Unharmed by denazification measures, he was still stirring up those ideas among church groups.[117]

Self-interest ensured that German Christians who took a public stance of defiance after 1945 were exceptions rather than the rule. But in more private contexts many expressed defiance of developments that had discredited their movement. In 1953, Buschtöns denounced denazification efforts, especially those in the church, with the words, "if the Nazis burned the Jews, so the others have not shown any less hatefulness."[118] Despite their own eager participation in efforts to expunge Jewish influences from Christianity, after the war Buschtöns and his Westphalian colleague Walther Fiebig decided they had not even been aware that concentration camps existed.[119] Buschtöns discounted the murder of the Jews as a rumor, one more indication of the "injustice" Germans now suffered.

After 1945, German Christians and their sympathizers could no longer fulminate openly against Jews. But the new situation provided its own possibilities for continuity. One of the most chilling illustrations of German Christian racial thought years after World War II comes from the former German Protestant bishop in Rumania, Wilhelm Staedel. Staedel's postwar comments on what he called the "race issue" revealed continued endorsement of chauvinistic biological determinism. In a telling sleight of hand, however, he adjusted the old Nazi dichotomy of "Aryan/non-Aryan" to a polarization he expected would find more resonance in the postwar world: "white/non-white."

To Staedel it was "an unprecedented tragedy of world history that the white people of the world called forth the two last wars with each other and thereby weakened each other and themselves." Hitler's involvement in the "race question," he theorized, reflected an assumption he presumed his reader shared as well, that, "contrary to the well-known enlightenment idea, and despite a basic similarity of structure, people are not all the same, but are different." Given that fact, he argued, "preservation of one's own Volk, of one's own race," became a "serious duty," and the "mixing of races" was to be "checked." Staedel closed his diatribe by citing none other than Martin Niemöller, then president of the Protestant Church in Germany, on the subject of race: "According to a report of the American newspaper *The Virginian* in October 1957, Niemöller said: 'The crucial issue was not whether the USA or the USSR would win the next war. The big question rather was whether there would still be a white race in thirty or forty years.'"[120]

It is tempting to dismiss Staedel's analysis as the bitter rantings of a disillusioned old man. Yet his comments show how the social construct of race itself provided some German Christians with a vehicle to normalize and legitimize their anti-Jewishness, casting it as part of a cosmic struggle for white, Western, Christian purity. At the same time, Staedel's diatribe suggests how easily old Nazi Christian ways of thinking could blend into revised strands of racism.

Conclusion

The German Christians rose to prominence in 1933. They survived their fall from political favor and endemic fragmentation to make a comeback by the mid-1930s. From then the German Christian Movement grew out of and fed back into the religious and social context of the Holocaust. During the war, activity intensified as the German Christian project of dejudaizing Christianity meshed with the Nazi assault on the Jews. After 1945, most former German Christians, including prominent spokespersons of the movement, were reintegrated into the church.

The German Christian Movement persisted for as long as it did because it was embedded in the culture around it. German Christians did not invent the core ideas that they represented. The ideal of a people's church, Christian anti-Jewishness, racial antisemitism, an antidoctrinal, romantic understanding of religion—those were all familiar themes to Germans of the 1920s and 1930s. German Christians pulled them together into a movement dedicated to the creation of a church that would provide spiritual expression to a racially pure nation. Defeat and the debacle of the Third Reich discredited some German Christian ideas, particularly their vehement anti-Jewishness. But even their ideas about race needed only a bit of tinkering to make them again appear to be within the mainstream. In some ways, the differences between the German Christians and many of their fellow Protestants were never very great after all.

The persistence of the German Christian Movement may also reflect a more general crisis of Christianity in modern Europe. The German Christians' retention of certain aspects of Christian practice and tradition meant that the movement appeared both revolutionary and familiar to fellow Protestants. In that way, it offered a welcome compromise for Germans who embraced the new Nazi ideology yet were unwilling to abandon completely their Christian heritage. German Christians jettisoned every inconvenient theological and moral aspect of Christianity and reduced it to a handful of cultural symbols and practices from their childhoods. Yet they clung to these with a tenacity that suggested both genuine dedication and profound spiritual confusion.

Historiography and Suggestions for Further Reading

The Protestant church struggle (*Kirchenkampf*) in Nazi Germany is extremely well-chronicled. Overviews by Klaus Scholder (in German) and John Conway (in English) have become staples on undergraduate and graduate reading lists.[121] Collections of documents, local studies, and hefty series on specific issues record and analyze developments in the Protestant church in Nazi Germany.[122] Until the 1980s, this abundant literature was notably one-sided; scholars examined the Confessing Church in meticulous detail but spent little time on the German Christian Movement, often dismissing it as a Nazi creation or assuming that its story ended with the Sports Palace Affair in November 1933. The myriad biographies and autobiographies of Confessing Church members contrast to the few firsthand accounts by German Christians. Only Guida Diehl, the nationalist women's leader in Eisenach; Christian Kinder, German Christian Reich leader in 1934 and 1935; and Franz Tügel, German Christian bishop in Hamburg, have published memoirs.[123] Diehl skims over the Nazi years, Kinder seeks to justify his involvement, and Tügel's account appeared after his death.

Throughout the 1950s, 1960s, and 1970s, secondary literature on the German Christians was equally sparse. Hans Buchheim's 1953 analysis of the movement discusses it together with neopagan groups as part of a broad spiritual crisis in National Socialist Germany.[124] But Buchheim pays little attention to the German Christians as part of the church. A number of dissertations have explored facets of the movement, from its propaganda to differences among splinter groups,[125] and regional studies such as Helmut Baier's 1968 work on Bavaria fill in more of the picture.[126] For decades, however, the definitive word on the movement remained Kurt Meier's *Die Deutschen Christen* (1964). Meier, a church historian, offered a detailed organizational study up to 1939. But not only did he leave out the war years, he devoted almost no attention to antisemitism or Christian-Jewish relations.

It is not surprising that studies of the German Christian Movement were rare while literature on the Confessing Church burgeoned. Many of the early chroniclers of the church struggle were themselves participants in the events they described; their personal and institutional interests lay in presenting the Protestant church in the most anti-Nazi light possible.[127] Former German Christians stood to gain little from exposure of the past and were reluctant to attract attention that might jeopardize chances of employment in the postwar church.[128]

The last decade and a half have seen the situation change as a number of works on the German Christian Movement have appeared. Several factors explain this development. The new, critical generation of Germans that came of age some thirty years after the war has shown less interest in continuing what John Conway once called the "hagiographical" tradition of writing about the church struggle.[129] Reijo E. Heinonen's 1978 study of the German Christians of Bremen, Hans-Joachim Sonne's 1982 exploration of the movement's political theology, and Thomas Schneider's recent account of Reich Bishop Ludwig Müller typify the work of such scholars.[130]

Even more transformative have been publications that brought to the forefront the centrality of antisemitism to German Protestant thought in the 1930s and 1940s. Studies by the Israeli scholar Uriel Tal, as well as by the Germans Detlef Minkner, Wolfgang Gerlach, and Hans Prolingheuer, have revealed how broad segments of German Protestantism, including the Confessing Church, were implicated in Nazi crimes against the Jews.[131] Suddenly the German Christians appeared as more than just a marginal aberration. The fifty-year commemoration of *Kristallnacht*—the November Pogrom of 1938— generated further interest in the relationship between the Christian churches and Jews in the Third Reich, a subject long neglected.[132] Susannah Heschel's discussion of the German Christian-dominated Institute for the Study and Eradication of Jewish Influence on German Church Life is a recent contribution in this area.[133]

Participation by scholars from outside Germany as well as methodological developments have enriched the field enormously. The American scholar Robert P. Ericksen broke new ground by focusing on the so-called neutrals in the church struggle.[134] At the same time, his 1985 work demonstrates the impact of German Christian ideas at the very centers of theological scholarship. Rainer Hering has made similar discoveries.[135] Studies by Sheila Briggs and Jochen-Christoph Kaiser introduce gender to the analysis of German Protestant theology in the recent past.[136] Shelley Baranowski's examination of the Confessing Church with an eye to social class and elitism has helped bring church history into social historical discussions of the Third Reich.[137] Germans like Manfred Gailus have followed her lead.[138] Rainer Lächele's 1993 look at the German Christian Movement in Württemberg indicates the extent to which the subject of Christianity under National Socialism has come out of isolation and into dialogue with cultural, social, intellectual, and political history.[139] My own work on the German Christians pays attention to gender while keeping the movement's racial antisemitism at the forefront of the analysis.[140] Taken together, all of these studies offer a complex, nuanced picture of German Protestantism in the Third Reich that breaks down a simple resistance-collaboration dichotomy and explodes the myth of the churches as passive victims of Nazi aggression.

When Jesus Was an Aryan

The Protestant Church and
Antisemitic Propaganda

Susannah Heschel

In Germany the combination of racial theory with religion, beginning in the nineteenth century and blossoming during the early decades of the twentieth, led to the creation of Aryan Christianity, a phenomenon Saul Friedländer has described as "redemptive anti-Semitism." Born, Friedländer writes, "from the fear of racial degeneration and the religious belief in redemption," Aryan Christianity advocated Germany's liberation from the Jews and from the Jewish.[1] An authentic Germany would be free of all Jewish accretions, those that had entered via modernity and those that had entered via Christianity. If the contemporary savior was Hitler, his mission was that of Christ. The redemption of Christianity itself was at stake, and could only be accomplished by purging Jesus of all Jewish associations and reconstructing him as he allegedly really was, as an Aryan.

The implementation of Aryan Christianity within the institutional Protestant church was the goal of the pro-Nazi German Christian Movement, described in chapter 3 by Doris Bergen. The movement reached its zenith in 1939 with the establishment of an antisemitic research institute, known as the Institut zur Erforschung und Beseitigung des jüdischen Einflusses auf das deutsche kirchliche Leben (Institute for the Study and Eradication of Jewish Influence on German Religious Life), named herein as "the Institute." Several of the major figures within the Institute had met as students of Gerhard Kittel and had worked under him at the University of Tübingen during the early 1930s on the *Theological Dictionary of the New Testament*. Data from church archives allow us to reconstruct the establishment, activities, membership, funding, and theology of the Institute, which was located in central Germany, in the town of Eisenach (Thuringia), and to trace the postwar careers of its leaders within the church and the theological faculties. Until now, the very existence of the Institute, from 1939 to 1945, was barely known as a result of postwar efforts to hide all of the church's pro-Nazi activities.

The significance of the Institute lies in its efforts to identify Christianity with National Socialist antisemitism by arguing that Jesus was an Aryan who sought the destruction of Judaism. Its members proclaimed, "We know that the Jews want the annihilation [*Vernichtung*] of Germany."[2] Even after they were aware of the deportations and murders, they continued to justify mistreatment of the Jews on Christian grounds. In 1942, Walter Grundmann, professor of New Testament at the University of Jena and academic director of the Institute, declared: "A healthy Volk must and will reject the Jews in every form. This fact is justified before history and through history. If someone is upset about Germany's treatment of the Jews, Germany has the historical justification and historical authorization for the fight against the Jews on its side!"[3]

Of the several research institutes in Nazi Germany, this one had the largest membership of academics and the largest list of publications. That it was run by theologians is highly significant; the site of academic expertise on Judaism lay within Protestant theological faculties, particularly among New Testament scholars, who had some training in post-biblical Hebrew and Greek Jewish sources. It is worth noting that precisely those German scholars who trained in early Judaism during the 1920s became active members in the Institute: Paul Fiebig, Karl Georg Kuhn, Georg Bertram, and Georg Beer, among others.

The efforts of these theologians to synthesize Christianity with National Socialism should be seen as motivated by political opportunism, to be sure, but another factor was the internal crisis within liberal Protestant theology that welcomed Nazi racial theory as its solution. The crisis arose in the late nineteenth century, as liberal Protestant New Testament scholars sought to define the historical figure of Jesus and identify Christianity with the faith *of* Jesus, not the faith *about* Jesus. The discovery that the historical Jesus was a Jew whose teachings were identical to those of other rabbis of his day led to the problem of determining the uniqueness of Jesus and the boundary between liberal Protestantism and liberal Judaism, as Uriel Tal has delineated.[4] That problem motivated Protestant theologians to embrace racial theory: While the content of Jesus' message may have been identical to Judaism, his difference could be assured on racial grounds. Thus, serious theological debates about whether Jesus was a Jew or an Aryan began long before Hitler came to power. What was innovative about the Institute was its goal of radically revising Christian doctrine and liturgy as practiced in churches throughout the Reich and bringing them into accord with racial antisemitism.

The theologians' embrace of National Socialism was an unrequited affection. Hitler showed little interest in church affairs after 1934, and the hopes of theologians for positions of power and influence within the regime met with disappointment. When Reich Bishop Ludwig Müller delivered the eulogy in Eisenach at the funeral of Thuringian Bishop Martin Sasse on 31 August 1942, he described the situation: "When Bishop Sasse was consecrated as bishop eight years ago in this church, it was absolutely obvious that the higher representatives of the Party and the State would take part. Today there is hardly a brown-shirt to be seen in the church."[5] Yet the postwar historiography presents the Protestant church as the persecuted victim of the Nazi regime—as argued by Kurt Meier and John Conway, among others—or as theologically intact, thanks to the rigors of the German theological method—as argued by Trutz Rendtorff.[6]

Such claims have to be radically revised in light of the control attained by members of the German Christian Movement within most of the regional churches in Germany and within the university theological faculties. Any persecution the church may have experienced reflects primarily the regime's lack of interest in church affairs. For example, archival documents show that in 1935 the official representative of the theological faculties submitted several formal petitions requesting membership in the SS for theology students and pastors; the petition was rejected by Heinrich Himmler.[7] Other evidence reveals that in 1936, when Nazi Party officials ordered the swastika removed from church altars and the mastheads of church newspapers, numerous church officials protested, claiming that the swastika on the altar was a source of profound inspiration to churchgoers.[8] During the regime, church leaders might have complained of neglect, but they could hardly complain of persecution.

Origins of the Institute

In order to enhance the role of the church within National Socialism, the League for German Christianity (Bund für deutsches Christentum) met on 26 January 1938. Organized by Berlin Church superintendent Herbert Propp, it hoped to illustrate a massive show of church support for the regime.[9] The government's renewed interest in anti-Jewish measures that began in late 1937 provided a focus for the group. The group decided that a thorough dejudaization of the church would be part of Hitler's "world struggle against world Jewry" ("Weltkampf gegen das Weltjudentum").[10] Hugo Pich, a church superintendent in Thuringia, prepared the league's report during the summer of 1938: "The Führer of our Volk has now been called to lead an international fight against world Jewry. . . . In order to lead the National Socialist German struggle against world Jewry, the quick and thorough implementation of the dejudaization of the Christian church is of high and essential significance.

Only when the dejudaization of the Christian church is completed can the German people join in carrying out the fight of the Führer within its Christian membership and within its religious beliefs, and can the divine commission of the German Volk assist in its fulfillment."[11] Pich proposed that the work be carried out by a special office within the church that would supervise the dejudaization process.

Shortly after the *Kristallnacht* pogrom in November 1938, church headquarters in Berlin circulated Pich's proposal to the regional churches and received favorable responses. To give the plan a broad backing of support, the Godesberg Declaration was formulated in the spring of 1939, signed by leaders of most regional churches, and adopted as official church policy. It stated that National Socialism carried forward the work of Martin Luther and would lead the German people to a true understanding of Christian faith. The centerpiece of the declaration was the statement: "What is the relation between Judaism and Christianity? Is Christianity derived from Judaism and is it its continuation and completion, or does Christianity stand in opposition to Judaism? We answer this question: Christianity is the unbridgeable religious opposition to Judaism."[12] The declaration, signed by representatives of eleven regional churches, was printed in the official *Gesetzblatt* of the German Protestant Church with an addendum stating the church's intention to implement the declaration by establishing an Institute for the Study and Eradication of Jewish Influence on the Church Life of the German Volk.[13]

Bishop Sasse of Thuringia, an early member of the Nazi Party,[14] supported the proposal energetically. In response to *Kristallnacht,* he published a small pamphlet titled, "Martin Luther über die Juden: Weg mit Ihnen" ("Martin Luther on the Jews: Get Rid of Them"), in which he argued that the pogrom was fully in accord with Luther's own intentions. Luther, Sasse noted, had also called for synagogues and Jewish books to be burned, and the eradication of Judaism was, he argued, one of Luther's own goals for the Protestant Reformation. Sasse called for the establishment of a dejudaization research institute at the University of Jena in Thuringia, where the theological faculty was dominated by members of the German Christian Movement. However, the rector of the university, Karl Astel, professor of medicine and an ardent Nazi, opposed any expansion of the theological faculty, so no formal linkage with the university was made. Eventually, the Institute was housed in the church's training seminary in Eisenach, independent of the university, but it was run by members of the university faculty as well as local ministers who were leaders within the German Christian Movement.

Grand opening ceremonies took place on the afternoon of Saturday, 6 May 1939, in the old, historic Wartburg castle in which Luther had once taken refuge. Quartets by Mozart and Schubert, the reading of congratulatory telegrams, and learned speeches filled the program. Julius Streicher's attendance was prevented only by recent surgery; his telegram declared: "I am convinced your work will yield much good for our field."[15] The audience was welcomed by the Institute's nominal director, Siegfried Leffler, one of the original founders of the German Christian Movement, now serving in the Thuringian Ministry of Education. The president of the Prussian Protestant Church, Friedrich Werner, also attended and welcomed the Institute, expressing the hope that it would distance itself from theological special-interest groups and bring honor to German theological scholarship.[16] Grundmann, the academic director of the Institute, had served since 1936 as professor of New Testament and *völkisch* theology at the University of Jena. His address at the Institute's opening, "The Dejudaization of the Religious Life as the Task of German Theology and Church," set forth his aspirations: "The elimination of Jewish influence on German life is the urgent and fundamental question of the present German religious situation." Theological scholarship had made apparent the "deformation of New Testament ideas into Old Testament preconceptions, so that now angry recognition of the Jewishness in the Old Testament and in parts of the New Testament has arisen, obstructing access to the Bible for innumerable German people."[17] Grundmann's lecture was printed in six thousand copies and distributed through the German Christian Movement's publishing house, run by Heinz Dungs, an Institute member.[18]

Membership in the Institute was open and soon became large, even larger than published records indicate. More than fifty professors of theology at universities throughout the Reich joined, including many distinguished figures, as well as dozens of instructors and graduate students.[19] The Institute also listed about one hundred pastors and bishops as members. Having studied theology in the late 1920s and 1930s, Most members were too young to have fought during World War I, and most had shown their Nazi sympathies through early membership in the National Socialist German Workers Party (NSDAP), the German Christian Movement, or the SA. Many were trained in the field of New Testament studies and assumed they were experts in what they called "late Judaism"—a term used by scholars to designate Judaism during the centuries just before the advent of Christianity. Numerous pastors, religion teachers, and laypeople also joined. The Institute established at least one branch—in Rumania in 1942—and built an alliance with faculty and students in Scandinavia, led by Hugo Odeberg, a distinguished scholar of Judaica at the University of Lund. In 1941 Grundmann and Wolf Meyer-Erlach formed a working group, Germanentum und Christentum, which brought Scandinavian theologians and writers to participate in two annual conferences in Germany.[20] Odeberg took the initiative among the Scandinavians, inviting thirty academics, students, and writers from Sweden, Norway, and Denmark to lecture at the conferences, which were held in Weissenfels and in Eisenach. Impressed by the high quality of scholarship practiced by Institute members, Odeberg sent seven Scandinavian students to Jena to write doctoral dissertations under Grundmann.

Work of the Institute

Of all the so-called research institutes that flourished during the Nazi era, the Eisenach Dejudaization Institute (Entjudungsinstitut), as the Institute was informally called during its heyday, proved the most prolific and had the largest membership. Its members were divided into working groups, rapidly producing publications. The Institute's dejudaized version of the New Testament, *Die Botschaft Gottes,* first appeared in 1940, and together with a small, abridged version, eventually sold around two hundred thousand copies."

A dejudaized hymnal, *Grosser Gott Wir Loben Dich,* also appeared in 1940, to great commercial success; and a catechism, *Deutsche mit Gott: Ein deutsches Glaubensbuch,* was published in 1941 to summarize the Institute's theological principles. All were sold to churches throughout the Reich, in small towns and villages as well as cities. Each eliminated Hebrew words, references to the Old Testament, and any links between Jesus and Judaism. For example, the hymnal expunged words such as *amen, hallelujah, Hosanna,* and *Zebaoth,* while the New Testament eliminated Jesus' descent from David, and the catechism proclaimed: "Jesus of Nazareth in the Galilee demonstrates in his message and behavior a spirit which is opposed in every way to that of Judaism. The fight between him and the Jews became so bitter that it led to his crucifixion. So Jesus cannot have been a Jew. Until today the Jews persecute Jesus and all who follow him with unreconcilable hatred. By contrast, Aryans in particular can find answers in him to their ultimate questions. So he became the savior of the Germans."[21]

The Institute's publications were not the first efforts to produce dejudaized Christian liturgical materials. For example, Bishop Heinz Weidemann of Bremen issued a dejudaized New Testament, composed with the assistance of the noted theologian Emanuel Hirsch.[22] Reich Bishop Müller issued a "germanized" version of the Sermon on the Mount in 1936 to eliminate what he considered inappropriate Jewish moral teachings.[23] Yet those publications were generally limited to local church usage, whereas the Institute's publications were in far more widespread use; one hundred thousand copies of both the *Die Botschaft Gottes* and *Grosser Gott Wir Loben Dich* were printed in the first edition to fill prepublication orders from parish churches throughout the Reich.[24]

Thanks to the success of its publications and to generous donations from regional churches, funneled through Berlin church headquarters, the Institute never suffered financially. Indeed, in 1943, the only year for which its accounts are extant, the Institute had a surplus income.[25] The Institute's costs were, in fact, minimal. It did not pay expenses for participants in its conferences; pastors who attended were reimbursed for travel expenses by their regional churches, since the conferences were considered to be work related.[26] Members drew their salaries as church officials, pastors, or university professors, not as contributors to the Institute. The publications of the Institute were generally self-supporting, printed by Dungs, an active Institute member who was also director of the German Christian Publishing House (Verlag Deutsche Christen), with headquarters in Weimar. The Institute itself was located rent-free in the large and elegant villa that housed the training seminary (*Prediger-seminar*) in Eisenach. A few surviving records, including financial receipts and letters, indicate extra financial contributions from church headquarters in Berlin and from regional bishops.[27] Relations with government ministries remained positive. Meyer-Erlach, professor of practical theology at the University of Jena and one of the leading forces within the Institute, was sent to lecture German troops during the war years; he explained that they were fighting a war against world Jewry.[28] Even England, he argued, had been judaized as a consequence of its Protestant Reformation, which placed too much emphasis on the Old Testament, and as a result it was waging war against Germany.

In addition to its liturgical materials, the Institute sponsored conferences and published books and articles delineating its view of Christian theology and history. The conferences were held in town halls and universities throughout the Reich, opening and closing with hymns, prayers, and the Nazi salute and attracting anywhere from thirty to six hundred participants. Most of its publications emphasized the degeneration, after the eighth century B.C.E., of Judaism, which supposedly reached its nadir during the second temple period; Judaism's final and utter destruction was the mission of Jesus. The degeneracy of Judaism served to explain why God sent Jesus and why the Jews failed to recognize him as divine; it also served to highlight the extraordinary nature of Jesus' own religious personality, compared with the Jews.

Jesus as Anti-Jewish

At one of the Institute's first conferences, held in July 1939, Heinz Eisenhuth, professor of systematic theology at the University of Jena, explained "The Meaning of the Bible for Faith." He argued that Luther's translation of the Bible had transmitted the meaning of the gospel for the German people, but new historical-critical scholarship would refine Luther's understanding. The tie between German Christians and the Bible was not legalistic, but ethical: "*Völkish* ethics also need an inner religious foundation." The Old Testament, however, was the expression of a racially foreign soul and a non-Christian religion.[29] Jewish influence had infiltrated Germany not only through the Old Testament, but also through secularization processes. Spinoza was one example of such a nefarious Jewish influence, explained Martin Redeker, professor of systematic theology at the University of Kiel. "Just as the Jew does not know and see the living God and his will, but only the Torah, the law, and its development in the Talmud, so for Spinoza nature is not a living reality, but rather he sees only rigid natural laws and seeks to explain them. Natural law takes the place of divine law for him. Jews lack the awe before nature that Germans have, and the sense of being bound up with nature; [the Jew] stands cold in relation to nature. The German experiences God as being in the background of all events and affecting all events; for the Jew there isn't this view of faith behind the superficiality of life and history, for him there is only the visible, material world."[30]

Exposing the dangers of the Jews for German society continued to be a major theme at Institute-sponsored conferences. At a meeting held in July 1941, the writer Wilhelm Kotzde-Kottenrodt argued that Jews had eliminated God from the world ("Juda hat die Welt entgottet"); they are unable to understand the higher thoughts of Nordics—that the world is filled with God. The Old Testament itself is an unreliable document, since Jews have used and distorted it to their own purposes through the centuries.[31]

The Institute's publications tried to prove that the Jews had always been aggressive and threatening. The Maccabees were cited as an example, as were the Hasmoneans generally, and the Zealots. Judaism continued to be violent and dangerous; Jesus' goal was clear: to save the world and fight against Judaism.[32] Subtle perversions of society characterize Judaism; Bertram argued that from Philo to the present day, Jewish assimilation had the goal of decomposing a society and then taking control over it.[33]

In their discussions of how to dejudaize Christianity, Institute members debated how to define Judaism. Eisenhuth argued that the entire Old Testament, including the prophetic literature, should be eliminated, while the New Testament should be purged of all texts except the four Gospels—Paul being considered a Jewish theologian. Heinz Hunger, a pastor who served as business director of the Institute, argued that dejudaization consisted of removing the gestalt of the Jew ("Entjudung heisse nur Ausmerzung der Gestalt des Juden"). Friedrich Wienecke, one of the German Christian leaders in Berlin, identified Jewishness with Pharisaism, in which depravity is religiously embellished and profane institutions like the stock market are transformed into religion—the "Jewish Trick." Wienecke was supported by Redeker and Grundmann. Redeker emphasized the materialist influence of the Jews on German society, even on some major theological figures, such as Karl Barth.[34]

The purging of everything Jewish from Christianity that was proposed by Institute members was perceived by many as radical and illegitimate. Grundmann defended his proposals by arguing that "[j]ust as people couldn't imagine Christianity without the Pope during the time of Luther, so, too, they can't imagine salvation without the Old Testament."[35] Dejudaizing Christianity was simply a continuation of the Reformation.

The problem of removing "Judaism" from Christianity was theologically complex. According to Grundmann, the very concept of God is radically different in Judaism and Christianity: "The Jewish concept of God is fundamentally determined through the Vergeltungsgedanken: God is the Judge who repays men. But Jesus sees God as One who forgives, in order to generate community."[36] The distinction is not an accident; Jesus undertook a fight against Yahweh as a tribal God and against Judaism.[37] In the Sermon on the Mount, Grundmann argued, Jesus expresses a sense of community between God and human beings, and elsewhere Jesus addresses God in intimate terms, as *Abba*, father, rather than the Hebrew term, *Yahweh*. Grundmann devoted a book to discussing the ethical implications of the divine relationship with humanity in Christ.[38] He concluded that Jesus introduced a new understanding of God and of divine expectations of human beings, a new situational ethic that overrode commandments such as the prohibition against murder. Jesus' authority was rooted in himself, rather than in the Bible, and it was insignificant that Jesus cited the prophets and psalms of the Old Testament, because "so much more that is in the Old Testament was not cited by Jesus."[39] Rather than being bound by the Old Testament's laws and commandments, which represent a Jewish outlook, Christians are to follow Jesus' example and make moral decisions by listening to the religiosity of their own hearts, which transcends commandments, even those prohibiting murder. Grundmann wrote: "With the proclamation of the kingdom of God as present, a new experience of God and a new understanding of God were linked. Internally, it had nothing to do with Judaism, but meant the dissolution of the Jewish religious world. That should be recognizable from the fact alone that the Jews brought Jesus Christ to the cross."[40]

Jesus as Aryan

The German Christians liked to claim that their mission was not to create a new Christianity, but to provide a Christianity appropriate to the German people. Christian missionaries in other parts of the world had not hesitated to synthesize elements intrinsic to the native culture with Christian beliefs and liturgies, and native Germanic expressions should be similarly included in a German Christianity, they argued. What is striking, however, is how they defined those native Germanic expressions: "German" was equated with the elimination of everything "Jewish." While purging Hebrew words from the liturgy or Scriptures was a fairly easy task, the greater problem was what to do with Gospel accounts describing Jesus as a Jew. What role could there be for a Jewish savior in a religion of German Christianity? Opening his address to the Institute's conference in March 1941, Grundmann, who served as academic director of the Institute, declared, "Our Volk, which stands above all else in a struggle against the satanic powers of world Jewry for the order and life of this world, dismisses Jesus, because it cannot struggle against the Jews and open its heart to the king of the Jews."[41]

That assumption was false, Grundmann argued; Jesus was not a Jew at all, but the great enemy of the Jews. Of Galilean, not Judean, origin, Jesus was "with the greatest probability" a member of one of the foreign peoples living in northern Palestine since the Assyrian conquest in the eighth century B.C.E., most likely an Aryan.[42] That Jesus was an Aryan was not a new idea; it had already been proposed during the nineteenth century by some German philosophers and scholars. Johann Fichte, in his *Addresses to the German Nation*, suggested that Jesus may not have been of Jewish origin, given that his genealogy is omitted in the Gospel of John.[43] The rise of racial theory in the nineteenth century provided a new vocabulary, allowing scholars such as Ernest Renan to distinguish between a Semitic Old Testament and an Aryan New Testament.[44] Renan sought to prove that Christianity was not Semitic in origin, because Jesus came from the northern Galilee, rather than Judea;[45] Jesus' Galilean origins provided a popular motif for German scholars writing on the life of Jesus in the 1860s and 1870s.[46]

Friedrich Delitzsch added the further suggestion that after the Assyrian conquest, the Galilee had been resettled with Babylonians of mixed Aryan descent.[47] Paul de Lagarde, one of Germany's great Semitic scholars, rejected Christianity's traditional understanding of Jesus as Jew as an "intolerable distortion."[48] Jesus was no Jew, but a rebel against Judaism who deliberately called himself a Son of man to escape any association with the Jews. In another kind of approach, Edmond Picard argued in 1899 that Jesus must have been an Aryan because of his antipathy to capitalism, the tool of the Jews.[49] Houston Stewart Chamberlain gave widespread popularity to the idea that Jesus was racially Aryan, and German professors of Protestant theology in the 1910s and 1920s found themselves debating the issue, granting the claim even greater legitimacy.[50] Ernst Lohmeyer developed the theory of a two-site origin of early Christianity: Galilee, where a universalistic, son-of-man eschatology prevailed, and Jerusalem, dominated by nationalistic, Jewish eschatology.[51] Rudolf Otto had made a similar claim, based on his phenomenological observations of Jewish and Christian religiosity.[52]

In his 1940 study of Jesus, *Jesus der Galiläer und das Judentum,* Grundmann was thus able to conclude that Jesus' rejection of the Jewish title of "messiah" in favor of the title 'Son of man' proved his Galilean, and thus his Aryan, origin. Although Grundmann declared Jesus to have been an Aryan, the troubling problem remained: to account for Jewish concepts and texts, attributed to Jesus, within the very body of the New Testament. But the explanation was simple: The image and message of Jesus had been falsified by the early Jewish Christians, who presented Jesus as "the fulfiller of the law and the new teacher of law, only sent to the house of Israel."[53] Furthermore, the Jews expected a messiah who would be their ruler, whereas Jesus' message was to be a server of God and the community.[54] Johannes Hempel, professor of Old Testament at the University of Berlin and one of the early organizers of the Institute, argued that Jesus' monotheism broke with the Old Testament's henotheism and that he similarly universalized the promise of salvation.[55]

The Institute took the argument a step further as it sought recognition within the institutional church. Grundmann argued that Jewish motifs in the New Testament represent falsifications of the original text, introduced by early Jewish Christians to distort the tradition in order to make Christianity serve the purposes of Judaism. Correcting this error was a suitable task for the German New Testament scholars, who were considered the finest in the world, fully capable of emending the biblical text to remove Jewish elements. As Gerhard Kittel's students, Grundmann, Bertram, and other leaders of the Institute were considered experts on Judaism, though their work shows limited awareness of the Hebrew Jewish sources of antiquity and a very narrow reading of Greek Jewish sources.

The eradication of Jewish influences from Christianity was viewed, in other words, as a restoration of the original message of Jesus and a recovery of his historical personage. Not the Aryan Jesus, but the Jewish Jesus was the falsification; the sophistication of modern theology's historical-critical methods finally enabled this recognition and the reformation of church life it engendered. Far from being a threat to religious faith, National Socialism was viewed as a great opportunity for the revival of true Christianity.[56]

The Theological Faculty at the University of Jena

Most of the theological faculties at German universities included professors who were supporters of the German Christian movement, or even members of the Institute, and they inevitably brought their anti-Jewish viewpoints to their scholarship and teaching. In some cases, such professors dominated and controlled the theological curricula. The faculty at the University of Jena, located just a short distance from the Institute's headquarters in Eisenach, was highly politicized, and the theologians were no exception. The theological faculty at Jena strove to create, in the words of one of its professors, Wolf Meyer-Erlach, "a stronghold of National Socialism."[57] To that end, only Nazi supporters were appointed professors, student dissertations had to comply with Nazi racial theory, and "Jewish" topics such as Hebrew language were eliminated. Several other theological faculties had also abolished the study of Hebrew or made Old Testament studies optional. In 1938, Grundmann urged eliminating the study of Hebrew from the curriculum at the University of Jena because, he argued, the early Christians had read the Greek Bible and because the Greek text of the Old Testament is older than the extant Hebrew manuscripts; the decision to make Hebrew study optional was announced by the dean, Eisenhuth, on 1 April 1939.[58]

Both Grundmann and Eisenhuth were appointed to the faculty in 1936. According to the recommendation written by Meyer-Erlach, who was then serving as rector of the university, Eisenhuth was "unquestionably a reliable party member who, out of deepest convictions, stands true to the Führer and to the Movement and with greatest earnestness works to bring a decisive recognition of National Socialism to his discipline."[59] Similarly, Meyer-Erlach recommended Grundmann as a longtime member of the NSDAP who expressed his loyalty to National Socialism in his theological scholarship, which "will be path-breaking for a National Socialist perspective in the field of theology."[60] On 17 December 1937, Eisenhuth was appointed tenured professor, on orders signed by Hitler. Identical orders making Grundmann a tenured professor were signed by Hitler on 5 October 1938.

This politicization involved students as well as faculty. Several students were active members of the Institute and used the Jena faculty to promote their antisemitism. During the Nazi era, approximately thirty-six students submitted doctoral dissertations in theology at Jena; of these, twelve were written under Grundmann's direction. Ten of the thirty-six were rejected, all on grounds that they had not paid sufficient attention to issues of race. Doctoral dissertations in theology frequently treated topics concerning Christianity's relationship to National Socialism, and the faculty evaluated student work on political grounds.

For example, although one student had been an active member of the NSDAP since 1931, his dissertation, "Notwendiger Christ," claimed that Jesus' ideas must be understood within an Old Testament context. It was rejected. Meyer-Erlach explained, "The theologian lacks the understanding of National Socialism that the racial question is the fundamental question for everything."[61] On the other hand, the 1941 dissertation by another student, on "Präexistenz und Unsterblichkeit," received a mixed review from Grundmann: "The author observes correctly that Judaism took over its ideas about the preexistence and immortality of the human soul from other perspectives and religions. This, however, did not lead him to the fundamental observation of the spiritual unproductivity of Judaism. . . . Judaism represents a level of human spirituality that has been left behind . . . and which has degenerate effects on higher perspectives."[62] A third student, although himself a member of the Institute as well as of the NSDAP, had to make revisions in his 1942 dissertation, "Die Wandlung der katholischen Kirche in ihrer Stellung zur Judenfrage seit der französischen Revolution," ("Transformation of the Catholic Church in Its Position Regarding the Jewish Question since the French Revolution") because he gave too much credit to the Roman Catholics for developing antisemitism, thereby unfairly denying adequate credit to the Protestants.[63]

The theological faculty at Jena was small, and the dominance of leading figures from the Institute fulfilled Meyer-Erlach's goal of creating a "stronghold of National Socialism." Through their academic work, Institute members were able to transform their antisemitic ideas into respectable teachings of Christian theology. Through theological faculties, the antisemitic Christian theology of the Nazi era was transmitted to the next generation of ministers and theologians.

The Final Years

The distinguished church historian Kurt Meier has argued that the Institute was established to defend Christianity against Nazism.[64] There is, however, no evidence that the churches were in any danger of being dissolved by the regime, nor does Meier's claim explain the enormous enthusiasm with which Institute members set about their tasks of dejudaizing Christianity. On the contrary, Institute members seem to have been sincerely committed to the work they were undertaking, even when it failed to achieve the anticipated goals. An exchange of letters between Grundmann and Institute member H. J. Thilo, written in November 1942, makes clear that Grundmann's commitment to Aryan Christianity overrode his commitment to Christianity: "I cannot go back to the old church . . . thus there remains nothing else but to go humbly into the corner and take up other work as a German literature scholar or historian."[65] Disappointed by the failure of the German Christian Movement to achieve its hoped-for recognition by the regime, Grundmann expressed his confidence that the Institute at least had broad popular support among German soldiers in a letter to another Institute member, Gerhard Delling, who was serving in 1942 as a military chaplain.[66] In this correspondence, Grundmann appears aware that his Christian support for National Socialism was an unrequited affection.

When Grundmann was drafted in the fall of 1943, he was replaced as director of the Institute by Bertram. Even as growing numbers of Germans came to believe that they would not win the war, and as Goebbels' total war propaganda became less and less convincing, Carl Schneider, a member of the Institute and professor at the University of Königsberg, called for an even more radical dejudaization of Christian theology, redefining early Christianity as itself an antisemitic movement. Bertram supported this in his report to Institute members in March 1944, where he described his goals as director: "'This war is the fight of the Jews against Europe.'" This sentence contains a truth, which is over and over confirmed by the research work of the Institute. However this work serves not only as a head-on attack, but also as a strengthening of the inner front to attack and defend against all clandestine Judaism and Jewish essence which has seeped into occidental culture during the course of the centuries."[67]

In the summer of 1944, church superintendent Pich, whose 1938 report had served as the basis for establishing the Institute, sent a proposal to church officials for a more thorough dejudaization of the Scriptures, titled "The Jew Saul and his Proclamation of Christ." Pich called for a thorough overhaul of the Pauline epistles, arguing they were infected with Jewish notions that had contaminated Christianity. But by this time both church and Institute officials were unsympathetic, given the war conditions.[68] Moreover, one German Christian church official argued, Pich's proposal would imply that for many centuries the church had been held hostage by a Jew: "I consider Pich's statements totally misguided and moreover an insult to our Volk, whom one indirectly insults by saying that in its miserable narrowness and lack of instinct for fifteen hundred years it was duped into servility by some stinking Jew."[69]

It is noteworthy that even at the end of the war, Institute members did not give up their efforts. In May of 1945, as Thuringia fell under Allied occupation, Bertram petitioned the Thuringian church, now run by former members of the Confessing Church, to retain the Institute on the grounds that its work was "neither politically determined, nor expressed politically." Rather, its goal was to demonstrate scientifically that "Jesus had taken up a fight against Judaism in all sharpness and had fallen as victim to [his fight]."[70] The Church Council of Thuringia met with Bertram on 24 May 1945 to decide whether the Institute should be retained as a research center. According to the minutes of the meeting, Pastor von Nitzsch thanked Bertram for his work but stated that such a worldwide project could not be supported by the small church of Thuringia. Church counsel Büchner stated the importance of retaining the

Institute, especially since the theological library at the University of Jena had been damaged by the bombings. Moritz Mitzenheim, soon to become bishop of Thuringia, urged dissolution of the Institute but retention of its property. Church counsel Phieler wanted the Institute retained but its goals changed to a historical study of the Luther Bible and its effects on German culture and the Protestant people. On 31 May 1945, Phieler wrote to Bertram with the decision that the Institute would not be reopened. Bertram was thanked for his service but rejected for future work within the Thuringian church.[71] He returned to Giessen.[72]

In the fall of 1945, Grundmann returned from a Russian prisoner-of-war camp and appealed to church officials to maintain the Institute, arguing that since non-German scholars had arrived at the same conclusions, the work of the Institute could not be seen as merely reflecting "tendencies of the era" ("Zeittendenzen") but was the result of serious scholarship that should be continued.[73] He explained that the Institute's research had concluded that Jesus was independent of the Old Testament and stood in opposition to the Judaism of his day. Moreover, he wrote, the Institute's goal had been to defend Christianity against National Socialism: "The National Socialist system led the fight against Christianity with all legal means at its disposal.' In the eyes of the Nazis, he continued, "Christianity is of Jewish origin, is Judaism for Aryans and must therefore be rooted out. As spiritual Judaism it poisons the German soul."[74] The Institute, Grundmann concluded, was a defense of the church.

But Grundmann's argument produced no effect, and his proposal to maintain the Institute was rejected in January of 1946. One church official, who shortly thereafter was appointed to the professorship in practical theology at the University of Jena once held by Meyer-Erlach, wrote that he regretted the curtailment of Grundmann's scholarship, which he respected, but that the church could not retain the Institute.[75] The Institute was closed, its extensive library was incorporated into the Thuringian ministerial training seminar (Predigerseminar), and the liturgical materials it had published were no longer used. Readings from the Old Testament were reintroduced into church services after the war, but no official condemnation of the Institute's antisemitism was ever issued by the Thuringian church.

Most institute members continued their careers unhampered after the war. Grundmann, Meyer-Erlach, and Eisenhuth lost their professorships at the University of Jena because of their early membership in the NSDAP, but all were given positions of distinction within the postwar church. Jena replaced them with other Institute members, Herbert Preisker and Rudolf Meyer. Other Institute professors and instructors retained their academic positions. Georg Bertram moved from Giessen to Frankfurt, Gerhard Delling left Leipzig for Greifswald, Rudi Paret left Heidelberg for Bonn and then Tübingen. Martin Redeker remained at Kiel, Johannes Leipoldt at Leipzig, Wilhelm Koepp at Greifswald, Fritz Wilke and Gustav Entz at Vienna. Other members who retained their professorships include Johannes Hempel, Hartmut Schmoekel, and Carl Schneider, among others. Grundmann, who had joined the NSDAP in December 1930, protested the loss of his professorship in a letter to the new rector, claiming that he had been not a perpetrator but rather the victim of a struggle by the Nazi party against his work and his person.[76]

Grundmann's return to the church came as a result of support from state officials. In January 1946, state officials in Thuringia had refused Grundmann's request for support in securing a church position.[77] Less than a year later, however, they reversed their stance. In the fall of 1946, the state urged Grundmann's retention by the church on the grounds that he had waged a "manly struggle" *against* National Socialist ideology. Testimony came from Grundmann's erstwhile colleagues, Eisenhuth and Meyer-Erlach, who declared that Grundmann had been persecuted by anti-Christian Nazi officials. His early membership in the NSDAP was dismissed as the error of an "unworldly" theologian who recognized his mistake soon after 1933. His value as an internationally recognized scholar was cited by pointing to his membership in the distinguished Society of New Testament Studies, which had offered him membership in 1938.

Like so many other leaders of the German Christians, Grundmann emerged from the denazification process relatively unscrutinized. Yet his Nazi-era activities were known to East German officials. As late as 1990 an East German secret police (*Stasi*) document lists his name among other Nazi supporters and war criminals who had eluded responsibility by receiving a church position. Gerhard Besier suggests that the information was used by the *Stasi* to control Grundmann.[78]

Few members of the Institute expressed any public repentance for their Nazi-era activities. In the later years of their lives, both Meyer-Erlach and Grundmann continued to present themselves as persecuted victims of the Nazi regime. Meyer-Erlach claimed that "despite threats and temptations," he had never abandoned the church and that he had "fought the Party" in his writings. Further, he had been mocked by regime officials because his name, Meyer, sounded Jewish and because he had once attended a synagogue service in Würzburg in 1929, which had led Nazi officials to mock him as "der Synagoge-Meyer."[79] He was no antisemite, he further stated, since he retained his Jewish family physician until November 1933 and once permitted a Jewish doctor to operate on two of his children.

By contrast, Grundmann's postwar defenses do not even mention anti-semitism, and in his 1969 unpublished autobiography he barely acknowledges that he erred during the Third Reich: "We attempted to pose the questions raised by the period and not to avoid them. I admit that in so doing we made [big (this word is crossed out in the manuscript)] mistakes." While most of the materials pertaining to Grundmann's denazification remain closed, he writes in his autobiography that he had stood in real danger of Nazi retribution as the result of his writings criticizing Alfred Rosenberg.[80] In meetings with church officials of Thuringia in late 1945, to clear himself of any Nazi suspicions, Grundmann had insisted that his fundamental commitment to Christ never wavered during the Nazi years. Church leaders asked him to express an acceptance of the Barmen Declaration as a sign that he accepted the ultimate sovereignty of Christ, rather than political leadership. Grundmann agreed. He was never asked to repudiate antisemitism, nor did he ever mention the Holocaust in his postwar publications.

In subsequent years Grundmann was appointed rector of the seminary in Thuringia that trained religion teachers and church organists, he taught at the ministerial seminary in Leipzig, and he served as adviser to the Protestant publishing house of the German Democratic Republic, a powerful position. He also continued to publish extensively and his commentaries on the Synoptic Gospels became highly regarded reference works in the postwar theological communities of East and West Germany. Shortly before his death in 1976, he was appointed *Kirchenrat* of Thuringia, an honorary position that indicates the esteem with which he was regarded by the postwar church in East Germany. Meyer-Erlach also escaped serious retribution for his antisemitism and his support of the Nazi regime. On the contrary, by January 1962, now living in Hesse, he received the Federal Republic of Germany's award, the *Verdienstkreuz*, First Class.[81]

Church Opposition to the Institute

The Institute was not without its critics within the church. The so-called church struggle refers to the ongoing clash for control of the church that developed between two Protestant factions, the German Christian Movement and the Confessing Church. Members of the Confessing Church came from a more conservative theological tradition that objected to alterations in the biblical text, liturgy, and catechism, although many were sympathetic to the Hitler regime. Their opposition to the Institute and its theology was based on its radical changes of traditional Christian teachings and was not directed primarily against its antisemitism. Indeed, Wolfgang Gerlach has documented the failure of the Confessing Church to take a stand in support of Jews other than those who had already converted to Christianity, and he has also exposed the theological anti-Judaism in the writings of many Confessing Church theologians.[82] For example, the Godesberg Declaration of April 1939, which created the Institute, evoked Confessing Church hostility and resulted in a counterdeclaration. However, that document—issued on 31 May 1939 and signed by leading neutral bishops, including Theophil Wurm (Württemberg), Hans Meiser (Bavaria), and August Marahrens (Hanover)—showed little respect for Jews or Judaism: "In the realm of faith there exists the sharp opposition between the message of Jesus Christ and his apostles and the Jewish religion of legalism and political messianic hope, which is already emphatically fought against in the Old Testament. In the realm of the *völkisch* life an earnest and responsible racial politics is required for the preservation of the purity of our people."[83] As argued in this statement, elimination of the Old Testament is unnecessary because it is not a Jewish book, but an anti-Jewish book. Racial policies are acceptable and necessary, according to these bishops, and Christianity stands in opposition to Judaism, as the Godesberg Declaration had also formulated.

Opposition to the Institute's publications also came from some of Grundmann's colleagues in the field of New Testament studies who sided with the Confessing Church. For example, Grundmann's 1940 study of Jesus' racial background, *Jesus der Galiläer,* which argued that Jesus could not have been a Jew, was reviewed negatively by Hans von Soden, professor of New Testament and church history at the University of Marburg and an active member of the Confessing Church.[84] Yet von Soden simply argued that the racial question was theologically irrelevant and criticized Grundmann for his sloppy scholarship; he did not fault Grundmann's negative presentation of Judaism.[85]

Most striking in the Confessing Church opposition to German Christian measures is the negative attitude toward Judaism shared by both sides. For example, in a pamphlet issued by the Confessing Church in 1939 to repudiate the Institute, von Soden distinguished between the historical phenomenon of Judaism, which formed the basis of early Christianity, and a spiritual "Jewishness," which fails to understand religion because it "confuses outward and inward." This "Jewishness," he wrote, "shudders before every Hebrew word in the liturgy or hymnal, but has itself fallen victim to the Jewish anti-Christian spirit."[86] The German Christian Movement was infected with this "Jewishness," according to von Soden, an infection illustrated by the dejudaization efforts called for in the Godesberg Declaration. That is, trying to dejudaize Christianity by banning the Old Testament and rewriting the hymnal and New Testament actually threatened "a spiritual Judaization" of the church. While von Soden, along with the majority of Confessing Church members, vigorously opposed German Christian measures, they agreed with the basic assumption that Judaization represented a real threat to Christianity. The difference between the two groups lay in their definition of what constitutes Judaization. For von Soden, the threat came not from the Old Testament, Hebrew words, and other elements within traditional Christian theology, but from what he saw as an antispiritual, materialistic theology promoted by Grundmann and his German Christian colleagues.

The response of the Confessing Church represents a tradition that does not repudiate antisemitism, but redefines it. Judaism is a recognizable religion that can be debated, opposed, or accepted. Jewishness, however, was seen as an evil that potentially can afflict all people, even Christians, and must therefore be opposed with the strongest means available. Just as German antisemitism toward the end of the nineteenth century considered the greatest danger to be assimilated Jews, because they could inflict a nefarious influence before they were ever recognized as Jews, this tradition of antisemitism feared that Jewishness could infiltrate Christian theology and poison it. The great danger for modern Christian anti-Judaism was not its opposition to the *religion* of Judaism, nor to Jews themselves, but rather the imaginary danger associated with the loosely defined but far more threatening concept of "Jewishness."

Historiographical Observations

The history of the Institute calls into question postwar interpretations of developments in the Protestant church during the Third Reich. The relatively few studies of the German Christian Movement have not examined its effective exploitation of antisemitism after 1938 to gain adherents and win support from the Nazi regime. Through the Institute, the German Christians achieved an effective structure for disseminating their theology and avoiding disintegration after the onset of the war. Moreover, the German Christian Movement can no longer be considered an insignificant element within the church, given the support it won through the Institute from professors of theology at prominent German universities and the popularity of its liturgical materials among churches throughout the Reich. The Institute's effectiveness is also shown by the individuals who at first kept themselves at a distance from the German Christians but who eventually became supporters of the Institute, such as Werner.

How should the Institute's relation to the Nazi regime be evaluated? On the one hand, viewing the Institute primarily as a creation of Nazi antisemitic ideology would sever its links to pre-1933 theological tendencies and would not explain why church members found its theology respectable. On the other hand, without the Third Reich and its intensification of anti-Jewish policies after 1938, German Christian leaders might well have developed a different ideology; they clearly realized antisemitism would be politically advantageous. The Institute made effective use of traditional Christian anti-Judaism to support Nazi policy, offering theologians for the service of the regime. Institute membership included a few well-known theologians, but also a large number of less-well-known but still influential scholars in all fields of theology representing universities from throughout the Reich. Finally, it is significant that Institute associates continued to work within the churches and university theological faculties after 1945. Many records of the churches' denazification proceedings remain closed to scholars; examining them would help determine just how admissible the Institute's theology remained even after the Third Reich collapsed.

The conventional treatment of the German Christians as a marginal phenomenon within the German churches is called into question by the accomplishments of the Institute. Its popular and academic publications, their wide distribution to churches throughout the Reich, and the representation on Institute membership rolls from the ranks of university faculties and church hierarchies all indicate that the German Christians attained a higher level of influence than has been previously recognized. Finally, the Institute's theology should be analyzed as a phenomenon parallel to Nazism itself, that is, one with roots within the history of German antisemitism and Christian theological anti-Judaism, taken to radical extremes out of both genuine conviction and the quest for political power. Within Christianity, the Institute undertook the goals of National Socialism: As the Nazi regime was creating an Aryan Germany, the Institute was creating an Aryan Christianity.

Conclusion

What motivated the Institute's members to seek the eradication of Jewish influence on German religious life? Two factors predominated. First, there were purely political interests: Nazi antisemitic policies were defined as Christian and given the support of the church, with the hope that the Nazi regime would respond by giving its support to the church. If the Nazis wanted a *Judenrein* Germany, the church would create a *Judenrein* Christianity. Church leaders never gave any thought of opposition to Nazi antisemitism, even though they were uncomfortable with some of the regime's other policies. On the so-called Jewish question, the church's response should be measured not in degrees of resistance, but of enthusiasm.

Second, for many German theologians racial theory was a gift, a way to solve a central dilemma raised by historical Jesus scholarship. Since the nineteenth century, New Testament historians had examined the gospels within the context of first-century Judaism and discovered that Jesus' teachings were not new, but repeated ideas common to the rabbis of his day. Yet that recognition led to a crisis: What was original and unique about Jesus and Christianity? One way of solving that dilemma was to draw on racial theory, insisting that although Jesus' teachings may not have been Jewish, his racial identity was Aryan, thus marking his difference from the Jews. Jesus' use of Jewish teachings, Institute members argued, did not demonstrate his Jewishness, but his clever manipulation of the enemies' ideas against them.

For some historians today, the Institute's activities remain a marginal phenomenon, limited to a small group of theologians. Yet the issue is not so much how many individuals were involved in the Institute, but how large a role was played by the collective literature they produced. To what extent did the Institute's theologians, by means of their epistemological tools and sense of scholarly and moral purpose as theologians, helped to effect the Nazification of Germany theologically?[87] At issue is not only the Nazi politics of each individual theologian, his party or SA membership, or whether his scholarship directly shaped Nazi decisions regarding the murder of the Jews, but the nature of the larger theological discourse Institute members helped to create. Theologians from a wide range of political backgrounds, ranging from Bultmann and Barth to Kittel and Grundmann, shaped a theologically based ideology of the degeneracy of "Judentum"—a German term designating Judaism, the Jews, and Jewishness. Their position as scholars gave their ideology the masquerade of Wissenschaft, giving substance to the politics and rhetoric of the state. As Sheldon Pollock has pointed out in his study of similar developments within the field of Indology in Germany, scholars produced "objective truth" that they asserted was independent of political interests and values. Whether theologians after 1933 were motivated by opportunism or cynicism is far less important than the role played by a broad group of theologians before and after the advent of Hitler. Theological Wissenschaft produced an accepted knowledge of "Judaism," and the imprimatur of Wissenschaft provided a warrant of objective truth that constituted it as scholarship. Under the protection of such claims, Protestant theologians could use Wissenschaft to disguise the racism of their depictions of "Judaism" as objective truth rooted in scholarship. After a while, it was no longer clear whether New Testament scholarship was a search for the historical Jesus and the origins of Christianity, or a scholarly legitimation of antisemitism and an ideological legitimation of National Socialism. The goals became so intertwined that at a certain point they could no longer be separated.

Postwar New Testament scholarship in Germany did not make a clean break with the theological writings of the Nazi era. While postwar German scholars may not have been self-consciously racist, many continued working within some of the same parameters as the literature produced by the Institute. Although certain terms, such as "Aryan," were dropped, the presentation of a degenerate Judaism that was anathema to Jesus remained vivid in postwar publications. Such continuities with the Third Reich are not surprising, since the halfhearted denazification program allowed most members of the Institute to retain their teaching posts, as well as their positions of authority within the church, so that they continued to train a new generation of ministers and theologians.

Friedrich Wilhelm Marquardt has analyzed in detail the use of Nazi language in the postwar writings of several major postwar theologians, including Gunter Bornkamm, Günter Klein, and Karl Barth.[88] Marquardt notes that Bornkamm, in his book on Paul, describes the "aggressive vehemence" of Paul's critique of Judaism as a "machine gun." In his 1956 book, *Jesus of Nazareth*, Bornkamm compares Jesus' aggressive assault on the Judaism of his day to that of the Nazis. Similar examples can be found in religious best-sellers in Germany, by Gerda Weiler, Christa Mulack, and Franz Alt, among others. Suggestions that Judaism is a violent religion, to which Jesus was opposed, repeats themes popularized by the Institute; what is new is that postwar writers claim that Judaism is analogous to National Socialism and even responsible for the blind obedience to authority that led to genocide.

On the other hand, the Holocaust has sparked other New Testament scholars in Germany, such as Peter von der Osten-Sacken and Dieter Georgi, to undertake an energetic repudiation of those traditions and demand of their students a commitment to serious study of early Judaism. Indeed, despite the continued perpetuation of anti-Jewish stereotypes in certain theological literature, Germany today is witnessing a widespread, concerted effort by scholars to overcome Christian theological anti-Judaism. Perhaps in a future generation, the influence of the Institute and all its theological forebears and offspring will diminish and theological affirmations of Christianity will take shape alongside an affirmation of Judaism.

1. (*left*) *The Gospel in the Third Reich, a Sunday Paper for German Christians,* featuring the heroic picture of Martin Luther as characteristic of the German Christians, the fruit of a centuries-old nationalist interpretation of Luther.

2. (*right*) The headline from Julius Streicher's anti-semitic newspaper reads "Was Christ Jewish?" Streicher, one of Hitler's earliest followers, published the paper from 1923 to 1945. During the Third Reich, *Der Stürmer* display cases were found all over Germany. Streicher was executed for crimes against humanity in 1946.

3. (*top*) A marked Jewish-run business.

4. (*above*) Tire cover reads "The Jews are our misfortune."

5. (*left*) A sign warning: "Jews in the Blossersberg community are not welcome. To know the Jew is to know the devil."

6. (*below*) The sign reads "The father of the Jews is the devil."

7. On leaving the Leonhardskirche in Stuttgart, Bishop Theophil Wurm, who had been rehabilitated by the Führer, was given a rousing welcome with shouts of "Heil!" from 450 Tübingen theological students, pleased that they could support both the Nazi state and their bishop.

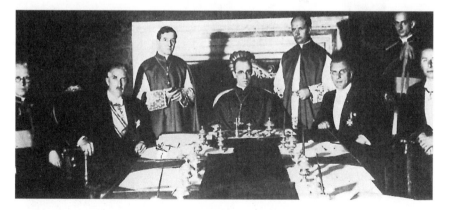

8. The signing of the Concordat between the German Reich and the Holy See on 20 July 1933 in the Vatican. From the left, Ludwig Kaas, Franz von Papen, Msgr. Pizzardo, Vatican Secretary of State Cardinal Evgenio Pacelli, Msgr. Ottaviani, Ministerial Director Rudolf Buttmann, Msgr. Montini, Counsellor Klee.

9 and 10. (*left and below*) The papal nuncio in Berlin, Cesare Orsenigo, leaving St. Hedwig's Cathedral, 17 September 1933, after a solemn service of thanksgiving to mark the ratification of the Concordat.

11 and 12. Campaign posters. At the election and plebiscite of 12 November 1933, Hitler reaped the fruits of the Reich Concordat by surprisingly high "yes" votes, above all in predominantly Catholic circles of the electorate.

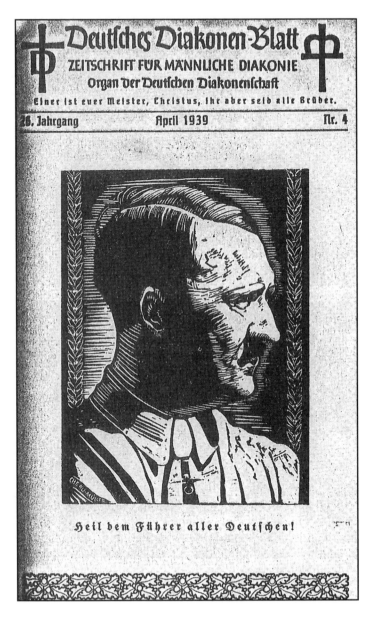

13. A favorable portrayal of Adolf Hitler in *German Deacon's Page*.
Caption reads: "Hail to the leader of all Germans!"

14 and 15. A cartoon from a Nazi children's book, *The Poisoned Mushroom* (*cover art in inset*). The book was published in Nurnberg by *Der Stürmer* in 1938. The caption reads "Baptism didn't make them into non-Jews."

16. A photomontage published in *AIZ* (*Worker's Illustrated Magazine*), January 1934: "The Bishop of the Reich rectifies Christianity," a response to the Protestant pastor Dr. Ludwig Müller calling for the Nazification of the church. The artist, John Heartfield, was German and created many political cartoons in opposition to Hitler. Heartfield fled Germany in 1933.

17.Christ and Christians flee from *The Nazi Priest* (1941). Pencil and sanguine by John Henry Amshewitz (1882–1942), an English Jew.

The Confessing Church and Antisemitism

Protestant Identity, German Nationhood, and the Exclusion of the Jews

Shelley Baranowski

The Confessing Church, so named because it claimed to be the "true" Evangelical church of Germany doctrinally grounded in the confessions of the Reformation, became the most prominent source of Protestant opposition to the Third Reich. Formed in mid-1934 as a coalition of pastors, higher clergy, and laypeople, the Confessing Church resisted the attempts of the Nazi-sympathizing German Christian Movement (*Deutsche Christen*) to restructure the loose federation of regional churches (*Landeskirchen*) known as the German Evangelical Church according to the "leadership principle" (*Führerprinzip*) and to infuse Protestant theology and doctrine with Nazi racism.[1] The most famous theological statement of the Confessing Church, the Barmen Declaration, was named after the Westphalian city where the Confessing Church was founded. The declaration condemned as "false doctrine" the nazified theology of the German Christians and their unbiblical "synchronization" (*Gleichschaltung*) of church institutions and ideas with the Nazi state. Yet as absolute as Barmen sounded in its censure of the German Christians, the Confessing Church limited its protests to maintaining the autonomy and theological integrity of the Evangelical churches against politicization by an adjunct of the Nazi Party. Although the Nazi intention to undermine the social influence of the Christian churches forced the Confessing Church into a broader defense of the allegedly Protestant foundations of German culture, the Confessing Church did not contest the legitimacy of the Third Reich itself.

The goals of the Confessing Church resonated deeply among the Evangelical Church leadership, both lay and clerical, and attracted much of the clergy from the *Landeskirchen,* whom the German Christians threatened to depose. The lay contingent of the Confessing Church drew disproportionately from the educated middle classes, the commercial and industrial sector, and the landed nobility of the eastern Prussian provinces, whose patronage supported the parish churches. As a vocal contingent in an institution with a huge, but largely nonobservant membership, the Confessing Church consisted of the "active" parishioners—those who regularly attended Sunday services and held church office.[2]

Because of its social composition, the Confessing Church typifies conservative elite opposition to National Socialism, that is, an ambivalence between opposition and support that persisted until the end of the Third Reich, despite the bitter disagreements that often erupted between elites and the Nazi Party. The overwhelming majority of those who joined the Confessing Church objected little to the regime's aggressive foreign policy, which they saw as regaining Germany's rightful place as a world power. Most approved of the suppression, exile, and imprisonment of leftists, believing that the communist "threat" warranted strong measures to contain "Marxism." Finally, although the Confessing Church protested the German Christians' violation of the biblical foundations of the Evangelical Church, its cultural conservatism marked its response to the Third Reich's racism. Thus, the efforts of oppositional pastors and theologians to stop the German Christians from "Aryanizing" the Evangelical Church—that is, expelling pastors, church officers, and parishioners with Jewish blood—could not conceal the instinctive antisemitism that continually prevented the Confessing Church from challenging anti-Jewish persecution, both within the church and without. Like most conservative groups, the Confessing Church supported the National Socialist regime as long as it respected the position of the institutions that had traditionally buttressed German politics and culture.

Remarkably, the Confessing Church did become a mass movement, even if its most prominent voices consisted of elites.[3] In 1934, popular demonstrations of significant size occurred in defense of ecclesiastical integrity and against the arbitrariness of a pro-Nazi church party that enjoined its secular standards on the church. In particular, large crowds protested the attempted removal of Bishops Theophil Wurm and Hans Meiser, who were unsympathetic to German Christian *Gleichschaltung*. In fact, the popular voices that the Confessing Church attracted persuaded the regime, by 1935, to withdraw its endorsement of the centralized German Christian Reich Church, an indication of the regime's vulnerability to domestic dissent.

However, the very ability of the Confessing opposition to unite elite and popular discontent in a potent protest movement betrays the true horror of National Socialist rule, because defiance against the nazification of the church coexisted with tacit consent for the militaristic and destructive core of

Nazism. Although preserving a culture receptive to the word as proclaimed in Scripture represented a less lethal conception of German nationhood than the rigidly integralist and racist version that the Third Reich promoted, the goals of the Confessing Church nonetheless militated against questioning the regime's racial hygiene, its *Drang nach Osten,* and its persecution of the Jews. The Confessing Church exemplifies the limits of the regime's ideological penetration of German society and its major institutions, yet it demonstrates as well how Nazism could orchestrate the racially defined reorganization of Germany and Europe without having to convert the majority of Germans to Nazi ideology.[4]

Revitalizing Protestantism: The German Evangelical Church and the Rise of Nazism

The political and social attitudes of Evangelical Church leaders during the Weimar Republic shaped the character of the Confessing opposition in the Third Reich. The regional churches had reluctantly accepted that they would have to negotiate with the Weimar government if they wished to prevent the left from effecting the separation of church and state. That possibility emerged most dramatically in the months immediately following the November Revolution and did not dissipate until the creation of the Weimar Constitution in the spring of 1919. Despite the generous terms of the constitution and of subsequent church-state agreements, however, most church leaders expressed little regret when the Weimar system later unraveled at the seams. Furthermore, most betrayed their sympathy with the political right.[5]

To be sure, the *Landeskirchen* did refrain from overtly proclaiming their distaste for parliamentary democracy, despite the conservatism of the upper-class clergy and lay church officials. Indeed, for some leaders the abdication of the Kaiser and the elimination of the Hohenzollern monarchy provided an opportunity to revitalize parish life, thus rolling back the decline in regular Sunday attendance that had become evident under the Second Empire, especially among the urban working class. Now that the *Landeskirchen* were no longer subject to an emperor who simultaneously served as supreme bishop (*Summus Episcopus*), the German Evangelical Church could transform itself into a genuine "people's church" (*Volkskirche*).

Legal and economic considerations also intervened to ensure that the church maintained tolerable relations with the Weimar system. If it was to preserve its status as a public corporation, with all the financial benefits that accrued to it thereby, the church could ill afford to appear anti-republican. Continued state support meant not only financial solvency for the church, but also the state's acceptance of the historic mission of the German Evangelical

Church to preach the word to German society. For Lutherans, who composed the majority of German Protestants, Luther's teaching on the two kingdoms, spiritual and secular, and two regiments, church and state, obligated the state to preserve public space for the church to accomplish its mission. The church, for its part, was obligated to maintain neutrality in political matters. Throughout the republican period, Evangelical Church consistories consistently intervened in cases where right-wing pastors aroused the ire of the left.[6] They often chastised pastors who, by propagating conservative views from their pulpits, thus compromised the official posture of political neutrality. In 1927, the Church Assembly (*Kirchentag*)—the legislative body for all Evangelical churches in Germany—urged parishioners to obey the state, albeit without affirming that the Weimar Republic had been legally constituted. Church leaderships thus steered a delicate course between the Scylla of alienating nominal Protestants, whom the church wanted to recruit, and the Charybdis of state disapprobation.

Although most Evangelical clergymen and lay officials of the church had grown resigned to the Weimar system, even as the Republic fell under increasing attack they nonetheless championed views that predisposed them to a positive view of Nazism. Despite the fact that a number of these church leaders would join the Confessing Church opposition to the German Christians after the Nazis took power, their outlooks fluidly accommodated much of the Nazi Party's electoral program. This boded ill for the formation of an anti-Nazi resistance of sufficient determination to destroy the Third Reich. During the Weimar crisis, the conservative outlook, characterized by a fear of cultural liberalization, adjusted to the right-radical Nazi movement, a movement that cloaked its extremes with issues having wide appeal.[7] For the Evangelical churches, and especially for their parish and synodical newspapers, cultural liberalization encompassed a variety of "ills," ranging from the Republic's persistent, if unsuccessful, attempts to secularize the public primary schools to the pressure to lessen the penalties for abortion, the spread of pornography, lewdness in the theater, and rising rates of divorce, alcoholism, and juvenile delinquency, as well as the emancipation of women. Church leaders associated such social problems with the Republic, and particularly the Social Democrats, the Communists, and the left-liberal Democratic Party.

Moreover, the Evangelical definition of cultural liberalization included religious pluralism, which under the Republic received a boost from the increasing proselytization by religious sects and the prominence of the Catholic Center Party in Weimar cabinets. Religious and cultural pluralism extended further to the widening avenues open to Jews, who now escaped the constraints on their professional opportunities that had existed during the Second Empire.[8] The anti-leftist attitudes of church leaders betrayed antisemitism as well, for clergymen often alluded to the number of Jews in the parties of the left, and these parties appeared most determined to dechristianize Germany. Antisemitism even surfaced in discussions regarding the spread of Christian sectarianism. In their attacks on the Jehovah's Witnesses, the most widely disliked of the "new" religious movements, the periodicals of the regional churches accused "international Jewry" of sponsoring the sect through generous infusions of American money.[9]

The electoral growth of the Nazi movement after 1928, especially in heavily Protestant regions, concerned Evangelical Church leaders, the majority of whom affiliated themselves with the German National People's Party (DNVP) or the German People's Party (DVP). The blatant anti-Christianity of prominent Nazi Party figures, notably Alfred Rosenberg and Heinrich Himmler, threatened the consignment of Christianity to the margins of life. The politicized theology of the Nazi-sympathizing German Christians, who performed very well in parish elections for the synods of the Old Prussian Union Church prior to the Nazi takeover,[10] also worried the church leadership, who felt that this development threatened to undermine the church's official stance of neutrality and to overthrow the church bureaucracies. Of course, according to the German Christian Movement, these bureaucracies hindered the development of a genuine *Volkskirche*.

Nevertheless, as a fluid amalgam of anti-republican radicalism and bourgeois conservatism, the Nazi Party allayed Evangelical concerns more often than not. In regions, such as the eastern Prussian provinces, where Lutheranism remained deeply embedded in the social fabric and where Luther and Bismarck appeared as the twin founders of the German nation, the Nazis affirmed the Christian foundations of German culture. The Hitler movement asserted that unlike the "Bolsheviks" who turned churches into cinemas, the Nazi Party respected the vital place of both major churches, Evangelical and Catholic, in German life. Furthermore, for all their irresponsible enthusiasm, the German Christians seemed to represent the revitalization of parish life because they appeared to draw nominal Protestants back to the church. Finally, National Socialism reinvented itself as the guardian of the "traditional" family and morality against the cultural liberalization of the Weimar era. Church periodicals praised the closure of abortion clinics and the outlawing of prostitution after Hitler came to power. After all, cultural liberalization and secularization merged in the minds of Evangelical church leaders. Conversely, solidifying the cultural importance of Protestantism meant ending the moral disintegration of the republican years. Moral recovery would in turn bring about Germany's revival in Europe.

Revitalization Backfires: The Confessing Church and the Preservation of Autonomy

In January 1933, the appointment of the government of "National Concentration," with Hitler as chancellor, spawned a nearly religious awakening, one that arose from the widespread belief that Germany would now recover from military defeat and national humiliation, parliamentary fragmentation, and economic catastrophe. Casting their nationalism in theological terms, the German Christians claimed that divine revelation worked through the emergence of Hitler. In fact, attendance at Sunday services dramatically increased, an encouraging sign for Evangelical clergy, who had long rued the declining commitment among Protestants beyond a minimal observance of baptism, marriage, and burial. For many devout Protestants, the March 1933 ceremony in the Potsdam Garrison Church that marked the opening of the newly elected Reichstag—in which the crown prince, Reich President Paul von Hindenburg, and the conservative general superintendent of the Brandenburg church, Otto Dibelius, accompanied Hitler—signified not only a resurgent Germany but also the resurrection of Germany's Evangelical heritage after the accelerated secularization and moral corruption of the republican years.[11] In order to adapt to the spirit of the "national awakening," the *Landeskirchen* composed a new constitution, ratified in July. The constitution created a stronger central administration under the leadership of a Lutheran Reich bishop and a four-member Spiritual Ministry, three theologians and one jurist with significant regulative powers, while preserving the autonomy of the regional churches in specifically confessional matters and liturgical practice.

The church leadership received more than it bargained for, however, because more so than Catholics, Protestants evinced a great attraction to the Nazi Party.[12] The German Christians, buoyed by the Nazi surge among a predominantly Protestant electorate, proposed a more radical ecclesiastical reorientation that, in the view of many, resulted in the subordination of the church to the rawest sort of politicization. Stunning victories for the German Christians in the parish elections of July 1933 went well beyond their impressive performance in Prussia during the previous fall, allowing them to supplant the incumbent leaderships in most *Landeskirchen,* including the largest, the Old Prussian Union. Nazi Party organizations, especially the paramilitary SA, contributed significantly to the German Christian cause. The "Brown Synod" that convened in Prussia in early September—so named because the newly elected German Christian members wore SA uniforms with swastika armbands—shouted down opposing delegates, dismissing them as the out-of-touch voices of the "old" bureaucratic church.

Several weeks later, the election of a German Christian Reich bishop, Ludwig Müller, at the national synod in Wittenberg accelerated the German

Christian *Gleichschaltung* of the *Landeskirchen* into an entity that conformed to the Nazi centralization of local and state government. The federation of churches, newly approved in July, would disappear into the streamlined and unified Reich Church. The location of the national synod at Wittenberg was no accident, for it symbolized the determination of the German Christians to drape themselves in the reforming zeal of Martin Luther. However, Müller's ham-handedness, which included the summary removal of church leaders in Prussia, provoked outrage. The German Christian regime replaced established church leaders with young, presumably unqualified German Christians, and it violated the synodical structure of the churches grounded in the Reformation's vision of a community of believers justified by faith. In short, Müller transferred *Gleichschaltung* from the political arena to a church that, despite its periodic attempts at achieving a coherent and effective national structure, preferred a federal system that acknowledged the basic autonomy of each *Landeskirche*.

The Pastors' Emergency League, founded in September 1933 in response to the postelection *Gleichschaltung*, set forth the theological concerns that would shortly animate the Confessing Church. According to the League, revitalizing the church could only come from preaching the word of God as revealed in Scripture and the Reformation confessions. The Pastors' Emergency League agreed with the German Christians that the Evangelical churches needed to be revivified through an energized laity and by de-emphasizing bureaucratic leadership that dispensed directives from on high to inert parishes. Yet authentic renewal would prosper only through a code of personal responsibility and service, through improved pastoral training, and through the involvement of a committed laity. The herdlike mobilization of masses of nominal Protestants in the German Christian style—the politicization of the uncommitted through the electioneering of the Nazi Party—would erode the faith that was the foundation of the church.

Moreover, *Gleichschaltung* with the aid of the state's coercive power threatened dechristianization by eliminating the church's special identity as a community of believers.[13] For one of the most prominent lay members of the League, the Pomeranian estate owner, Reinhold von Thadden-Trieglaff, "the mere registration and mobilization of the laity for the purpose of better church-political utilization can under no circumstances be the end in itself of a church renewal movement, which is really intended to serve our *Volk* in its struggle of destiny." Increased lay participation "makes sense then only if it arises from the living congregation, which is conceived in faith and in the promise of the coming redemption."[14]

The opposition that crystallized in Barmen in mid-1934 embraced considerable diversity and latent conflict. Put at its simplest, the Confessing

Church represented an alliance between elements of the "destroyed" churches whose administrations and synods the German Christians now controlled—particularly members of the Pastors' Emergency League—and the "intact" Lutheran churches of Hannover, Bavaria, and Württemberg, whose bishops remained in command. The disproportionately Prussian composition of the Pastors' Emergency League disturbed the bishops, who could never entirely suppress their ingrained anti-Prussian regionalism and Lutheran confessionalism.[15] In fact, the Confessing Church only converged when the threat of German Christian *Gleichschaltung* became a truly national danger. Reich Bishop Müller's decision in January 1934 to merge Evangelical youth groups into the Hitler Youth, his decree forbidding the "misuse" of church services for attacks on the German Christian administration (the so-called Muzzling Decree), and the attempt during the same month to depose the bishop of Württemberg Theophil Wurm, provided the catalyst for a coherent national response.

The Barmen Synod, the defining moment of the Confessing Church, testified to the crisis atmosphere that prevailed among active Protestants, who believed that the German Christian Reich Church had abandoned all pretense of a revitalization grounded in the Gospel, becoming instead all but indistinguishable from the Nazi political movement. Bishop Müller's recent actions had placed the survival of the church as an autonomous entity at stake. The synod produced the declaration that has become one of the defining theological Protestant statements regarding the identity and mission of the church. Although often referred to as the Barmen "confession," the Barmen Declaration did not achieve confessional status because the doctrinal differences among the member churches prevented a unified understanding of the sacraments.[16] Nonetheless, the declaration defined clear boundaries between church and state, which the state could not cross. It further asserted that the word of God as mediated through Scripture could not be reduced to prevailing political ideologies. Nor could it be mediated through the great moments of German history independently of Christ—a common German Christian assertion. The declaration rejected as unbiblical the imposition of Nazi organizational principles on the church. Its firm Christocentrism and rejection of syncretism becomes clear in the retrospective of Heinrich Vogel, a Confessing Church pastor who later recalled the declaration's attack on the relativism of the German Christians: "We hear from Jesus, whom the Scripture reveals as the Christ, not only words *about* God, but God himself. This is the Word which was made flesh (John 1:14) and therefore the one word which we must hear. Unlike, indeed, in opposition to all the words *about* God, we are encountered here by the one word of God in person, in the person of one who speaks to us as a brother, as one of us, with the mystery of His divinity fully hidden.

It is the majestic mystery of the Truth of God in Christ which is revealed to us in the word of Holy Scripture, indeed, which makes itself heard in this word. This says everything!"[17]

The Confessing Church reached its high-water mark at its synod in Berlin-Dahlem in the fall of 1934, after Bishop Müller's legal administrator, August Jäger, otherwise known as *Kirchenjäger* ("Church Hunter"), placed Bishops Wurm of Württemberg and Meiser of Bavaria under house arrest. Whereas the Barmen Declaration rejected as "false doctrine" the diverse manifestations of German Christian politicization, the Dahlem Declaration urged complete separation from the German Christian Reich Church.[18] After the Nazi government withdrew its patronage of Bishop Müller in 1935, however, the Confessing Church could not long survive. By 1936 it had permanently fragmented into bitterly divided factions that mirrored sharp doctrinal and regional fault lines. "Moderates," led by the intact churches, and "radicals," found mainly in Prussia, grew hopelessly deadlocked over the issue of whether to cooperate with the "church committees" that the regime's new Ministry for Church Affairs designated to force negotiations between the German Christians, their opposition, and the growing number of undecided. The moderates, especially the extraordinarily compliant bishop of Hanover, August Marahrens,[19] sought a coalition with moderate German Christians and the numerous independents, who had grown weary of ecclesiastical polarization. The radicals, who included such luminaries as Martin Niemöller and Dietrich Bonhoeffer, rejected any compromise as "fellow-traveling" with "heresy."[20]

Ironically, the Confessing Church had become a victim of its own success. Following a raft of unfavorable foreign press reports, a number of court decisions that devastated the German Christian claims, and a good deal of popular outrage, the incompetence and unpopularity of the German Christian national administration rendered the Reich Church a political liability for the Nazi regime. The Confessing Church presented the worst possible combination for the Gestapo. It amounted to an opposition with considerable participation from political elites, whose support the regime could never completely spurn, and from ordinary parishioners, especially the peasantry, whom the Third Reich claimed to favor. The arrests of Bishops Wurm and Meiser, neither of whom could have been accused of disloyalty to the Third Reich, brought petitions, public rallies, and even physical attacks on local Nazi Party officials by angry laypersons. A number of parishioners resigned from the party in protest.[21]

The regime's solution to these problems—the naming of a Reich minister for church affairs, Hanns Kerrl—presented innumerable problems to the Confessing opposition and exposed its already latent internal divisions. It also subjected the *Landeskirchen* to the ever more intrusive regulation of their internal affairs, ranging from the management of their finances to the training and ordination of pastors. Moreover, the German Christians did not simply disappear. They remained as leaders of many *Landeskirchen* and exerted an insidious influence in the theological faculties of the universities.[22] At the same time, however, the survival of the Confessing Church illustrates the regime's dread of losing popular legitimacy, and it testifies to the limits of repression, even in a terroristic dictatorship. That lesson is worth remembering as we consider crucial issues that confronted the Confessing Church, especially Nazi racism and antisemitism. The muted protests of the Evangelical opposition to the persecution of the Jews and other "undesirables" contrasts markedly to its spirited defense of ecclesiastical autonomy. The ubiquity and severity of Nazi repression cannot suffice as the sole or decisive explanation.

Militant Accommodation: The Confessing Church and the Jews

After the Nazi "seizure of power," the Evangelical Church leadership made no secret of its antisemitism, just as it did not conceal its relief at the Nazi "national renewal." The Aryan Paragraph of the April 1933 Reich Civil Service Law that resulted in the dismissal of Jews from the bureaucracy, the SA-initiated boycott of Jewish businesses, and the suppression of the left, which Evangelical Church leaders saw as harboring an "excessive" number of Jews, engendered approval and apologetics. The alleged Jewish influence in journalism, the universities, and the arts was believed to have threatened the Christian faith and family life. The large number of relatively poor, unassimilated Jews from eastern Europe living in Germany's largest cities were said to personify an unhealthy "foreign" presence. Few Evangelical Church spokespersons, lay or clerical, departed from the conviction that a Jewish "problem" or "question" existed and that it required restrictions upon the "excessive" influence of Jews. In fact, Protestant leaders tended to recast the regime's anti-Jewish measures not as persecution but rather as retribution for Germany's "victimization" at the hands of Jews. The "corrosive effects" of Jews on German culture through their role in the professions, the civil service, and the media allegedly contributed to Germany's weakness.[23]

Despite its protean character, antisemitism in Evangelical church circles had two intersecting strands, one subtle, the other blatant, that stood out. The first resided in the cultural pessimism that swelled after World War I. This pessimism wove the fear of the erosion of Germany's Christian heritage due to urbanism, secularization, and the influence of the left with a "crisis" mentality, prominent among theologians, arising from the loss of certainty regarding basic tenets of the faith. The disillusion that materialized with the failure to recover the historical Jesus and the debate over the accessibility of God (or lack thereof) resulted in a loss of confidence in the claims of the Enlightenment that Evangelical theologians had tried to accommodate throughout the nineteenth century. They became less convinced of the primacy of reason and the perfectibility of human beings. Yet even as they lost confidence in that body of thought, which presupposed the desirability of recovering a uniformly Christian culture and the certitude of faith, many theologians retained an implicit hostility to religious and ethnic difference. In that view Jews inevitably remained "foreign" by definition, a people whose very existence personified the erosion of Christianity in Germany.[24]

The second and much older strand of antisemitism consisted of the "traditional" theologically based anti-Judaism drawn primarily from the New Testament, a tradition that assigned to Jews the responsibility for the trial and execution of Jesus. Moreover, it condemned the Jews for having rejected Christianity—the religious tradition arising in the name of Jesus that, according to God's design, had superseded Judaism. Thus, cultural antisemitism, with its integralist and antipluralist conception of German nationhood, exacerbated the centuries-long proclivity of Christians, rooted in the New Testament canon itself, to stake their identity on the chastisement of the Jews.[25] Ironically, the rapidly spreading opposition to the German Christians, which used the word as revealed in Scripture to condemn German Christian syncretism, could neither cast away the anti-Judaism of the New Testament nor overcome its own peculiar blend of secular and religious antagonism toward Jews.

To be sure, there were significant differences between the cultural and biblically based antisemitism of the church establishment and that of the extreme Church Movement of German Christians led by Siegfried Leffler, who called for the complete elimination of all traces of Jewish influences from Scripture.[26] Yet the growing polarization within the German Evangelical Church throughout 1933 did nothing to minimize the common Evangelical abhorrence of Judaism and the Jews. Dibelius, who would soon join the opposition to the German Christian *Gleichschaltung*, complained during an interview that unfavorable foreign news coverage of the antisemitic boycott was the result of Jewish influence.[27] Martin Niemöller, pastor of a prestigious congregation in Berlin-Dahlem and one of the founders of the Pastors' Emergency League, would become the very symbol of unyielding Protestant resistance, yet he found the regime's curtailment of the Jews tolerable, given what he saw as the disproportionate number of Jews in the liberal professions.[28] Both betrayed a more fundamental problem that the Confessing Church would never overcome, the conviction that the Jews constituted an alien presence in a culture that the Evangelical Church insisted should remain captive to the Evangelical message.

Even Dietrich Bonhoeffer, the young Lutheran theologian who was executed for his role in the 20 July 1944 assassination attempt against Hitler and who became the most forceful opponent of Nazi racism in Evangelical Church circles, could not escape the rhetoric of the Jews as a "problem." In an essay written in April 1933, titled "The Church and the Jewish Question," Bonhoeffer allowed the state room to address the Jewish "question" on its own terms. Although he insisted on the obligation of the church to stop injustice rather than merely aid the victims of injustice, admittedly a novel position for a German Lutheran pastor to take, Bonhoeffer's reserve toward the Jews settled in the Lutheran framework of the two kingdoms. God willed the state to preserve law and order in a godless world, and the state alone had the power to make history: "Without a doubt the Jewish question is one of the historical problems with which the state must deal, and without a doubt the state is justified in blazing new trails here [*hier neue Wege zu gehen*]."[29]

Nevertheless, the German Christians were determined to insert the Aryan Paragraph of the Civil Service Law into the church constitution, forcing their opponents to limit the penetration into the church of the Nazi regime's racially driven antisemitism. When the Prussian Brown Synod met in the fall of 1933, it acted on the pledge of the German Christian national convention of the previous April to rid the church of Jewish influences. Seven other German Christian-dominated *Landeskirchen* followed suit. Baptized Jews, Protestants with Jewish ancestry, and Protestants married to "non-Aryans" were forbidden to hold church office or serve as pastors. Ultimately, the German Christians envisioned that non-Aryan parishioners would be confined to separate congregations. Several weeks later the national synod in Wittenberg imposed the Aryan Paragraph on the Reich Church as a whole. The integrity of the church as a biblically grounded institution, with its own unique criteria for membership, baptism, and ordination, demanded a response to this variant of German Christian politicizing, just as *Gleichschaltung* demanded a defense of ecclesiastical autonomy. Yet although the Aryan Paragraph became a major catalyst for the formation of a coherent Protestant opposition to the German Christians—the ensuing uproar delayed the final implementation of the clause until August 1934—it also underscored the ambiguity of the oppositional movement, the primary aim of which was to preserve an Evangelical culture and the role of the church in maintaining it.

To be sure, the Aryan Paragraph became one of the most important issues for the Pastors' Emergency League. For the clergy and laity who joined the League, the Aryan Paragraph desanctified the rituals by which individuals joined the community of believers in Christ. Baptism, not race, determined one's entry into the fellowship of Christians. One's oath to God, not race, determined one's fitness as a pastor. The use of racial criteria meant that the church could no longer *be* the church, because unambiguously secular standards had replaced ecclesiastical ones. The Pastors' Emergency League pledge card obligated its members to show solidarity with the Aryan Paragraph's victims.[30] Moreover, other initiatives that indicated to what extent the German Christians were prepared to "Aryanize" the church stimulated the rapid growth of the Pastors' Emergency League to seven thousand strong by early 1934. In fact, prominent spokesmen for the German Christians attempted to rewrite Scripture itself. At a German Christian rally in the Berlin Sports Palace in November 1933, Dr. Reinhold Krause, a German Christian district leader, demanded that the church rid itself of all things un-German, including the Old Testament "with its Jewish system of wage morality [*Lohnmoral*]."[31]

Yet beneath the Pastors' Emergency League's apparently forthright display of opposition to the German Christians, its own lurking antisemitism created ambivalence to resistance against antisemitism, within the church and without. Protecting the Old Testament's place in the Christian canon became less controversial than contesting Aryanization.[32] Few became as resolute as Bonhoeffer, who despite his tacit acknowledgment of the state's freedom to effect Jewish policy in the secular kingdom, adamantly rejected the removal of non-Aryan Christians from church offices, the segregation of non-Aryans into separate congregations, and the Nazi regime's violent persecution of unbaptized Jews.[33] Antisemitism predisposed the Pastors' Emergency League not only to refrain from criticizing the Civil Service Law and other evidence of Nazi antisemitism in the political realm, but even to restrain its protests on behalf of non-Aryan victims of the German Christians.

Some in the Pastors' Emergency League turned the tables on non-Aryan Protestants, tacitly assenting to the notion that, regardless of their numerical insignificance,[34] the very presence of Christians of Jewish heritage in the church victimized their Aryan brethren. According to Niemöller, non-Aryans should avoid seeking positions of leadership in the church so as not to give offense.[35] Similarly, others concluded that non-Aryans who asked for the support of their brothers and sisters in Christ burdened the consciences of Christians, who in aiding non-Aryans would ineluctably place themselves in opposition to the state. The very supersessionism that expected Jews to convert to Christianity in order to assure their salvation also resulted, when combined with cultural antisemitism, in the "guest status" of baptized Jews and Christians with Jewish ancestry. Thus even baptism and ordination, supposedly the keys to equality in Christ, and the primacy of Christian identity over race and ethnicity coexisted with the belief that the church could not separate itself from the (justifiable) effort to limit Jewish "influence."

Furthermore, periodicals associated with the Pastors' Emergency League, such as *Junge Kirche,* could not avoid incorporating antisemitic language and concepts even when protesting the German Christians' employment of the Aryan Paragraph. Establishing separate Jewish-Christian congregations was nothing less than "Judaistic" and "pagan."[36] Bonhoeffer's arguments against the Aryan Paragraph, although strongly worded, made little dent in the stack of theological opinions that expressed more compromising positions. Even had Bonhoeffer remained in Germany instead of leaving for London in the fall of 1933 in search of German-speaking congregations untainted by German Christian heresy, it is doubtful that his views could have modified attitudes that were so deeply entrenched.[37]

The Barmen Synod proved even more reluctant to contest the antisemitism of the German Christians, much less that of the Nazi regime. Instead, it elevated the anti-pluralist concerns of the Evangelical opposition even as it crisply denounced "heresy." Incorporated in the declaration was the vision of the church as a public corporation of privileged status, entrusted with assuring the proclamation of the word to the surrounding culture. The synod's deliberations—supported by the contributions of several distinguished jurists, among them the Reich court justice, Wilhelm Flor—repeatedly stressed the legal continuity of the Confessing Church with the Evangelical Church as defined by the constitution of July 1933, approved just days before the German Christian victories in the parish elections. Although the Confessing Church repudiated the politicization of the church, its characterization of German Christian policy as illegal, unbiblical, and arbitrary showed that it was equally concerned to avoid the appearance of a sectarian breakaway.[38] The majority in the Confessing Church interpreted the Barmen Declaration as a way to protect the Evangelical church against the German Christians, whose manipulation of political standards compromised the church's identity as a community of believers in Christ. Those so inclined could draw inferences about Barmen's broader implications. Nevertheless, the Barmen statement avoided any direct reference to the Aryan Paragraph's impact in the church, much less to the Nazi regime's repression and racism.[39]

Ironically, the author of the declaration, Karl Barth, one of the foremost theologians of the twentieth century, often criticized the Confessing Church for focusing so narrowly on preserving its corporate legal status. Barth's leftist politics, although not easy to deduce from his Christocentric dogmatics, consistently complicated his relationship to the Confessing Church, even after 1935, when he was forced to return to his native Switzerland because of his opposition to the regime. Yet Barth's politics, which were so alien to the conservatism of the majority in the Confessing Church, cannot by themselves explain the inability of the Barmen meeting to address the persecution of the

Jews and non-Aryan Christians, for Barth's leadership in formulating the Confessing Church's opposition to the German Christians was not seriously challenged. Although Barth abhorred the conservative nationalism that blinded his compatriots in the Confessing Church, and although he later condemned the mass murder of the Jews, his theology of the word embraced the anti-Judaism constitutive of the New Testament itself.[40] Not only did Barth have difficulty delineating the ethical implications of the Aryan Paragraph (the relationship between theology and ethics has always been problematic in Barth), he could never put aside his own supersessionism.[41] Thus, if Barth's politics appeared idiosyncratic, his anti-Judaism did not.

The Aryan Paragraph's significance for the opposition declined as the Confessing Church more sharply formulated its identity as the guarantor of the Evangelical sociocultural mission to preach the word to an unredeemed world. Subsequent attempts to address the regime's escalating persecution of the Jews succumbed to the overwhelming desire to avoid a confrontation with a regime whose secular policies won nearly unanimous approbation. Once the Nazi government withdrew its endorsement of the Reich Church, a painful dilemma confronted the Confessing Church: continued opposition to Nazi church policy now meant direct opposition to the Nazi government itself. The Prussian Confessing Synod at Steglitz, held in the fall of 1935 after the promulgation of the Nuremberg Laws, illustrated this problem acutely. Pressed by a few militants—among them Bonhoeffer, Vogel, Martin Albertz, and Marga Meugel—to produce a public statement expressing solidarity with the regime's victims, the synod instead heeded the advice of Bishop Meiser of Bavaria, who from the seat of his diocese in Munich urged the avoidance of self-inflicted martyrdom. Recognizing only the church's supersessionist obligation to establish missions to the Jews, it passed a resolution that narrowly concentrated on the right of the church to baptize Jews who sought conversion.[42] After the Steglitz gathering dispensed its decision, it devoted most of its time to dealing with the threat that Kerrl's Ministry for Church Affairs posed for the financial autonomy of the church.

Given the antisemitism that shaped the outlook of this overwhelmingly conservative movement, the persecution of the Jews could not generate sustained protest from an opposition focused principally on the preservation of the church. Even the Steglitz synod's tepid endorsement of baptism would not have occurred had not some congregations refused to baptize Jews, thus threatening the integrity of the sacraments. Suspicion of baptismal candidates' motives was common, as the candid remark of Dibelius reveals: "I therefore became increasingly firm and exact in my demands [of Jews asking to be baptized]. This gradually became known, and in the end I was spared such externally motivated requests for baptism."[43] Although thereafter small groups of Confessing clergy and laity, notably women, did rescue Jews, as well as non-Aryan Christians—hiding them, caring for them, and providing false papers so that they could emigrate—the various wings of the Confessing movement directed their attention to threats that they believed had a direct impact on the social and cultural relevance of the church.[44]

The regime's tolerance of Nordic cults, such as the German Faith Movement, and of the anti-Christian pronouncements of Rosenberg, its attempt to secularize the schools, and its apparent encouragement of a consumer and leisure culture through its organization "Strength through Joy" appeared to the Church as a dechristianization campaign that threatened what the Confessing Church most wanted to preserve: a culture receptive to a Christianity rooted in the Reformation.[45] Furthermore, although the Confessing Church continued to attack German Christian theologians' attempts to "dejudaize" Christianity through the Institute for the Study and Eradication of Jewish Influence on German Church Life, it frequently cast its criticisms in antisemitic terms.[46]

The tortuous policy of the Confessing Church regarding the Jewish "question" conformed to the attitudes of Evangelical Church circles generally and to other aspects of the Nazi "racial state." The regime's comprehensive program of racial hygiene and politicized reproduction included the mandatory sterilization of the genetically "diseased" and the "euthanasia" of "lives unworthy of life." The Inner Mission, the predominantly lay, Protestant organization that supervised a nationwide network of hospitals and social welfare services, delivered a significant share of the health care in Germany. It maintained 512 asylums and homes containing beds for over thirty-five thousand patients. Thus the Inner Mission was directly confronted with the implications of the state's population policy.[47] It wrestled with the regime's sterilization program, initiated in July 1933—not to mention the killing of mental patients and the chronically ill that the regime introduced in 1939 as the threat of war became palpable.

Although disturbed by the relentless coercion of the Nazi programs and skeptical of eugenics decisions based solely on the grounds of a patient's social and economic utility, the Inner Mission nonetheless accepted many of the premises of the Nazi regime's racial hygiene. It agreed to the necessity of sterilization, albeit in carefully restricted circumstances (severe mental retardation, for example), as a means of maintaining a healthy population. In turn, that healthy population was essential to Germany's resurgence as a world power. Moreover, given the cost-benefit analysis that characterized medical and scientific discussion during the interwar period, especially after the Depression forced cutbacks in public welfare expenditures, the Inner Mission found it difficult to refute arguments that Germany could no longer afford to support patients who had little prospect of becoming economically productive. The lengths to which the regime went to eliminate "undesirables" unsettled a good many consciences, but not enough to inspire a categorical denunciation of Nazi racism. Even the 1941 protests against euthanasia by Bishop Wurm and, on the Catholic side, Bishop Klemens August von Galen failed to discourage the Nazi regime from expanding its killing program. In any case, the considerable time that elapsed before the churches chose to speak out reveals the ambivalence of the churches' resistance to the destruction of "lives unworthy of life."[48]

Like the Confessing Church's "defense" of non-Aryan Christians, the Inner Mission's protection of those under its care was analogous to erecting an earthen dam against a tidal wave. It did not help matters that the Evangelical Church itself, as it unraveled into bitter factionalism, took no position on sterilization and euthanasia, leaving the directors, doctors, and nurses of the Inner Mission to construct ad hoc, provisional, and wholly reactive policies. Inside the Inner Mission, the divisions between German Christian sympathizers, Confessing Church loyalists, and the neutral were not the decisive issue, although they certainly inhibited the prospects for resistance. To a remarkable degree, the Inner Mission managed to distance itself from the church struggle, putting its institutional goals ahead of participation in ecclesiastical factionalism. Rather, the Inner Mission's determination to overtake its Catholic counterpart, *Caritas*, in the Nazi restructuring of social welfare—a determination based in no small measure on the hope that the Third Reich would spawn the revival of a Protestant Germany—constituted a sizable mortgage against the integrity of the organization.[49]

The Limits of Repression, the Consequences of Consent

The pervasiveness of anti-Jewish attitudes exhibited in the Confessing Church was by no means uncommon among institutions in Germany during the Third Reich. The Confessing Church fused Christian anti-Judaism and the arrogance of supersessionism with a cultural antisemitism that saw the Jews as a danger to the integrity and Protestant foundations of the nation. To be sure, the Confessing Church was "only" guilty of silence, of limiting its resistance so as to preclude a forthright strategy against the Nazi regime's racism. By contrast, the army, the bureaucracy, the SS, not to mention the Nazi Party, directly orchestrated the Final Solution.[50] Like most middle- and upper-class civilians, the clergy and laity of the Protestant opposition did not condone violence, nor did they advocate extermination. In fact, the Prussian Confessing Synod held at Breslau in the fall of 1943 condemned the killing of persons "because they are judged unworthy of life or because they belong to another race,"[51] thus asserting the intrinsic worth of each human being. Yet the failures of the Confessing Church due to the entrenched antisemitism in its ranks helps explain why National Socialism could pursue its murderous policies with relatively little public interference. The Confessing Church's acceptance of discourse about "another race" demands that we probe the relationship between the initiators of mass murder and those on the sidelines.

To grasp the full impact of the "mild" antisemitism of the Confessing Church (mild only in comparison to the Nazi regime), we must not merely catalog examples of antisemitic attitudes or even identify those issues in which the Confessing Church found common ground with the Nazis. Criticism of the Protestant opposition assumes that it had the power to limit the Third Reich's devastating brutality, power that church historians still persist in doubting. How much did the Third Reich's seemingly massive apparatus of repression contribute to the Confessing Church's failures? Is it enough to argue, as some have, that the Nazi police state and the sheer scale of its empire in eastern Europe rendered meaningful resistance impossible?[52]

Two characteristics of Nazi repression come to mind in response to these questions. First, the Nazi police network was highly selective in its implementation. Although no sector of German society escaped it, repression disproportionately affected the political left, religious and ethnic minorities, the racially and genetically suspect, and the socially marginalized. Second, the effectiveness of repression depended upon the cooperation of numerous volunteer informants. The Gestapo's paid professional staff was in reality quite small.[53] Both points demonstrate the degree to which police action depended on legitimacy among the populace. The Nazi terror was not some alien force imposed upon Germany. Rather, it evolved from the bitter antagonisms in a population beset by numerous interlocking crises: economic hardship, military defeat, international sanction, and internal conflict. Although Italian fascist repression should not be minimized, the relative lack of support that the Mussolini government encountered in its belated campaign to persecute Italian Jews provides a sobering comparison to the Third Reich. To give another example, an outspoken eugenics movement existed in Italy, but the Catholic Church mounted a far more sustained and vigorous denunciation of it than did either of the two German churches. The coercive power of the state that could be brought to bear against domestic and foreign enemies was not only less developed in Italy, but it also received less public sanction.[54]

The Gestapo did rein itself in when German popular opinion reacted negatively, and collectively, against Nazi Party attacks on the churches. The church and its clergy maintained a significant role in the lives of many parishioners, shaping their values and views of the world. Therefore, actions such as arresting bishops, removing crucifixes from the schools, and secularizing the schools found little public support. As Ian Kershaw notes, the leadership of the churches was most evident, and most effective, when church leaders championed issues that resonated with their parishioners. The protests of both churches against euthanasia, for example, formally articulated the dismay that spread among their parishioners as rumors of the killings circulated.[55] Nazi measures that represented dechristianization found few volunteer informants willing to denounce others, because the discontent against such measures was widespread enough to provide security in numbers. For example, the party backed away from removing crucifixes from primary schools in Bavaria, when outraged Catholics demonstrated en masse. This retreat is stunning evidence of the limits of police repression in a supposedly "totalitarian" state, especially since it came at the height of the regime's popularity in the summer and fall of 1941 when the invasion of the Soviet Union seemed to be proceeding on schedule.[56] Demonstrations of dissent arising from groups that otherwise supported the Third Reich (or at least Hitler's leadership),[57] showed that effective opposition did not have to come from the regime's most obvious domestic foes, such as the left. Therefore it will not do to speak of a progressive decline of once powerful social institutions against the expanding power of the Nazi regime, as some suggest.[58] The Third Reich's power, although uncontestable, never grew so absolute as to defy popular and elite sentiment. Rather, the determination of the Nazi regime to create a harmonious *Volksgemeinschaft* presupposed the maintenance of at least a passable degree of consent.

When we move from Nazi church policy to Nazi racial policy we find noticeably less popular discomfort. There was indeed an outcry against euthanasia from ordinary Germans as well as clergy, and it undoubtedly was heartfelt; but it nonetheless revealed sympathy for the premises behind "containing" the hereditarily ill and genetically "inferior," the mentally retarded, the severely disabled, the alcoholic, and the "work shy." Disturbingly, opposition to euthanasia was often confined to questioning whether the regime could *legally* justify terminating life. It did not go further to avow the unconditional preservation of life itself.[59] Furthermore, opposition to euthanasia focused exclusively on protecting racially untainted Germans.

There was a virtual absence of mass protest against the deportation and extermination of Jews, and this absence then increased the risks for the few who did come to their aid. Furthermore, because those who helped or consorted with Jews were often social "misfits," persons whose lifestyles did not meet "normal" bourgeois expectations, the regime had little to fear in punishing them for disobeying the regime's racial laws.[60] Repression succeeded when the regime knew it would not face public disapprobation and, in fact, the Gestapo arrested rescuers of Jews precisely because their neighbors denounced them.The suppression of the left and the deportation of the Jews, both of which drew responses ranging from approbation to studied igno- rance, testify not merely to the fanaticism of the Nazi leadership, but even more so to the broad tolerance that allowed the regime to pursue its racial and political goals.

Thus, the combined unwillingness and inability of the Confessing Church to expand its mission beyond preserving the "true" Evangelical church in a culture where the church sought a captive audience for its mes- sage had grave consequences. Staking claim to an institution with substantial reserves of popular and elite loyalty, the Confessing Church failed to chal- lenge Nazi brutality, thus showing that the viciousness of Nazism did not depend on German civilians becoming equally rabid about racial purity. The Confessing Church is a disturbing and negative demonstration of two char- acteristics of modern Europe and Germany that historians have recently acknowledged: the strong, if fluctuating, influence of the Christian churches and the relative lack of secularization in the modern era, at least until the end of World War II.[61] The insistence of the Confessing Church on preserving a Germany linked to its Reformation heritage, by exposing the continuing, deeply problematic relationship between Christianity and Judaism, facili- tated the isolation, deportation, and extermination of minorities, especially Jews, who did not "belong" to the German nation. To be sure, the Nazi "national community" bore little resemblance to the national vision of the Confessing Church, yet neither tolerated "alien influences."

Dietrich Bonhoeffer and Hitler's Persecution of the Jews

Kenneth C. Barnes

Introduction

Post-Holocaust Christians have generally tried to make Dietrich Bonhoeffer into a saint, a hero, and a martyr. Of all the leaders of the Confessing Church, Bonhoeffer consistently called for the most assertive response to Nazi inroads into church affairs. Moreover he was eventually imprisoned and executed for taking a further step, in his involvement with the German Resistance movement. Bonhoeffer's biographer, Eberhard Bethge, who not by chance was his best friend and student, as well as his relative by marriage, has complied with attempts to heroize by detailing almost every moment in Bonhoeffer's life and editing almost every word that fell from his pen. Along with Bethge's edited collected works of Bonhoeffer, his long biography of Bonhoeffer's short life, lacking though it is in objectivity, nonetheless remains the lodestone of Bonhoeffer studies. Bonhoeffer's Boswell, as Michael Goldberg has called Bethge, has provided Protestants with what they desperately wanted in the cold, dark, gray world after Auschwitz: the sound of a courageous moral voice.[1]

Yet the iconoclasts did not wait for long. Within a decade after the discovery of Bonhoeffer in Anglo-America, both Christian and Jewish authors pointed out that, like most heroes, Bonhoeffer had feet of clay. Perhaps Bethge had done his work too well, for there, along with the courageous statements, readers could find writings easily labeled as ambiguous, contradictory, acquiescent, and even antisemitic. The most strident of his critics, Stanley Rosenbaum, eventually dismissed Bonhoeffer as merely "the best of a bad lot." The "bad lot" to which Rosenbaum referred was not just German Protestants or the German people, but all of European Christianity.[2]

This study examines Bonhoeffer's response to the persecution of Jews in Nazi Germany. It presents Bonhoeffer as somewhere between the two impassioned portraits fashioned in the last thirty years. Bonhoeffer was an utterly human figure who vacillated, but also a young man who grew up and began to think more for himself. By the end of his life, he acted courageously on behalf of the oppressed.

By virtue of his early background, Bonhoeffer was less disposed than many of his contemporaries to the virulent forms of German antisemitism. Born in 1906 in Breslau, Silesia, where his father was a professor of neurology and psychiatry, Dietrich grew up in western Berlin's fashionable Grunewald neighborhood after his father received a promotion to the medical faculty at the University of Berlin in 1912. The Bonhoeffer children—Dietrich had seven brothers and sisters—lived in an atmosphere of bourgeois privilege complete with a private governess, music lessons, and a vacation home in the Harz Mountains. With the highly educated university crowd as their social circle, the Bonhoeffer family held to liberal democratic views and enthusiastically supported the Weimar Republic.[3]

Young Dietrich had several associations with assimilated Jews in his neighborhood and school. Grunewald had the highest percentage of Jewish residents of any neighborhood in Berlin, a city in which the proportion of Jews was nearly five times greater than in Germany as a whole. Four out of the ten members of Dietrich's graduating class (his *Abiturklasse*) at the gymnasium came from Jewish households.[4] In the mid-1920s, while he studied theology at the University of Berlin, Dietrich's twin sister, Sabine, announced her engagement to Gerhard Leibholz, a Christianized Jew. Some members of the extended family raised eyebrows at the union, but the nuclear family, especially Dietrich, appeared enthusiastic about the marriage when it took place in 1926. Three years later, while Dietrich studied for his doctorate in theology, he became especially close to a young theologian of Jewish ancestry, Franz Hildebrandt. With both a best friend and a brother-in-law of Jewish descent, the liberal Bonhoeffer thought Jewishness was of absolutely no consequence, and that Franz and Gerhard were no different from any other Germans. The Bonhoeffer family utterly disregarded racial origins, as long as one embraced Christian German culture. Their liberal view could be said to embody a subtle form of antisemitism, however, for failing to affirm Jewishness. Neither Dietrich nor his family apparently had any contact with religiously observant Jews or Jews of the ghetto.[5]

In Dietrich's rather sheltered world of suburban Berlin and the theological hothouse of the University, there appeared to be no Jewish "problem."

After his ordination as a Protestant pastor and then further study to complete his habilitation as lecturer at the University, in 1931 Bonhoeffer took a nine-month leave of absence to study at Union Theological Seminary in New York City. In America he appears to have encountered racism for the first time. Spending his free time in neighboring Harlem, Bonhoeffer acquired a taste for jazz and a true love for the African-American Christian culture. He wrote to his elder brother, Karl-Friedrich, about his interest in the race issue. Karl-Friedrich, a brilliant physicist, had refused a position at Harvard, he told his brother, because he could not bear thinking that his children would grow up in this American culture of racism. Reflecting the naïveté of German liberals, he wrote to Dietrich: "At all events, our Jewish question is a joke in comparison; there cannot be any people left who maintain they are oppressed here."

Of course, while Dietrich studied in New York, from September 1930 to June 1931, the situation changed rapidly back home. As the Great Depression arrived in Germany, the Nazi Party made great gains in the Reichstag and the streets. The winds of change blew even through the hallowed halls of the University of Berlin. Around the same time as Karl-Friedrich's letter to his brother in January 1931, a group of nationalist students, shouting "Death to the Jews," grabbed several Jewish students and threw them out of the entrance hall of the university onto the courtyard below.[6]

When Dietrich returned to Germany in the summer of 1931 and resumed his post as lecturer at the university, he would witness firsthand the growth of the Nazi Party and the spread of antisemitism. No record survives of any writings or speeches by Bonhoeffer from this time directed against the movement. The accession of Hitler to power in January 1933, however, required a response. His brother-in-law, his best friend, and other acquaintances suddenly found themselves labeled as "non-Aryans." The Civil Service Law of April 7, which purged government employees who were of Jewish descent, threatened Leibholz, Dietrich's brother-in-law, who was a professor of law at the University of Göttingen. He was spared from dismissal only when President Hindenburg intervened to exempt non-Aryan government employees who had fought in the war.[7]

Bonhoeffer's response in this critical year, 1933, was hesitant and tentative, a far cry from the Bonhoeffer of later fame, the author of *Letters and Papers from Prison*. In the early months of the Third Reich, the strongest stand in the family was taken by Dietrich's ninety-one-year-old grandmother (Julie Bonhoeffer). During the boycott of Jewish businesses throughout Germany that took place on 1 April 1933, she went shopping as usual to buy her butter from a Jewish shopkeeper. An SA man posted outside the store reportedly asked her, "Do you really have to buy from this Jew of all people?" She rapped her cane on his high boots, shoved him aside, and said in her Swabian dialect, "I will buy my butter where I always buy my butter." According to Emmy Bonhoeffer, Dietrich's sister-in-law who told this story, Grandmother Bonhoeffer was the shopkeeper's only customer of the day.[8]

On the other hand, Dietrich's father, Karl Bonhoeffer, embarrassed the family by his involvement in the celebrated Reichstag fire case. When Martin van der Lubbe, the mentally impaired Dutch communist youth branded by the Nazis as the arsonist, went on a hunger strike in prison, authorities called in Karl Bonhoeffer, the eminent psychiatrist, and one of his colleagues to examine the accused. While many observers outside and within Germany believed, as many historians do today, that Nazis themselves burned down the Reichstag, the two psychiatrists who visited van der Lubbe seven times in 1933 made no mention of guilt or innocence in their final report.[9]

In the heady days of spring 1933, Dietrich likewise took the cowardly way out when Leibholz asked him to conduct funeral services for his father, who died on April 11. Unlike Gerhard, the elder Leibholz had never been baptized. Under the tense atmosphere of the time, the general superintendent of Dietrich's Old Prussian Union Church (the Old Prussian Union was a component, the largest one, of the German Evangelical Church) advised him against conducting a funeral for a Jew, and he heeded the advice. He later regretted his inaction and asked forgiveness of Gerhard.[10]

"The Church and the Jewish Question"

With his pen and voice, Bonhoeffer did much to address the situation of Jews. His outrage in 1933, however, was directed primarily toward the discriminatory measures aimed at assimilated "Christian Jews," like Gerhard Leibholz and Franz Hildebrandt. By March of that year, the German Christian Movement, the fanatically pro-Nazi party of Protestant clergy, began plans to apply the Aryan Paragraph to the Church, which would result in the suspension of non-Aryans from the rosters of the Protestant clergy. As a result of the victory of the German Christians in the church elections during the summer of 1933, the Aryan Paragraph became official policy in the Prussian church in early September. Bonhoeffer spent much of his energy between April and September 1933 combating the German Christians and working against the enactment of this Aryan Paragraph.[11]

By the end of March 1933, Bonhoeffer had drawn up six theses about the situation of Christian Jews for a pastoral discussion group that met in the home of Gerhard Jacobi, the pastor of the Kaiser Wilhelm Memorial Church in Berlin. After the boycott of Jewish businesses began and the Civil Service Law was decreed in early April, Bonhoeffer added to his six theses a lengthy preamble that discussed the church's attitude about state actions toward the

Jews. The essay then addressed both the Jewish and the Christian-Jewish "problems." He continued to rework the essay, and by April 15, just a few days after he had refused to conduct the funeral for Gerhard Leibholz's father, he finished the article, titled "The Church and the Jewish Question," which was published in the following June issue of *Der Vormarsch*. Of all Bonhoeffer's writings, this short essay has been perhaps the most scrutinized, by both his hagiographers, who wish to find in this essay the basis of a strong defense of the Jews, and his detractors, who find the essay anti-Jewish. These varying assessments are possible because Bonhoeffer contradicts himself throughout the essay.[12]

Nevertheless, in this essay lies the blueprint for Bonhoeffer's response to the persecution of the Jews for the rest of his short life. The essay outlined three positions that he would take in successive phases of his career, which I will term (1) a call to qualified obedience, which characterizes his stance in 1933–1934; (2) a call to suffering, which describes his views from 1935 to 1939 and is most visible in his work *The Cost of Discipleship*; and (3) a call to resistance, which eventually brought him to prison and his death in 1945.

First, in his call to obedience, Bonhoeffer legitimated the state's right within the political realm to enact measures dealing with the Jews, drawing the line at the state's intervention in church affairs affecting Christian Jews. Consistent with traditional Lutheran distinction between the two kingdoms, spiritual and secular, his attention for the next two years focused on action within the ecclesiastical arena, not on political action. His second position, a call to suffering, picked up on the theme that Christians should stand in solidarity with the Jews in their suffering. From 1935 to 1939, he tried to persuade the Confessing Church to take a strong public stand on the persecution of Jews and be willing to accept the consequences. Then after 1939, when he lost confidence in the Confessing Church, he returned to the third theme of this early essay, direct political action, and applied this idea through his own association with the Resistance movement. He articulated the idea of active resistance more clearly in his theological works from this period, *Ethics* and *Letters and Papers from Prison*.

In his conservative Lutheran persona, expressed in the 1933 essay as the call to obedience, Bonhoeffer clearly distinguished between the positions of baptized and non-baptized Jews and took a strong stand in support of Christian Jews. He categorically dismissed the exclusion of Jews by race from the Christian church as impossible. In the view of the church, he said, Jewishness was not a racial concept, but a religious one. While Bonhoeffer had doubtless heard Nazis refer to the words of Martin Luther to justify antisemitic measures, he ended his essay by quoting the Reformer: "There is no other rule or test for who is a member of the people of God or the church of Christ than this: where there is a little band of those who accept this word of the Lord, teach it purely and confess against those who persecute it, and for that reason suffer what is their due." The baptized Jew who professed Christ was a member of the church, Bonhoeffer concluded, and the church could not allow the state to determine its membership on the basis of race.[13]

While Bonhoeffer stood firm and unwavering on behalf of Christian Jews, his remarks about Jews *as Jews* sound more ambivalent. He accepted the traditional Lutheran distinction between the two kingdoms and granted enormous jurisdiction to the state to act politically, free from any limitation or intervention by the church. He went even further than Luther by echoing the neoconservative Lutheran arguments of the 1920s. Theologians such as Paul Althaus and Emanuel Hirsch had posited the national state as the embodiment of God's law, as an entity that both functioned as a divine order to preserve human life on earth and revealed God's action in history. Bonhoeffer conceded that the "Jewish question" was a real historical problem that came under the domain of the state to resolve, and he instructed the church never to criticize the history-making actions of the state. Concerning the Jews specifically, Bonhoeffer said, the church "cannot in the first place exert direct political action" or demand that the state act differently.[14]

As if to explain, if not justify, recent measures against Jews, Bonhoeffer's essay reiterated the old-fashioned, Christian, antisemitic belief that the suffering of the Jews throughout history came as a punishment for their crucifixion of Christ. He quoted Luther again on this point: "Jews are the poorest people among all nations upon earth, they are tossed to and fro, they are scattered here and there in all lands, they have no certain place where they could remain safely and must always be afraid that they will be driven out." This pattern of suffering would only end, for Bonhoeffer as well as for Luther, with the conversion of the Jews to Christianity. So the Jewish "problem" would continue until all the Jews became Christians. These views, of course, were common among Christians before the Holocaust and have persisted within conservative Christian circles even well afterward.[15] The theological world of the 1950s that so enthusiastically embraced Bonhoeffer would find the Bonhoeffer of this essay a stranger.

Fortunately, Bonhoeffer did not stop with obedience in his famous essay of 1933. He went on to make bolder calls for charitable action toward and empathy with the Jews. He instructed the church to assist victims of the state's discriminatory acts, to stand with them in their suffering regardless of their religious profession. He again quoted Luther—the early Luther, not the vengeful older man—who called in 1523 for merciful treatment of the Jews: "If the Apostles, who also were Jews, had dealt with us Gentiles as we Gentiles deal with the Jews, there would have been no Christians among the Gentiles.

But seeing that they have acted in such a brotherly way toward us, we in turn should act in a brotherly way toward the Jews in case we might convert some. For we ourselves are still not yet fully their equals, much less their superiors. . . . But now we use force against them . . . what good will we do them with that? Similarly, how will we benefit them by forbidding them to live and work and have other human fellowship with us, thus driving them to practise usury?" For Bonhoeffer, Christian kindness and charity toward Jews meant sharing in their suffering.[16]

But Bonhoeffer's words went beyond a call for charitable actions toward victimized Jews. He articulated a principle by which the church could speak out against and even engage in direct action to resist anti-Jewish laws or state programs. While he accepted the conservative view of the state as a divine order of preservation, Bonhoeffer called for the church to ask if recent state actions, namely, the laws against non-Aryans, were actually in accordance with this role. When the state terrorized Jews and denied them basic civil liberties, Bonhoeffer asked, did it preserve law and order or undermine it? Using this logic, the church could speak out on political issues from its traditional theological perspective. Even more radically, Bonhoeffer argued that the church might need to resort to political action against the state if the state failed to preserve law and order. He described the church's political role with the image of the church not only bandaging the victims crushed under the wheel of the state, but at some point throwing itself into the spokes of the wheel. However, Bonhoeffer backed off from this third response by saying in regard to the Jewish problem, the "compelling demands of the hour" called for charitable assistance and speaking out. He did not yet call for direct political action in 1933; this he left open, to be decided if necessary in the future by an evangelical council.[17]

As with Luther, who was never a paragon of consistency, the force of Bonhoeffer's argument cancels itself out by his contradictory presentation. For each argument for church action he presented a counter-argument which invalidated that action. With his expression of Christian solidarity with the suffering of Jews came the Christian antisemitic rationale used for centuries to justify persecution of the Jews. While in April 1933 he aimed to focus attention on injustices perpetrated against Jews and rally support for Christian Jews, his views smacked of the very attitudes and prejudices that made the Nazi Party successful and the Holocaust possible. While on the one hand he called for the church to question Nazi policies aimed at Jews as to whether they fulfilled the state's role as an order of preservation, and even suggested the church might actively resist such state policies, elsewhere in his essay he had forbidden the church to speak or act in such a way. Bonhoeffer's essay reflects a humane, concerned, well-intentioned, and—in the environment of

April 1933—courageous individual. But the young Bonhoeffer was very much a creation of the sheltered, upper-middle-class, Lutheran milieu in which his parents raised him. In a time of such extraordinary and rapid change, and with his penchant for language obscured by theological abstractions, the twenty-seven-year-old Bonhoeffer probably was not aware of the contradictions inherent in his essay.

A Call to Obedience

As Bonhoeffer's life progressed, he passed eventually through all three themes introduced in his essay of 1933. However, during the next two years, his work centered on the church's stand regarding Christian Jews. Historians are now beginning to recognize that the German church struggle, as it progressed in 1933 and 1934, took place not because Protestant church leaders repudiated the politics of the Nazi regime. It involved instead a power struggle over who would control the church. The key test concerned the application of Nazi racial policy to the personnel and membership of the Protestant churches. As the summer of 1933 progressed, Bonhoeffer took a stronger position than anyone in his church in opposition to these measures against Christian Jews. In June, before a large crowd of students at the University of Berlin gathered to debate contemporary church politics, Bonhoeffer countered the German Christian Professor Fabricius, who insisted on the need to maintain the purity of the German gospel and to resist "judaizing." Bonhoeffer responded that only those who were weak in their faith need to eject people from their congregation; the weak need a racial law, he said, the strong do not.[18] Also in June, the Gestapo threatened to arrest Bonhoeffer and his friend Gerhard Jacobi if they would not stop canvassing for the upcoming July church elections against the German Christians and their plan to base the church on race.[19]

After the disastrous church elections in July, in which German Christians took over leadership in Bonhoeffer's church, the Old Prussian Union, the new leaders made good on their threats and proposed that the Aryan Paragraph become church law. Bonhoeffer drafted a leaflet, circulated among pastors and congregations in his district, in which he spoke in strong language against the exclusion of non-Aryan clergy from the church and denounced the German Christian proposal to segregate Jewish Christians into their own congregations.[20] Shortly after he wrote the pamphlet, the Young Reformation Movement, the association of pastors who had opposed the German Christians in the church elections, chose Bonhoeffer and Hermann Sasse, a theology professor at Erlangen University, to draft a confessional statement for the national synod planned for later in the fall. The two met in August at Bethel, near Bielefeld. Bonhoeffer had never before visited Bethel, the most famous home in Germany for the mentally and physically handicapped, and was stunned by the experience. From Bethel he wrote prophetically to his grand-mother: "It is sheer madness to believe, as is done today, that the sick can or ought to be legally eliminated. It is virtually the same as building a tower of Babel, and is bound to bring its own revenge."[21]

The purpose of this Bethel Confession, authored by Bonhoeffer and Sasse, was to force a confrontation with the German Christians over the intrusion of racist, nationalistic ideology into the traditional Lutheran theol-ogy of the church. Part of the confession would respond to the Aryan Para-graph. Wilhelm Vischer, a teacher at the Bethel School of Theology, assisted Bonhoeffer and drafted the article on the Jewish question. The confession, completed by August 25, took a strong stand against the German Christian plan to remove Christian Jews from the mainstream of the church and isolate them in their own congregations. The document called for gentile Christians to suffer persecution rather than abandon their Jewish-Christian brothers and sisters.

However, more conservative leaders of the church opposition, under Martin Niemöller's direction, edited the confession significantly, watering down the passages about Jews and even striking the section calling for soli-darity in suffering with the Jews. Bonhoeffer refused to sign the version that was sent on to the synod. Thus by August 1933, before the Confessing Church had even been organized, Bonhoeffer had already begun to split from the other leaders, such as Niemöller, who were either more willing to compro-mise or less concerned about the plight of the Jews.[22]

Bonhoeffer's worst fears were realized when the general synod of his Prussian church, now dominated by German Christians elected in the July church elections, voted at its meeting in Berlin on 5–6 September to imple-ment the Aryan Paragraph. When one Young Reformation leader, Karl Koch, rose to speak on behalf of the defrocked pastors, he was shouted down from the stage. The dissenting group, which by now included Niemöller, left the hall in protest. At gatherings afterward at the homes of Niemöller and Jacobi, Bonhoeffer and Hildebrandt called for mass clergy resignations to protest the clause. Hildebrandt, who had just been ordained in July, would lose his job under the new law. Bonhoeffer wrote to Sasse and Karl Barth for advice about whether to leave the church or stay. Barth advised him to wait. On 7 Septem-ber, Bonhoeffer and Niemöller drafted a statement declaring that anyone who assented to the Aryan Paragraph excluded himself from the communion of the church. An edited version of this statement became the manifesto of the Pastors' Emergency League, the first organized dissent against Nazi efforts to control the churches.

From these frantic efforts in Berlin, Bonhoeffer went in late September directly to an international ecumenical meeting to present the problems in the German church to the world Christian community. At this meeting in Sophia, Bulgaria, of the World Alliance for Promoting Friendly Relations among the Churches, Bonhoeffer explained the Jewish situation in Germany, the Aryan Paragraph, and the divisions within the German Protestant Church. Most important, he called for the ecumenical movement to withhold recognition of the new church government in Germany. As a result, the Sophia conference passed the following resolution: "We deplore the fact that the State measures against the Jews in Germany have had such an effect on public opinion that in some circles the Jewish race is considered a race of inferior status. We protest against the resolution of the Prussian General Synod and other Synods which apply the Aryan paragraph of the State to the Church, putting serious disabilities upon ministers and church officers who by chance of birth are non-Aryan, which we believe to be a denial of the explicit teaching and spirit of the Gospel of Jesus Christ."[23]

Bonhoeffer returned home to Berlin feeling rather vindicated, confident that the world Christian community had heard and responded to Germany's distress. He returned just in time for the national synod meeting of the Protestant Church Federation in Wittenberg. Although he was not a delegate—because all the Young Reformers had stormed out of the hall in protest at the Berlin synod in September, none were elected to the national meeting—he had his father's chauffeur drive him and Hildebrandt to Wittenberg to observe the meeting. They took with them a stack of handbills against the Aryan Paragraph to pass out and plaster along the streets. However, the new German Christian *Reichsbishof*, Ludwig Müller, allowed no discussion of the issue, and Bonhoeffer left the meeting feeling like an abject failure. The mass resignations from the church for which he had called earlier did not materialize. He himself did not resign, but chose flight instead.[24]

By the fall of 1933, Bonhoeffer had emerged within the ecumenical community as the chief spokesperson for the dissenting German pastors. Within his own church, the Old Prussian Union, he pushed hardest for an active opposition to the German Christians, even advocating that dissenters withdraw into a separate free church, unencumbered by any ties with the Nazi government. Foreshadowing his future role within the Confessing Church, he found himself increasingly isolated from his peers who were more willing to compromise with the German Christian church leadership. He wrote in October to Barth: "I felt that I was incomprehensibly in radical opposition to all my friends, that my views of matters were taking me more and more into isolation, although I was and remained in the closest personal relationship with these men."[25] However, while in the thick of the German church conflict and his defense of Christian Jews, Bonhoeffer made the decision to withdraw.

In October the young theologian, lecturer at the university, and leader of the clerical opposition to the new German church, left Germany for London, where he became the simple parish pastor for two congregations of German expatriates, mostly businessmen and their families. As he explained to Barth, "I simply did not any longer feel up to the questions and demands which came to me . . . so I thought that it was probably time to go into the wilderness."[26] He remained in England until April 1935.

For the year and a half he lived abroad, Bonhoeffer stayed in constant touch with his family and church connections back in Germany and used his presence in England to keep news of the German church situation before the eyes of the world. He became especially close to the Anglican bishop of Chichester, George Kennedy Allen Bell, whom he knew from his ecumenical contacts and who became the chief advocate for the Confessing Church within the ecumenical movement. Nevertheless, Bonhoeffer seemed ashamed of his decision to leave Germany, feeling that he had run away from the critical battle. He was cheered somewhat by the presence of Hildebrandt, who, now that he had been made unemployed by the Aryan Paragraph, could stay with Dietrich in the cold, damp parsonage for months at a time. Yet Bonhoeffer's flight to England at the height of the conflict at home suggests an uncertainty and ambivalence reminiscent of the contradictions in his April 1933 essay about the church and the Jewish question. This first phase in his struggle with the Nazi regime was marked by paradox: courageous fight and then a cowardly flight, a stand of solidarity with the Jewish people but then a theological profession that identified them as second-class citizens.

A Call to Suffering

The second phase of Bonhoeffer's personal struggle began while he was in exile in England, when he responded to the call to suffering in Germany. From London he watched the birth of the Confessing Church in May of 1934 at Barmen. Here, finally, was an evangelical council akin to what he proposed in April 1933, one that could call for action against the state. However, the Barmen Declaration said nothing about the Jews. Two months later, in August 1934, Bonhoeffer traveled to Fanø, Denmark, to attend the annual meeting of the Life and Work Movement, one of the early ecumenical organizations under the leadership of his Anglican friend, Bishop Bell. At Fanø, the ecumenical movement—under Bonhoeffer's urging and to the disgust of the official delegation from the German Evangelical Church—recognized the Confessing Church as the genuine church of Germany. Thus, despite his hand-wringing about leaving the battle by his escape to England, Bonhoeffer stayed involved from the sidelines. In the spring of 1935, he returned to Germany to lead a seminary for the Confessing Church, temporarily housed at Zingst on the Baltic Coast and then later at Finkenwalde, near Stettin in quiet, remote Pomerania. Here he met Eberhard Bethge, one of his first seminarians, and they became lifelong friends.

Bonhoeffer concentrated his energies during the next years on the practical work of running a seminary. But his broader goal was building up the Confessing Church as the true church of Jesus Christ in Germany, in opposition to the national church. However, during these years the Confessing Church found itself bitterly divided, with some of its members supporting various degrees of compromise with the Nazi regime and the German Evangelical Church. Bonhoeffer and his Finkenwalde students made up the radical wing of the church, consistently opposing the concessions made by more conservative leaders.

In September 1935 the state enacted the harsh Nuremberg Laws, which laid the basis for so many later state actions against Jews. Shortly thereafter Bonhoeffer learned from Hildebrandt that leaders of the Confessing Church from the Old Prussian Union were preparing a statement for their upcoming regional synod in the Berlin suburb of Steglitz. According to Hildebrandt, although the leading committee planned to reaffirm the Confessing Church's rejection of the Aryan Paragraph, as a concession it would recognize the state's right to legislate in the political realm about the Jewish question, thus seeming to condone the Nuremberg Laws. In response, Bonhoeffer brought the entire population of the seminary to Berlin to pressure the Steglitz assembly to take a public stand against the Nuremberg Laws. As a result of Bonhoeffer's efforts, the synod chose not to adopt the offensive clause. Instead, as Bonhoeffer had done in his essay of 1933, the synod called for missions to the Jews.[27]

The next year, Bonhoeffer strongly supported a memorandum to Hitler, drawn up by the Provisional Church Administration of the Confessing Church. Hildebrandt had helped draft the letter, which expressed concern, among other things, that Nazi ideology forced people into the hatred of Jews. Around this time, while he was the leader of the Finkenwalde seminary, Bonhoeffer apparently uttered his oft-quoted words, "Only he who cries out for the Jews may sing Gregorian chants."[28]

Of all the parties within the Confessing Church in the mid-1930s, Dietrich Bonhoeffer and his close associates pushed hardest for Christian solidarity with the suffering Jews. Yet in his own writing from these years, Bonhoeffer remained strangely silent about the Jewish question itself. While at Finkenwalde, he wrote the now famous book, *The Cost of Discipleship;* in fact, his seminary lectures of 1935–37 formed much of the book. Although it does not speak directly of the Jews, this book presented the theory underlying Bonhoeffer's call for a strong stand by the Confessing Church. In it, he argued that the call of Christ summons true disciples to suffering, to communion with the crucified. He emphasized the costly, the radical, the dangerous side of Christian discipleship, not an acquiescent, easy, guarded, and safe Christian life.

However, even with this focus on the call to suffering, Bonhoeffer did not yet depart from the traditional Lutheran political philosophy. Luther had called for Christians passively to disobey a government that required acts inconsistent with God's law, pointing out that they must be prepared to accept the consequences of such a stand. For his part, Bonhoeffer emphasized the challenge in this difficult teaching, rather than the more conventional Lutheran preoccupation with grace and forgiveness. *The Cost of Discipleship*, with its call to suffering, was Bonhoeffer's answer to the events since 1933.[29]

Soon after the publication of *The Cost of Discipleship* in 1937, authorities closed down Bonhoeffer's seminary at Finkenwalde. The state stepped up its actions against the Confessing Church in the summer of 1937, arresting Niemöller and forbidding German church delegates to attend the ecumenical meeting coming up in Oxford. Several of Bonhoeffer's former students, who by now had scattered throughout northern Germany, were arrested and interrogated, their houses searched, and so on. To replace the Finkenwalde Seminary, Confessing Church leaders worked out a system of "collective pastorates," whereby students were assigned to different parishes as assistants to the pastors but lived communally in two vicarages. Bonhoeffer divided his time for instruction between these two sites.

For most of the years 1938 to 1941, Bonhoeffer lived in remote Outer Pomerania trying to conduct his pastoral training under increasingly difficult circumstances. For him this period was similar to late 1933 and 1934, a time of uncertainty and soul-searching. He began to lose confidence in the Confessing Church, as it became stymied by internal divisions and held to a conservative, defensive strategy, refusing to take risks. The willingness of most Confessing pastors, around 85 percent, to take the loyalty oath to Hitler in 1937 and 1938 greatly disheartened him.[30] Bonhoeffer seemed not to know what route his life should take.

All this occurred just as the state stepped up its persecution of Jews. As formal and informal restrictions against Jews tightened in 1938, the Bonhoeffer family decided that the Leibholzes should leave Germany. Hildebrandt had already fled to London. Dietrich and his friend Bethge accompanied Gerhard and Sabine and their children on a "visit" to Switzerland in September, and from there the family traveled on to England. Bonhoeffer used his friendship with Bishop Bell, who had recently been appointed to the House of Lords, to secure Gerhard a position at Oxford University. The flight of his twin sister's family from antisemitism affected him deeply.[31]

The Leibholzes arrived in England just in time to read in the newspapers about the savagery of *Kristallnacht* in November. The violence reached the small village world of Bonhoeffer's Outer Pomerania; the synagogue in Köslin, one of the two towns between which Bonhoeffer divided his time, was burned. As soon as possible he made a trip to Berlin to survey the situation there for himself. According to Bethge, *Kristallnacht* marked a turning away for Bonhoeffer from some of the views he had expressed in 1933. No longer did he connect the suffering of Jews to a punishing curse. When some of his seminarians uttered this view after watching the Köslin synagogue burn, he corrected them saying, "When today the synagogue are set afire, tomorrow the churches will burn." In a circular letter sent to former Finkenwalde students in the week following the violence, Bonhoeffer pointed them to Scripture verses about which he had thought much, he said, in the last few days: Psalm 74, Zechariah 2:12, Romans 9:3f; 11:11-15. All these passages referred to Jews not as potential converts, as in his language of 1933, but as God's special people, the apple of God's eye. In Bonhoeffer's own Bible, Bethge notes that he had marked verse 8 of Psalm 74: "They say to themselves: Let us plunder them! They burn all the houses of God in the land," and had written in a marginal notation: *9 November 1938,* followed by an exclamation mark.[32]

A few Confessing pastors used their pulpits to denounce the violence. Bishop Theophil Wurm of Stuttgart, one of the more conservative leaders of the Confessing movement, made a protest. But the church largely remained silent about the atrocities of November 1938. Disgusted by the timidity of the Confessing Church and the inhumanity of the Third Reich toward the Jews and fearing he would be called up for military service, Bonhoeffer by 1939 again contemplated flight from Germany. He and Bethge spent five weeks in England in March and April of 1939, during which time the Nazis invaded Czechoslovakia, making a mockery of the Munich Agreement of the previous fall.

Through a visit with Reinhold Niebuhr, who was on holiday in London for a few weeks, Bonhoeffer received an invitation to visit New York. Upon his arrival in June, the Federal Council of Churches offered him a three-year post as coordinator of church work with German refugees. He had found his window of escape. However, he searched his soul, as he had while serving in the London pastorate in 1933, and decided flight from Germany was wrong. Regretting that so many had gone to so much trouble to find him a place of refuge, he wrote to Niebuhr in July explaining his decision to return to Germany: "I made a mistake in coming to America. I must live through this difficult period of our national history with the Christian people of Germany. I will have no right to participate in the reconstruction of Christian life in Germany after the war if I do not share the trials of this time with my people."[33]

A Call to Resistance

Just as flight six years earlier had prompted Bonhoeffer to move into a new phase of his life and work, so again he began a new course when he arrived back in Germany. In his writing and actions, this last phase of his life exemplified the call to resistance he had articulated in his 1933 essay. He returned to the loneliness of Pomerania to lead what was to be the final group of seminarians through instruction at one of the collective pastorates. In March 1940 the Gestapo closed this pastorate down, and he tried to continue his instruction through personal visits and correspondence. By September authorities forbade him to speak in public or publish any of his writings. With his work now virtually shut down, Bonhoeffer spent much of his time in 1940 and 1941 writing *Ethics,* an unfinished work published eventually after the war. Also in these years he drew away from the institutional church and into the movement of resistance against Hitler, a decision that would bring about his death.

Bonhoeffer had been introduced to members of the conspiracy against Hitler as early as 1938 through his brother-in-law, Hans von Dohnanyi, who had married Dietrich's older sister Christine. Dohnanyi was in the thick of the conspiracy led by Admiral Wilhelm Canaris and Major General Hans Oster in the *Abwehr,* the counterintelligence office of the High Military Command. In 1939, Canaris had made Dohnanyi a staff lawyer in the *Abwehr.* Dietrich's older brother, Klaus Bonhoeffer, and Rüdiger Schleicher, another brother-in-law, both legal advisers for Lufthansa, also became involved with a Resistance circle there.

With his work taken away from him and still fearing being drafted into military service, Dietrich managed to secure an appointment as a civilian agent on Dohnanyi's staff in the *Abwehr* by November 1940. This post kept him safe both from military draft and arrest. Frequently during the next two years, he used his cover in the *Abwehr* and his accompanying travel permit to visit Spain, Norway, Sweden, and Switzerland, smuggling out information on behalf of the Resistance movement. Bonhoeffer and Dohnanyi even traveled to Italy, where they made contact with the Italian Resistance. Bonhoeffer especially used his contacts in the ecumenical office in Geneva, particularly Willem Visser't Hooft, to transmit information.[34] In 1942 he arranged to meet his friend Bishop Bell in Sweden to pass on plans drawn up by the Canaris-Oster Resistance circle for an impending putsch, plans that Bell transferred to the British foreign minister, Sir Anthony Eden. The British Cabinet chose, however, to ignore the plans, which went awry in any case.[35]

Bonhoeffer's work for the Resistance coincided with the heightened persecution of Jews in 1941. Soon after he joined the *Abwehr,* Jews were forced to wear the yellow star for the first time. By the fall, deportation of Jewish families from Berlin had begun. The Bonhoeffer family in Berlin, in fact, helped a sixty-eight-year-old friend to pack when she received notification of her deportation to Theresienstadt. In October, Dietrich, along with Friedrich Justus Perels, the legal adviser to the Confessing Church, wrote up a report containing all the facts they could ascertain about the Jewish deportation. They presented the report via Dohnanyi to Oster and General Ludwig Beck, the leading conspirators in the German command, in the vain hope that the military would intervene or speed up the plans for the overthrow.[36]

Bonhoeffer also became involved that fall in an *Abwehr* plan to rescue several Jews from deportation by getting them out of Germany. Called Operation Seven, the scheme involved sending a group of twelve to fifteen Jews, mostly personal friends of Admiral Canaris, to Switzerland on an *Abwehr* propaganda program to demonstrate to the foreign press that there was no persecution of Jews in Germany. It was a complicated affair, for the *Abwehr* actually had to employ the Jews, which required circumvention of the law and enormous amounts of red tape. Bonhoeffer worked with Dohnanyi, who was largely in charge of the plan, for over a year before the refugees all arrived safely in Switzerland.[37]

Operation Seven became the downfall for the Bonhoeffer family, for through a Gestapo investigation of the misuse of funds within the *Abwehr*, the plan was uncovered. Bonhoeffer and Dohnanyi were arrested in April 1943. The Gestapo had not yet uncovered, however, the *Abwehr* plot to overthrow Hitler, which culminated in the famous bombing attempt that nearly succeeded on 20 July 1944. Although the Gestapo found little hard evidence against him, Bonhoeffer remained under arrest until his execution with fellow conspirators Oster and Canaris on 9 April 1945 at Flossenburg concentration camp.

Bonhoeffer spent most of his last two years in Tegel Prison in Berlin, where because of family connections, he received special treatment, better food, and visitor privileges. At Tegel he was able to write letters, essays, and poetry, all edited later by Bethge as *Letters and Papers from Prison*. This work— along with his *Ethics*, begun while in Pomerania early during the war and continued while he worked for the *Abwehr*—reveal his state of mind during this last phase of life. They show that his call to resistance meant more than his personal involvement with the conspiracy against Hitler. It meant also new theological views that moved away from the traditional Lutheran stance he had taken earlier.

While working with the Resistance to circumvent, in what limited way he could, the deportation of the Jews in the early 1940s, Bonhoeffer, in his *Ethics*, denounced the program as theologically wrong: "Jesus Christ was the promised Messiah of the Israelite-Jewish people, and for that reason the line of our forefathers goes back beyond the appearance of Jesus Christ to the people of Israel. Western history is, by God's will, indissolubly linked with the people of Israel, not only genetically but also in a genuine uninterrupted encounter. The Jew keeps open the question of Christ. He is the sign of the free mercy-choice and of the repudiating wrath of God. 'Behold therefore the goodness and severity of God' (Rom. 11:22). An expulsion of the Jews from the west must necessarily bring with it the expulsion of Christ. For Jesus Christ was a Jew."[38]

In this intriguing passage, which has been much and variably interpreted, Bonhoeffer as never before linked Christianity with the Jews *as Jews,* not as potential Christians. Bethge, as always, wishes to put the most positive construction on Bonhoeffer's words by suggesting Bonhoeffer meant the Jews were the church; "they themselves 'constitute' the church as church."[39] But this passage contains the characteristic ambivalence of Bonhoeffer's work. The ultimate importance of Jews for Bonhoeffer's Christianity lay in their rejection of Christ, their role as a sign both that belief is a choice and that God punishes unbelievers. This latter idea came close to Bonhoeffer's 1933 view about a punishing curse.

In his 1933 essay on the Jews, Bonhoeffer had articulated the possibility of political action against the state but stopped short of actually calling for it. By the early 1940s, when he wrote his *Ethics,* his thinking had changed. Now he said, "an apocalyptic view of a particular government would necessarily have total disobedience as its consequence, for in that case every single act of obedience obviously involves a denial of Christ." Breaking the laws of the state through the use of violence would be the lesser of two evils, he said, in extraordinary situations. Breaking the law might be the only way to preserve the law. The only evil greater than violence, he concluded, came when violence served as the law and standard, as Bonhoeffer certainly believed had become the case in the Third Reich. In such an extraordinary situation, "there can only be a complete renunciation of every law, together with the knowledge that here one must make one's decision as a free venture, together also with the open admission that here the law is being infringed upon and violated and that necessity obeys no commandment."[40] Read in the light of what we know now about Bonhoeffer's involvement in the conspiracy to assassinate Hitler, these words sound like an attempt to convince himself or theologically justify to others a violent political revolution.

At about the moment he entered the *Abwehr* and thus came into a more active role in the Resistance movement, Bonhoeffer confessed his personal guilt and that of the church for what they had failed to do under the Nazi regime: "I am guilty of cowardly silence at a time when I ought to have spoken. I am guilty of hypocrisy and untruthfulness in the face of force. I have been lacking in compassion and I have denied the poorest of my brethren."

He saved his sharpest words, however, for his indictment of the church: "The Church confesses that she has witnessed the lawless application of brutal force, the physical and spiritual suffering of countless innocent people, oppression, hatred and murder, and that she has not raised her voice on behalf of the victims and has not found ways to hasten to their aid. She is guilty of the deaths of the weakest and most defenceless brothers of Jesus Christ."[41] Bonhoeffer's use of the phrase "brothers of Jesus Christ" indicates that he spoke here of the suffering and murder of Jews, a year before the Wannsee Conference sanctioned such brutality as official policy. Elsewhere in his *Ethics*, however, he broadened his scope by denouncing euthanasia of the physically and mentally ill and deficient.[42]

Bonhoeffer's last writings, published in *Letters and Papers from Prison*, are perhaps the most famous and widely read of his works. These works show a decisive theological turn toward what Bonhoeffer called "secular" or "religionless Christianity," catchphrases that would keep theology students talking for the next four decades. While Bonhoeffer's work from prison took a greater interest in the Old Testament, it says little explicitly about the Jews. However, the historical context that framed his work—a criminal regime that persecuted Jews—doubtless shaped the meaning of Bonhoeffer's concept of religionless Christianity.

In his younger years, Bonhoeffer had followed Luther and Barth's lead in distinguishing between the church and the world, between theology and science and, to use H. Richard Niebuhr's words, between Christ and culture. During Bonhoeffer's early or ecclesiastical phase, his concern was that the church be the church by making an authentic confession of the truth about Jesus Christ. Bitterly disappointed when the Confessing Church fell into division and especially after most Confessing pastors took the loyalty oath to the Führer, Bonhoeffer finally realized that the church itself was a victim of culture, that religion *was* a culture. This realization meant that Christians must move out of their sanctuary, the church, into a godless world; they must confront the world; they must be part of the world. Instead of remaking the world into a Christian culture in a medieval fashion, Bonhoeffer's new Christianity offered redemption to a godless world by taking it seriously. Perhaps Bonhoeffer's preoccupation with "this worldliness" reflects the theological explication of his move, as a Protestant pastor, into active resistance against the state. In any case, Bonhoeffer came to his new theological insights in prison, without doubt through his consideration of the political situation at hand and the suffering of the Jews.[43]

Conclusion

Bonhoeffer's theology, like his short life, had its twists and turns. In a decade's time he passed through three distinct stages: his call to obedience to the state that nonetheless preserved the integrity and autonomy of the church, his call to suffering for the cause of justice and truth, and last, his call to resistance and active participation in the life of the world. In comparison, Bonhoeffer's Confessing Church did not get past the first stage. The German Protestant Church failed to protect its own turf; much less did it take a united stand on behalf of Jews or other victims of Nazi persecution; even less did it resist the state.

For those who come to Bonhoeffer through a study of the German church struggle, adulation might indeed seem the appropriate response to his life. However, those who arrive at Bonhoeffer from a study of the Holocaust most likely have a different view, one that describes Bonhoeffer's ideas as part of the problem rather than part of the solution. Truly in the shadow of the Holocaust, Bonhoeffer's words and actions appear small, tentative, restrained, and ambivalent. Yet his life was like a small candle in the black hole of his time. The Bonhoeffer phenomenon, the public reception of this man, illustrates that people would rather huddle around one point of light, no matter how feeble and flickering the flame, than sit alone in darkness.

Pius XII, The Jews, and the German Catholic Church

Guenter Lewy

Rolf Hochhuth's controversial "Christian tragedy," dealing with the failure of Pope Pius XII to protest publicly against the incredible horrors that Nazi Germany was inflicting upon the Jews of Europe, has dramatized a problem that is as old as Christianity itself. Hochhuth, to be sure, relates this failure to the personality of Pius XII himself, who is portrayed in *The Deputy* as a cold, unfeeling politician worried only about the interests of the Church. But the truth is that the Pope's stand cannot adequately be understood in terms of personalities. For one thing, we must remember that the Nazi assault upon the Jews of Europe took place in a climate of opinion conditioned by centuries of Christian hostility to Jews and Judaism. And for another, we must realize that in acting—or failing to act—as he did, Pius XII was to a considerable extent influenced by the behavior of his "constituency" within Germany itself. Consequently, it is with German Catholicism that any effort to explain the Pope's silence must begin.

1. The Weimar Period

From the time the National Socialist movement appeared in the '20s, organized German Catholicism came into repeated conflict with it, but antisemitism was not one of the primary bones of contention. On the contrary, many Catholic publicists—like the Franciscan Father Erhard Schlund— agreed with the Nazis on the importance of fighting "the destructive influence of the Jews in religion, morality, literature and art, and political and social life," and objected only to the extremist tone of the movement.[1] Thus, for example, the Jesuit Gustav Gundlach, writing in a reference work edited by Bishop Buchberger of Regensburg, argued that a political antisemitism, directed against the "exaggerated and harmful influence" of the Jews, was permitted so long as it utilized morally admissible means.[2] And Bishop Buchberger himself, while deploring racialism, concluded that it was "justified self-defense" to ward off the rule of "an overly powerful Jewish capital."[3]

Concentrating its fire upon liberals and free thinkers, many of whom were of Jewish descent, the Church did practically nothing to stem the inroads antisemitism was making on German life throughout the period of the Weimar Republic. Though the German bishops during these years spoke up against Hitler's glorification of race and blood, they rarely found anything specific to say about the virulent antisemitic propaganda the Nazis were spreading or about the acts of violence against Jews that were becoming more and more common. So far as individual Catholic clerics in the pre-Hitler years were concerned, the *Verein für die Abwehr des Antisemitismus,* an organization of Christians and Jews struggling against the rising antisemitic agitation, counted two Catholic priests as members of its board of sponsors, while only a few Catholic laymen—like the journalist Franz Steffen and the editor Felix Langer—ever raised their voices against the antisemitic tirades of the Nazis and their allies.[4]

2. The Prewar Hitler Years

On April 26, 1933, shortly after coming to power, Hitler had a talk with two dignitaries of the German church, Bishop Berning and Prelate Steinmann. In the course of this talk he reminded his visitors that the Church for 1500 years had regarded the Jews as parasites, had banished them into ghettos, and had forbidden Christians to work for them; he, Hitler said, merely intended to do more effectively what the Church had attempted to accomplish for so long.[5]

The reaction of the two Church dignitaries to Hitler's attempt to identify his brand of antisemitism with the age-old anti-Judaism of the Church is not known. What we do know, however, is that from the time Hitler came to power all the German bishops began declaring their appreciation of the important natural values of race and racial purity, and they limited their dissent to insisting that this goal be achieved without resort to immoral means. The article on "Race" in an authoritative handbook on topical religious problems, edited by Archbishop Gröber, expressed this position in the following words:

> Every people bears itself the responsibility for its successful existence, and the intake of entirely foreign blood will always represent a risk for a nationality that has proven its historical worth. Hence, no people may be denied the right to maintain undisturbed their previous racial stock and to enact safe-

guards for this purpose. The Christian religion merely demands that the means used do not offend against the moral law and natural justice.[6]

Similarly, in his celebrated Advent sermons of 1933, Cardinal Faulhaber observed that the Church did not have "any objection to the endeavor to keep the national characteristics of a people as far as possible pure and unadulterated, and to foster their national spirit by emphasis upon the common ties of blood which unite them." To what, then, did the Church object? To hatred of other nations, said Faulhaber, and to setting loyalty to race above the obligations one owed to the Church.[7]

Faulhaber was severely criticized by the Nazis for these qualifications, and his palace was fired upon—a fact that has been taken as proof that German Catholicism actually did condemn the Nazi persecution of the Jews. Yet in the same series of sermons, in his eloquent vindication of the sacred character of the Old Testament (which Rosenberg had attacked as the "Jewish Bible"), Faulhaber went out of his way to make clear that he was not concerned with defending the Jews of his time. We must distinguish, he told the faithful, between the people of Israel before the death of Christ, who were vehicles of divine revelation, and the Jews after the death of Christ, who have become restless wanderers over the earth. But even the Jewish people of ancient times could not justly claim credit for the wisdom of the Old Testament: "People of Israel, this did not grow in your own garden of your own planting. This condemnation of usurious land-grabbing, this war against the oppression of the farmer by debt, this prohibition of usury, is not the product of your spirit."[8]

Whatever ambiguity may still have attached to his position after these pronouncements, Faulhaber soon acted to dispel. In the summer of 1934 a Social Democratic paper in Prague published a sermon against race hatred that Faulhaber had allegedly preached. The Basel *National-Zeitung* in Switzerland reprinted excerpts from this sermon, and the World Jewish Congress at a meeting in Geneva praised the Cardinal's courageous stand. But the sermon turned out to be a fabrication, and Faulhaber had his secretary write a widely publicized letter to the Jewish organization protesting against "the use of his name by a conference that demands the commercial boycott of Germany, that is, economic war." The Cardinal, the letter continued, "in his Advent sermons of the previous year has defended the Old Testament of the Children of Israel but not taken a position with regard to the Jewish question of today."[9]

Lesser Church dignitaries quite naturally took the cue from their Archbishop. An article written by a canon of the cathedral chapter of Regensburg, and published in *Klerusblatt*, the organ of the Bavarian priests' association, advised Catholic teachers to point out to pupils that the sacred books of the Old Testament were not only beyond the Jewish mentality but in direct conflict with it. "The greatest miracle of the Bible is that the true religion could hold its own and maintain itself against the voice of the Semitic blood."[10]

The embarrassing fact that Jesus had been a Jew was handled in a similar manner. In a pastoral letter of 1939 Archbishop Gröber conceded that Jesus Christ could not be made into an Aryan, but the Son of God had been fundamentally different from the Jews of his time—so much so that they had hated him and demanded his crucifixion; and "their murderous hatred has continued in later centuries."[11] Jesus had been a Jew, admitted Bishop Hilfrich of Limburg in his pastoral letter for Lent 1939, but "the Christian religion has not grown out of the nature of this people, that is, is not influenced by their racial characteristics. Rather it has had to make its way against this people." The Jewish people, the Bishop added, were guilty of the murder of God and had been under a curse since the day of the crucifixion.[12]

The attempt to swim with the antisemitic tide was even more pronounced in the previously cited *Handbook* of Archbishop Gröber. Marxism here was defined as "the materialistic socialism founded primarily by the Jew Karl Marx,"[13] and Bolshevism was characterized as "an Asiatic state despotism, in point of fact in the service of a group of terrorists led by Jews."[14] The Führer had correctly described the struggle against this evil force as a defense of European civilization against Asiatic barbarism: "No people can avoid this clash between its natural tradition and Marxism which is opposed to national ties and led mostly by Jewish agitators and revolutionaries."[15] And in yet another article, the *Handbook* asserted that most of the unhealthy and un-German developments in art since the nineteenth century had been the work of "the uprooted and atheistically perverted Jew," or those under Jewish influence.[16]

If such language could be endorsed by an archbishop, it is no wonder that lower ranking figures in the Church felt free to express their antisemitic sentiments still more openly. Thus the theologian Karl Adam spoke of the need to purge the press, literature, science, and art of the "Jewish mentality," adding the usual caveat that "the Christian conscience must insist that these legal ordinances be implemented in a spirit of justice and love."[17] Thus also an article on the revolution of 1918 in the paper of the Bavarian priests accused the Jew [sic] Karl Liebknecht of treason, and told how "the Jew Emil Barth equipped his *Untermenschen* [inferior humans] with hand grenades and automatic pistols in order to attack the national defense from the rear."[18]

And so it went. The Jews had had a "demoralizing influence on religiosity and national character."[19] The Jews, as a spiritual community, had brought the German people "more damage than benefit."[20] The Jews had been "the first and most cruel persecutors of the young Church."[21] The Jews had killed

Jesus and in their boundless hatred of Christianity were still in the forefront of those seeking to destroy the Church.[22]

If we take into account this climate of opinion within the Church—all the sentiments just cited were published between 1933 and 1939 in journals edited by priests or in books bearing the *Imprimatur*—we will find it easier to understand how it happened that the Church retreated in the face of the Nazis' antisemitic legislation, even where these ordinances touched upon vital domains of ecclesiastical jurisdiction such as matrimony.

According to canon law, the Church had exclusive jurisdiction over the marriage of Catholics. In practice, however, the Church in many countries had recognized the right of the state to impose certain conditions on marriage, so long as these did not conflict with natural law. Thus in Germany, the Church had long agreed to the provision that a civil marriage ceremony normally had to precede the ceremony conducted by the priest,[23] and this agreement was ratified by the Concordat of 1933 between the Nazi government and the Vatican.

As early as 1934 the Church had made clear to the Nazi government that the enactment of a law forbidding racially mixed marriages would create a very difficult situation. In the eyes of the Church, the German bishops pointed out in a memorandum, every Catholic, whether born to a pure German or to a racially mixed marriage, whether baptized as a child or as an adult, was equally entitled to the sacraments. Hence if two baptized persons of racially mixed stock insisted on being married by a priest, the latter would have to comply, even if the state were to have prohibited such a union.[24]

This, however, is precisely what the state soon did, for one of the practical results of the so-called Nuremberg laws of September 15, 1935, was to make it illegal for two Catholics to marry when one was considered racially "non-Aryan" under the standards set up by the law. (Since the persecution of the Jews had led to many new conversions to the Catholic religion, the number of such marriages was undoubtedly rising at the time.) The central office of information of the German episcopate in Berlin reported in September 1935 that earlier Catholic couples of racially mixed descent had been traveling to England to get married there, but now even those marriages had become illegal, and the Church had a very serious problem on its hands.[25] What did it do? In some instances priests circumvented the law by using a provision of the Concordat of 1933 which, in cases of "great moral emergency," permitted a church marriage without a preceding civil ceremony,[26] but by and large the Church conformed to the law, bowing to what earlier it had termed an inadmissible infringement of its spiritual jurisdiction.

For some elements in the Church, to be sure, bowing was unnecessary, for they actually welcomed the Nuremberg laws. While a distinguished

German Catholic in exile, Waldemar Gurian, was denouncing the Nuremberg ordinances as violations of natural law and of the moral teachings of the Church, and declaring that they were "only a stage on the way toward the complete physical destruction of the Jews,"[27] an article in the *Klerusblatt* of January 1936 was justifying the new anti-Jewish statutes as indispensable safeguards for the qualitative makeup of the German people.[28] So, too, Bishop Hudal, the head of the German Church in Rome, said that the Nuremberg laws were a necessary measure of self-defense against the influx of foreign elements. The Church in her own legislation, the Bishop contended, had held a radical position on the Jewish question "until the walls of the Ghetto had been torn down in the nineteenth century by the liberal state first and not by the Church." Consequently, from the point of view of the Church, there could be no objection to laws containing discriminatory provisions for Jews. "The principles of the modern state [based on the rule of equal treatment before the law] have been created by the French Revolution and are not the best from the standpoint of Christianity and nationality."[29]

The Church surrendered in a similar fashion when the so-called Aryan Clause was applied to clerical teachers of religion. This ordinance, enacted in 1938, meant that priests teaching religion in the public schools had to submit proof of their Aryan descent before they could continue in their posts. However, the policy in question affected very few clerics and had no further ramifications. Such was not the case when the Church agreed to supply data from her own records on the religious origin of those under her care. A decree of April 7, 1933, which resulted in the discharge of numerous Catholic civil servants, had also provided for the dismissal of all Jews, except veterans of the First World War, from the civil service. Henceforth, anyone applying for government employment—and soon for various other positions as well—had to submit proof that he was not a Jew. Since prior to 1874–76 births had been registered only by the churches, the latter were asked to help in determining who was or was not fully Aryan, for under Nazi law this depended on the racial (i.e., religious) status of parents and grandparents. The Church cooperated as a matter of course, complaining only that priests already overburdened with work were not receiving compensation for this special service to the state.[30] The very question of whether the Church should lend its help to the Nazi state in sorting out people of Jewish descent was never debated. On the contrary. "We have always unselfishly worked for the people without regard to gratitude or ingratitude," a priest wrote in the *Klerusblatt* in September of 1934. "We shall also do our best to help in this service to the people."[31] And the cooperation of the Church in this matter continued right through the war years when the price of being Jewish was no longer dismissal from a government job and loss of livelihood, but deportation and outright physical destruction.[32]

The bishops sometimes showed concern for these non-Aryan Catholics, for whom the Church felt a special responsibility. Already in September 1933, Archbishop Bertram inquired from the Papal Secretary of State whether the Holy See could not put in a good word with the German government for the Jewish converts to the Catholic religion who were being made destitute on account of their non-Aryan descent.[33] Soon the *St. Raphaelsverein,* a Catholic organization founded in 1871 for the protection of German émigrés, and presided over by Bishop Berning, began to take care of these Catholics. In the years 1936–37 the *St. Raphaelsverein* helped 516 Catholic non-Aryans to emigrate; in 1938 it facilitated the emigration of 1,850 such persons.[34]

But what of non-Aryans who were not members of the Catholic faith? During these years prior to the adoption of the Final Solution, a few instances are on record where individual churchmen did speak up in defense of the Jews. In March 1933, a priest in the Rhineland in a sermon characterized the vilification of the Jews as unjust and was fined 500 marks for abuse of the pulpit.[35] In 1934 another priest, who for reasons of safety chose to remain anonymous, took his Church to task for not helping the Jews.[36] And yet another priest, in Bavaria in 1936, declared that the stories being told in Germany about the Jews were a pack of lies.[37] In Berlin on the morning after the *Kristallnacht* pogrom of November 1938, Provost Bernhard Lichtenberg prayed for the persecuted non-Aryan Christians and Jews and added, "What took place yesterday, we know; what will be tomorrow, we do not know; but what happened today, that we have witnessed; outside [this church] the synagogue is burning, and that also is a house of God."[38]

There probably were other such statements, and here and there acts of Samaritanism may have taken place that have remained unrecorded. But the Church as such, speaking through the voice of its bishops, extended neither aid nor sympathy to other than Catholic non-Aryans, and remained silent in the face of anti-Jewish legislation, burning temples, and the first roundups of Jews.

3. The Final Solution

In a speech delivered on January 31, 1939, the Führer served public notice of his intentions: "If international Jewry should succeed, in Europe or elsewhere, in precipitating nations into a world war, the result will not be the bolshevization of Europe and a victory for Judaism, but the extermination of the Jewish race."[39] A few months later Hitler attacked Poland and World War II began. On July 31, 1941, Reinhard Heydrich was charged "with making all necessary preparations . . . for bringing about a complete solution of the Jewish question in the German sphere of influence in Europe."[40] The machinery of destruction went into action.

It began with a decree, dated September 1, 1941, that provided that no Jew was to leave his place of domicile without special permission, and could appear in public only when marked with a yellow star. The idea of marking the Jews had first been applied in Poland, and now the system of identification was extended to the entire Reich. The decree covered so-called Mosaic Jews as well as baptized Jews; only those who had converted before September 15, 1935 (the date of the Nuremberg laws), and non-Aryans married to Aryan partners were exempt.

The wearing of the yellow star had a paralyzing effect upon those who were forced to do so. Many were afraid to leave their houses, and this fear created a special problem for the Catholics affected. In a number of towns, these non-Aryan Catholics applied to the police for permission to remove the yellow star while going to and attending church services, and they asked their bishops to support the request.[41] Accordingly, Bishops Wienken and Berning in Berlin tried to obtain permission from the Gestapo for the "Jewish" Catholics not to wear the Star of David while in church. But their efforts failed—the Gestapo was adamant.

Meanwhile, on September 17, Cardinal Bertram addressed a letter to the episcopate in which he counseled the avoidance of such "rash measures that could hurt the feelings of the Jewish Catholics as the introduction of special Jewish benches, separation when administering the sacraments, introduction of special services in specific churches or private houses." The segregation of the Catholic non-Aryans would violate Christian principles and therefore should be avoided as long as possible. (Priests might, however, advise Jewish Catholics to attend early mass whenever possible.) Admonitions to the faithful to exercise brotherly love toward the non-Aryans similarly should be postponed until disturbances resulted; and "Only when substantial difficulties result from attendance at church by the non-Aryan Catholics (like staying away of officials, party members and others . . .), should the Catholic non-Aryans be consulted about the holding of special services."[42]

Mass deportations of German Jews to the East began on October 15, 1941. Bishop Berning, in a letter of October 27, informed Cardinal Bertram that while discussing the question of the Jewish star with the Gestapo he had also pointed to the harshness accompanying "the evacuation of the non-Aryans" and had requested some amelioration. He had been told that Christian non-Aryans would be evacuated only in exceptional cases (such as where earlier conflicts with the Gestapo had occurred). For the time being non-Aryans in mixed marriages would not be affected by these measures.[43]

The promises made by the Gestapo to Bishop Berning were, of course, not honored. On October 27, Bishop Hilfrich of Limburg informed Bishop Wienken, the episcopate's troubleshooter in Berlin, that the transport of Jews from Frankfurt earlier in the month had included Catholic non-Aryans to whom no preferred treatment had been granted. Their fate was especially sad since they were being regarded by their *"Rassengenossen"* (fellow Jews) as apostates. Hilfrich inquired whether for this reason it might not be possible to secure their exemption; if that could not be done, they should at least be put into special settlements where they could be given religious care more easily.[44] Wienken replied a few days later that negotiations in the matter of the deportation of Catholic non-Aryans had been started at the highest level.[45] The bishops of the Cologne and Paderborn church provinces, meeting in November 1941, also suggested that the government be petitioned in the matter of the deportations. They furthermore recommended that non-Aryan or half-Aryan priests and nuns volunteer to accompany the deportees in order to hold services for them and provide religious instruction for the children.[46]

Meanwhile, rumors were spreading about the fate of the Jews in the East. These rumors had been making the rounds ever since the attack upon Russia on June 22, 1941, which had brought in its wake the employment of special detachments (*Einsatzgruppen*) assigned to the job of machine-gunning Jews. By the end of 1941 the first news had also trickled back about the fate of the deported German Jews who had been shot by mobile killing detachments near Riga and Minsk.[47] And in the spring of 1942 the "White Rose," an organization made up of a group of students and a professor of philosophy at the University of Munich, distributed leaflets telling of the murder of 300,000 Jews in Poland and asking why the German people were being so apathetic in the face of these revolting crimes.[48]

In December 1941, the first death camp had begun operations near Lodz. Sobibor, Treblinka, and Auschwitz went into operation in the course of the year 1942. By the end of 1942 more than 100,000 German Jews had been sent to their death in the East, and the vague rumors about their fate had been replaced now by hard and persistent reports that included details of the mass gassings. In August, 1942, Colonel Kurt Gerstein, who had joined the SS to investigate the stories of extermination for himself, tried to tell the Papal Nuncio in Berlin about a gassing he had witnessed near Lublin. When Monsignor Orsenigo refused to receive him, he told his story to Dr. Winter, the legal adviser of Bishop Preysing of Berlin, and to a number of other persons. He also requested that the report be forwarded to the Holy See.[49] During the same period, other reports about the extermination of the Jews reached the bishops through Catholic officers serving in Poland and Russia.[50] For a long time Dr. Joseph Müller, an officer in Canaris's Military Intelligence Service and also a confidant of Cardinal Faulhaber, had kept the episcopate well informed about the systematic atrocities committed in Poland.[51] Another source of information was Dr. Hans Globke, a Catholic and a high official in the Ministry of the Interior entrusted with handling racial matters. It is clear, then, that by the end of the year 1942 at the latest, the German episcopate was possessed of quite accurate knowledge of the horrible events unfolding in the East.

Until 1942, half-Jews and quarter-Jews, the so-called *Mischlinge,* as well as non-Aryans married to Aryans, had been exempt both from wearing the yellow star and from deportation. (The number of such persons in the Reich-Protektorat area was estimated at above 150,000.[52]) Though the Nuremberg laws had forbidden marriages between Jews and Aryans, they had not annulled existing mixed marriages. With the progress of the Final Solution, however, this loophole was now to be closed. A conference of experts in March 1942 decided upon the compulsory dissolution of racially mixed marriages, to be followed by the deportation of the Jewish partner. If the Aryan partner failed to apply for a divorce within a certain period of time, the public prosecutor was to file a petition for divorce which the courts would have to grant.

The bishops heard of the contemplated measure through Dr. Globke in the Ministry of the Interior, and they reacted promptly. On November 11, 1942, Archbishop Bertram in the name of the episcopate addressed a letter of protest against the planned compulsory divorce legislation to the Ministers of Justice, the Interior, and Ecclesiastical Affairs. The intervention of the bishops, he insisted, was not due "to lack of love for the German nationality, lack of a feeling of national dignity, and also not to underestimation of the harmful Jewish influences upon German culture and national interests." The bishops merely felt called upon to emphasize that the duty of humane treatment also existed toward the members of other races. Among the persons affected by the contemplated measure, Bertram went on, were many thousands of Catholics whose marriages, according to Catholic doctrine, were indissoluble. Respect for the religious rights of the Catholic Christians was an indispensable condition for the peaceful cooperation of church and state, which had never been as necessary as in the present situation. The bishops therefore hoped, the letter ended, that the government would withdraw the planned divorce ordinance.[53]

Despite the fact that the ordinance was still tied up in bureaucratic difficulties, the Gestapo in February 1943, in the course of deporting the last German Jews, seized several thousand Christian non-Aryans, partners of mixed marriages. In Berlin alone about 6,000 such men were arrested on February 27. But then something unexpected and unparalleled happened: Their Aryan wives followed them to the place of temporary detention and there they stood for several hours, screaming and howling for their men. With the secrecy of the whole machinery of destruction threatened, the Gestapo yielded, and the non-Aryan husbands were released.[54]

A few days after this unique event, Bertram composed another letter. This time he also sent copies to the chief of the Reich Chancellery and to the

Reichssicherheitshauptamt (RSHA), Himmler's headquarters. About 8,000 non-Aryan Catholics, Bertram complained, had been seized and deported. The episcopate could not silently accept these measures. He then repeated what he had said in November 1942 about the illegitimacy of compulsory divorce.[55] On April 16 Bishop Preysing informed his fellow bishops that the contemplated divorce decree was soon to be made public. He urged that for the time being the matter be treated as strictly confidential; but in the event that the order should be issued, a statement drawn up by Bertram was to be read from the pulpits. The statement reaffirmed the indissolubility of Christian marriage and the validity of this principle even in the case of racially mixed marriages, and it asked for prayer for the unfortunates affected by the decree.[56]

About two months later Preysing sent word to his colleagues through a messenger that the threatened decree had been postponed. The bishops were asked to write letters to all the ministries; they should inquire in strong language as to the whereabouts of the deportees, demanding pastoral care for the Christians and threatening a public protest. The point of departure should be concern for the Christian Jews, "but beyond this one should speak clearly about the outrages inflicted upon the Jews generally."[57] We do not know how many bishops acted upon Preysing's request.

In November 1943, Bertram sent out another appeal in the name of the entire episcopate to the Minister of the Interior and to the RSHA. The episcopate, he wrote, had received information according to which the non-Aryans evacuated from Germany were living in camps under conditions that would have to be called inhuman. A large number of the sufferers had already succumbed. "In view of the reputation of the German name at home and abroad," and in view of the commands of the Christian moral law concerning the duties owed fellow men even of foreign races, the bishops considered it necessary to plead for an amelioration of conditions in these camps. In particular, Bertram continued, the bishops wished to demand the benefit of pastoral care for the imprisoned Catholics. The episcopate would gladly designate priests for divine services and the administration of the sacraments in the camps.[58]

Bertram's letter neither employed strong language nor said anything very definite about the outrages against the Jews, as Bishop Preysing had suggested. Such vagueness was typical of the few public pronouncements the bishops made on this matter in the years following the adoption of the Final Solution. They spoke of the right to life and liberty, not to be denied even those "who are not of our blood,"[59] to "men of foreign races and descent," and to "the resettled,"[60] but the word "Jew" never once appeared in any of these documents.

In his next and last letter to the government, dispatched in January 1944, Bertram wrote that reports had been received to the effect that measures which had previously been applied only to Jews were now to be applied also to the *Mischlinge*. These Christians had already been barred from military service and institutions of higher learning, but now, it seemed, they were to be conscripted into special formations for labor service. "All these measures," Bertram continued, "aim clearly at segregation, at the end of which extermination threatens." In the name of the episcopate he felt obligated to point out that any change in the meaning of the term "Jew"—when the Nuremberg statutes had been accepted as the final word on this question for almost ten years—would seriously undermine confidence in the law. The *Mischlinge* were Germans and Christians and had always been rejected by the Jews. "The German Catholics, indeed numerous Christians in Germany," Bertram warned, "would be deeply hurt if these fellow Christians now had to meet a fate similar to that of the Jews." The bishops would not be able to reconcile it with their conscience to remain silent in the face of such measures.[61]

As against the case of the euthanasia program of the early war years, then—when the episcopate did not mince words and succeeded in putting a stop to the killings [Ed. note: we now know the killing did not stop, even though the regime changed its public face on euthanasia policy]—the bishops continually played it safe where the Jews were concerned. Such public protests as they did register could, indeed, have been seen as referring to the Jews, but any Catholic who chose to interpret them otherwise (as referring, say, only to Slavs) was left free to do so. Close to half the population of the Greater German Reich (43.1 percent in 1939) was Catholic and even among the SS, despite all pressures to leave the Church, almost a fourth (22.7 percent on December 31, 1938)[62] belonged to the Catholic faith. Yet while the episcopate had in the past issued orders to deny the sacraments to Catholics who engaged in dueling or agreed to have their bodies cremated, the word that would have forbidden the faithful, on pain of excommunication, to go on participating in the massacre of thc Jews was never spoken. And so Catholics went on participating conscientiously, along with other Germans.

There was, however, at least one Catholic churchman in Germany for whom the Christian duty to love one's neighbor amounted to more than a pious formula—the sixty-six-year-old Provost Lichtenberg of Berlin, who, right through the stepped-up antisemitic agitation, continued to say a daily prayer for the Jews. He was finally arrested on October 23, 1941, a week after the first of the mass deportation of Jews had begun. During questioning by Himmler's henchmen, the Provost asserted that the deportation of the Jews was irreconcilable with the Christian moral law, and asked to be allowed to accompany the deportees as their spiritual adviser. Sentenced to two years imprisonment for abuse of the pulpit, Lichtenberg was seized by the Gestapo upon his release in October 1943 and shipped off to the concentration camp at Dachau. He died during the transport on November 5, 1943.[63]

The passivity of the German episcopate in the face of the Jewish tragedy stands in marked contrast to the conduct of the French, Belgian, and Dutch bishops. In Holland, where the Church as early as 1934 had prohibited the participation of Catholics in the Dutch Nazi movement, the bishops in 1942 immediately and publicly protested the first deportations of Dutch Jews,[64] and in May 1943 they forbade the collaboration of Catholic policemen in the hunting down of Jews even at the cost of losing their jobs.[65] In Belgium members of the episcopate actively supported the rescue efforts of their clergy, who hid many hundreds of Jewish children.[66] And in France, the highest dignitaries of the Church repeatedly used their pulpits to denounce the deportations and to condemn the barbarous treatment of the Jews.[67]

Throughout western Europe untold numbers of priests and members of the monastic clergy organized the rescue of Jews, hid them in monasteries, parish houses, and private homes. Many lay Catholics in France, Holland, and Belgium acted in a similar fashion, thus saving thousands of Jewish lives. The concern of the Gentile populations of these countries for their Jewish fellow citizens was undoubtedly one of the key factors behind the bold public protests of the French, Dutch, and Belgian bishops—just as the absence of such solicitude in Germany goes a long way toward explaining the apathy of their German counterparts. In France, Belgium, and Holland, declarations of solidarity and help for the Jews were almost universally regarded as signs of patriotism; in Germany, on the other hand, the bishops in so acting would have incurred new charges of being un-German and of being in league with Germany's mortal enemies. Their own parishioners, moreover, would probably have failed to understand or support any signs of sympathy for the Jews—whom the Church, after all, had herself long been branding as a harmful factor in German life. Consequently, at the very moment when the bishops might perhaps have wanted to protest the inhuman treatment of the Jews, they found themselves the prisoners of their own antisemitic teachings. Indeed, in Germany only a handful of Jews were hidden by the clergy or otherwise helped by them in their hour of distress.[68] In Freiburg there was Dr. Gertrud Luckner, an official of the *Caritas* (the large Catholic philanthropic organization) who helped Jews get across the Swiss border, sent packages to deportees, and distributed money from a special fund established by the episcopate for non-Aryans. She was arrested in November 1943, while trying to bring a sum of money to the few remaining Jews in Berlin, and spent the rest of the war in a concentration camp.[69] A few cases are also recorded of individual Catholics hiding and saving Jews,[70] but only in Berlin did a significant number of Jews find refuge with friends and neighbors; according to Provost Grüber, most of these courageous people were workers, many of them were unconnected with any church.[71]

There were, then, exceptions, but the overall picture was one of indifference and apathy. "Among the Christians," a group of German Protestant and Catholic theologians concluded in 1950, "a few courageously helped the persecuted, but the large majority failed disgracefully in the face of this unheard-of provocation of the merciful God."[72]

4. The Role of the Papacy

In April 1933 a communication reached Pope Pius XI from Germany expressing grave concern over the Nazis' antisemitic aims and requesting the Supreme Pontiff to issue an encyclical on the Jewish question. The letter was written by the philosopher Dr. Edith Stein, a Jewish convert to Catholicism and later known as Sister Teresia Benedicta a Cruce of the Order of the Carmelites.[73] Edith Stein's request was not granted and nine years later, in August 1942, she was seized by the Gestapo from a Dutch monastery in which she had sought refuge, and sent to Auschwitz to be gassed. The debate over whether the Papacy could have prevented or should at least have vigorously protested the massacre of the Jews of Europe, of which Edith Stein was one of the victims, has been going on ever since and has acquired new vigor as a result of the Hochhuth play.

In response to Hitler's antisemitic drive, Pius XII's predecessor, Pius XI, like the German episcopate, seems to have limited his concern to Catholic non-Aryans. At the request of Cardinal Bertram, the Papal Secretary of State in September 1933 put in "a word on behalf of those German Catholics" who were of Jewish descent and for this reason suffering "social and economic difficulties."[74] In the years that followed, the Holy See often took issue with the Nazis' glorification of race, but the Jewish question specifically was never discussed. In 1934 the influential Jesuit magazine, *Civilta Cattolica*, published in Rome and traditionally close to Vatican thinking, noted with regret that the antisemitism of the Nazis "did not stem from the religious convictions nor the Christian conscience . . . but from . . . their desire to upset the order of religion and society." The *Civilta Cattolica* added that "we could understand them, or even praise them, if their policy were restricted within acceptable bounds of defense against the Jewish organizations and institutions . . . "[75] In 1936 the same journal published another article on the subject, emphasizing that opposition to Nazi racialism should not be interpreted as a rejection of antisemitism, arguing—as the magazine had done since 1890—that the Christian world (though without un-Christian hatred) must defend itself against the

Jewish threat by suspending the civic rights of Jews and returning them to the ghettos.[76]

Pius XI's encyclical "Mit brennender Sorge" of March 1937 rejected the myths of race and blood as contrary to revealed Christian truth, but it neither mentioned nor criticized antisemitism per se. Nor was antisemitism mentioned in the statement of the Roman Congregation of Seminaries and Universities, issued on April 13, 1938, and attacking as erroneous eight theses taken from the arsenal of Nazi doctrine.[77] On September 7, 1938, during a reception for Catholic pilgrims from Belgium, Pius XI is said to have condemned the participation of Catholics in antisemitic movements and to have added that Christians, the spiritual descendants of the patriarch Abraham, were "spiritually Semites." But this statement was omitted by all the Italian papers, including *L'Osservatore Romano*, from their account of the Pope's address.[78]

The elevation of Cardinal Pacelli to the Papacy in the spring of 1939 brought to the chair of St. Peter a man who, in contrast to his predecessor, was unemotional and dispassionate, as well as a master of the language of diplomatic ambiguity. "Pius XII," recalls Cardinal Tardini, "was by nature meek and almost timid. He was not born with the temperament of a fighter. In this he was different from his great predecessor."[79] But whether, as Hochhuth has speculated, Pius XI would have reacted to the massacre of the Jews during World War II differently from Pacelli, is a question to which no definite answer is possible.

That the Holy See had no intrinsic objection to a policy of subjecting the Jews to discriminatory legislation again became clear when in June 1941 Marshal Petain's Vichy government introduced a series of "Jewish statutes." The Cardinals and Archbishops of France made known their strong disapproval of these measures, but Leon Berard, the Vichy ambassador at the Holy See, was able to report to Petain after lengthy consultations with high Church officials that the Vatican did not consider such laws in conflict with Catholic teaching. The Holy See merely counseled that no provisions on marriage be added to the statutes and "that the precepts of justice and charity be considered in the application of the law."[80] In August 1941 the consequences of this discriminatory policy could not yet be clearly seen, but when mass deportations from France got under way in 1942, the Papal Nuncio, without invoking the authority of the Holy See, requested Laval to mitigate the severity of the measures taken against the Jews of Vichy France.[81] By that time, however, such pleas could no longer halt the machinery of destruction.

Meanwhile, there was growing criticism of the Pope's failure to protest publicly against Nazi atrocities, and especially against the murder of the Jews in the Polish death factories. In July 1942, Harold H. Tittmann, the assistant to

Roosevelt's personal representative at the Holy See, Myron C. Taylor, pointed out to the Vatican that its silence was "endangering its moral prestige and . . . undermining faith both in the Church and in the Holy Father himself."[82] In September 1942, after authorization by Secretary of State Hull, Tittmann and several other diplomatic representatives at the Vatican formally requested that the Pope condemn the "incredible horrors" perpetrated by the Nazis. A few days later Taylor forwarded to the Papal Secretary of State, Luigi Maglione, a memorandum from the Jewish Agency for Palestine reporting mass executions of Jews in Poland and occupied Russia, and telling of deportations to death camps from Germany, Belgium, Holland, France, Slovakia, etc. Taylor inquired whether the Vatican could confirm these reports, and if so, "whether the Holy Father has any suggestions as to any practical manner in which the forces of civilized opinion could be utilized in order to prevent a continuation of these barbarities."[83] On October 10 the Holy See, in reply to Taylor's note, said that up to the present time it had not been possible to verify the accuracy of reports concerning the severe measures that were being taken against the Jews. "It is well known," the statement added, "that the Holy See is taking advantage of every opportunity offered in order to mitigate the suffering of non-Aryans."[84] After the Western Allies in December 1942 had vigorously denounced the cold-blooded extermination of the Jews, Tittmann again asked the Papal Secretary of State whether the Holy See could not issue a similar pronouncement. Maglione answered that the Holy See, in line with its policy of neutrality, could not protest particular atrocities and had to limit itself to condemning immoral actions in general. He assured Tittmann that everything possible was being done behind the scenes to help the Jews.[85]

Two days later, in the course of a lengthy Christmas message broadcast by the Vatican radio, Pope Pius made another of his many calls for a more humane conduct of hostilities. Humanity, the Pope declared, owed the resolution to build a better world to "the hundreds of thousands who without personal guilt, sometimes for no other reason but on account of their nationality or descent, were doomed to death or exposed to a progressive deterioration of their condition."[86] Again, addressing the Sacred College of Cardinals in June 1943, the Pontiff spoke of his twofold duty to be impartial and to point up moral errors. He had given special attention, he recalled, to the plight of those who were still being harassed because of their nationality or descent and who without personal guilt were subjected to measures that spelled destruction. Much had been done for the unfortunates that could not be described yet. Every public statement had had to be carefully weighed "in the interest of those suffering so that their situation would not inadvertently be made still more difficult and unbearable." Unfortunately, Pius XII added, the

Church's pleas for compassion and for the observance of the elementary norms of humanity had encountered doors "which no key was able to open."[87]

The precise nature of these interventions has not been revealed to this day. We do know, however, that Nuncio Orsenigo in Berlin made inquiries several times about mass shootings and the fate of deported Jews. (Ernst Wörmann, the director of the Political Department of the German Foreign Ministry, recorded on October 15, 1942, that the Nuncio had made his representation with "some embarrassment and without emphasis."[88]) State Secretary Weizsäcker told Monsignor Orsenigo on another such occasion that the Vatican had so far conducted itself "very cleverly" in these matters, and that he would hope for a continuation of this policy. The Nuncio took the hint and "pointed out that he had not really touched this topic and that he had no desire to touch it."[89]

The Pope's policy of neutrality encountered its most crucial test when the Nazis began rounding up the 8,000 Jews of Rome in the fall of 1943. Prior to the start of the arrests, the Jewish community was told by the Nazis that unless it raised 50 kilograms of gold (the equivalent of $56,000) within 36 hours, 300 hostages would be taken. When it turned out that the Jews themselves could only raise 35 kg, the Chief Rabbi, Israel Zolli, asked for and received a loan from the Vatican treasury to cover the balance. The Pope approved of this transaction.[90] But the big question in everyone's mind was how the Supreme Pontiff would react when the deportation of the Jews from the Eternal City began.

The test came on the night of October 15/16. While the roundup was still going on, a letter was delivered to General Stahel, the German military commander of Rome. Bearing the signature of Bishop Hudal, the head of the German Church in Rome, it said:

> I have just been informed by a high Vatican office in the immediate circle of the Holy Father that the arrests of Jews of Italian nationality have begun this morning. In the interest of the good relations which have existed until now between the Vatican and the high German military command . . . I would be very grateful if you would give an order to stop these arrests in Rome and its vicinity right away; I fear that otherwise the Pope will have to make an open stand which will serve the anti-German propaganda as a weapon against us.[91]

A day later, Ernst von Weizsäcker, the new German Ambassador at the Holy See, reported to Berlin that the Vatican was upset, especially since the deportations had taken place, as it were, right under the Pope's window:

> The people hostile to us in Rome are taking advantage of this affair to force the Vatican from its reserve. People say that the bishops of French cities,

where similar incidents occurred, have taken a firm stand. The Pope, as supreme head of the Church and Bishop of Rome, cannot be more reticent than they. They are also drawing a parallel between the stronger character of Pius XI and that of the present Pope.[92]

Contrary to Hudal's and Weizsäcker's apprehensions, however, the man in the Vatican palace remained silent. On October 18, over one thousand Roman Jews—more than two-thirds of them women and children—were shipped off to the killing center of Auschwitz. Fourteen men and one woman returned alive. About 7,000 Roman Jews—that is, seven out of eight—were able to elude their hunters by going into hiding. More than 4,000, with the knowledge and approval of the Pope, found refuge in the numerous monastaries and houses of religious orders in Rome,[93] and a few dozen were sheltered in the Vatican itself. The rest were hidden by their Italian neighbors, among whom the anti-Jewish policy of the Fascists had never been popular. But for the Germans, over-whelmingly relieved at having averted a public protest by the Pope, the fact that a few thousand Jews had escaped the net was of minor significance. On October 28 Ambassador Weizsäcker was able to report:

Although under pressure from all sides, the Pope has not let himself be drawn into demonstrative censure of the deportation of Jews from Rome. Although he must expect that his attitude will be criticized by our enemies and exploited by the Protestant and Anglo-Saxon countries in their propaganda against Catholicism, he has done everything he could in this delicate matter not to strain relations with the German government, and German circles in Rome. As there is probably no reason to expect other German actions against the Jews of Rome, we can consider that a question so disturbing to German-Vatican relations has been liquidated.

In any case, an indication for this state of affairs can be seen in the Vatican's attitude. L'Osservatore Romano has in fact prominently published in its issue of October 25–26, an official communique on the Pope's charitable activities. The communique, in the Vatican's distinctive style, that is, very vague and complicated, declares that all men, without distinction of nationality, race, or religion, benefit from the Pope's paternal solicitude. The continual and varied activities of Pius XII have probably increased lately because of the greater suffering of so many unfortunates.

There is less reason to object to the terms of this message . . . as only a very small number of people will recognize in it a special allusion to the Jewish question.[94]

Since the end of World War II, Pius XII has often been criticized for his silence. It has been argued—and most recently by Hochhuth—that the Pope could have saved numerous lives, if indeed he could not have halted the machinery of destruction altogether, had he chosen to take a public stand, and had he confronted the Germans with the threat of an interdict or with excommunication of Hitler, Goebbels, and other leading Nazis belonging to the Catholic faith. As examples of the effectiveness of public protests, it is possible to cite the resolute reaction of the German episcopate to the euthanasia program. Also, in Slovakia, Hungary, and Rumania, forceful intervention of Papal nuncios, who threatened the Quisling governments with public condemnation by the Pope, was able, albeit temporarily, to stop the deportations.[95] At the very least, it has been suggested, a public denunciation of the mass murders by Pius XII, broadcast widely over the Vatican radio, would have revealed to Jews and Christians alike what deportation to the East actually meant. The Pope would have been believed, whereas the broadcasts of the Allies were often shrugged off as war propaganda. Many of the deportees who accepted the assurances of the Germans that they were merely being resettled, might thus have been warned and given an impetus to escape; many more Christians might have helped and sheltered Jews, and many more lives might have been saved.

There exists, of course, no way of definitively proving or disproving these arguments. Whether a papal decree of excommunication against Hitler would have dissuaded the Führer from carrying out his plan to destroy the Jews is very doubtful, and revocation of the Concordat by the Holy See would have bothered Hitler still less. However, a flaming protest against the massacre of the Jews coupled with an imposition of the interdict upon all of Germany or the excommunication of all Catholics in any way involved with the apparatus of the "Final Solution" would have been a more formidable and effective weapon. Yet this was precisely the kind of action which the Pope could not take without risking the allegiance of the German Catholics. Given the indifference of the German population toward the fate of the Jews and the highly ambivalent attitude of the German hierarchy toward Nazi antisemitism, a forceful stand by the Supreme Pontiff on the Jewish question might well have led to a large-scale desertion from the Church. When Dr. Eduardo Senatro, the correspondent of *L'Osservatore Romano* in Berlin, asked Pius XII whether he would not protest the extermination of the Jews, the Pope is reported to have answered, "Dear friend, do not forget that millions of Catholics serve in the German armies. Shall I bring them into conflicts of conscience?"[96]

The Pope knew that the German Catholics were not prepared to suffer martyrdom for their Church; still less were they willing to incur the wrath of their Nazi rulers for the sake of the Jews, whom their own bishops for years had castigated as a harmful influence in German life. In the final analysis, then, "the Vatican's silence only reflected the deep feeling of the Catholic masses of Europe."[97]

Some Catholic writers have suggested that a public protest by the Pope would not only have been unsuccessful in helping the Jews but might have caused additional damage—to the Jews, to the *Mischlinge,* to the Church, to the territorial integrity of the Vatican, and to Catholics in all of Nazi-occupied Europe. So far as the Jews are concerned, it is tempting to dismiss this argument by asking what worse fate could possibly have befallen them than the one that actually did. But in any case, the Catholic bishops of Holland tried the gamble and failed. In July 1942, together with the Protestant Church, they sent a telegram of protest against the deportation of the Dutch Jews to the German *Reichskommissar* (commissioner) and threatened to make their protest public unless the deportations were halted. The Germans responded by offering to exempt from deportation non-Aryans converted to Christianity before 1941 if the churches agreed to remain silent. The Dutch Reformed Church accepted the bargain, but the Catholic Archbishop of Utrecht refused and issued a pastoral letter in which he denounced the wrong done to the Jews. The Germans retaliated by seizing and deporting all the Catholic non-Aryans they could find, among them Edith Stein.[98] There was thus some basis for the fear that a public protest, along with any good that could come of it, might make some things worse, if not for the Jews, at least for the *Mischlinge* and the Catholics themselves.

The Pope had other, perhaps still weightier, reasons for remaining silent. As Mr. Tittmann was told by highly placed officials of the Curia, the Holy See did not want to jeopardize its neutrality by condemning German atrocities, and the Pope was unwilling to risk later charges of having been partial and contributing to a German defeat.[99] Moreover, the Vatican did not wish to undermine and weaken Germany's struggle against Russia. In the late summer of 1943, the Papal Secretary of State declared that the fate of Europe depended upon a German victory on the Eastern front;[100] and Father Robert Leiber, one of Pius XII's secretaries, recalls that the late Pope had always looked upon Russian Bolshevism as more dangerous than German National Socialism.[101]

Finally, one is inclined to conclude that the Pope and his advisers—influenced by the long tradition of moderate antisemitism so widely accepted in Vatican circles—did not view the plight of the Jews with a real sense of urgency and moral outrage. For this assertion no documentation is possible, but it is a conclusion difficult to avoid. Pius XII broke his policy of strict neutrality during World War II to express concern over the German violation of the neutrality of Holland, Belgium, and Luxembourg in May 1940. When some German Catholics criticized him for this action, the Pope wrote the German bishops that neutrality was not synonymous "with indifference and apathy where moral and humane considerations demanded a candid word."[102] All things told, did not the murder of several million Jews demand a similarly "candid word"?

Joseph Lortz and a Catholic Accommodation with National Socialism

Michael B. Lukens

The Dramatic Shift in Catholic Position

On 30 September 1930, the vicar general of the diocese of Mainz, Monsignor Mayer,[1] wrote a response to an inquiry that had come three days earlier from the Nazi district office in Offenbach. The question was whether a Catholic could be enrolled in the National Socialist German Workers Party (NSDAP). The Nazi inquiry was prompted by a sermon given in the village church of Kirschhausen by a certain parish priest, Fr. Weber, who had absolutely denied the possibility that a person in that parish could be both a Catholic and a Nazi. Further, Fr. Weber had proclaimed that Nazis could not attend church functions in uniform or in formations and that a Catholic who acknowledged belief in Nazi principles would be denied access to the sacraments. In his response to the complaint of the Nazi office, the vicar general, with the obvious approval of the bishop of Mainz, first confirmed that these judgments were in accord with Mainz diocesan instructions.

Mayer then inveighed in general against the Nazi program's understanding of religion in its infamous Article 24.[2] He criticized specifically the Nazi notion of "positive Christianity," the Nazi Party's conceptual umbrella for understanding not only Christianity but also, in fact, all religion as being necessarily in accord with both state policy and accepted social rules and cultural norms. For Mayer, true Catholic moral and theological beliefs transcended particular times and historical movements, and therefore, it would be "a great error to demand that the Christian creed be made to conform with the ethical and moral sense of the Germanic race." He went on to attack the concept of a German God and a German Christianity and any understanding of a national church that was somehow distinctive in its Germanic character. National Socialism and Catholicism were wholly incompatible, and hence, there was no way a person could be both a Nazi and Catholic.[3]

Three years later, on 10 November 1933, this same vicar general of Mainz, Monsignor Mayer, wrote to the same Nazi district office offering a church burial for Peter Gemeinder, a Nazi *Gauleiter* (district chief) who had died in 1931 and who had been denied a Catholic funeral. Mayer offered not only to bless the grave but also to hold a special funeral mass in which representatives of the district NSDAP in Nazi uniform would have a special place of honor. In a very short time, Mayer had completely reversed his previous decision.

The jarring discrepancy between these two incidents within the local history of but one diocese reflects the larger history of German Catholicism in relation to the National Socialist movement in the critical years between 1930 and 1934. In 1930 Mayer was simply reflecting the wider judgment of the German Catholic bishops in resisting National Socialism, taking a tough stand not only against Nazi beliefs but also against any compromise on Catholic membership in or adherence to the Nazi movement. Certainly his stance did not reflect the unanimous judgment of the German episcopacy, for a few bishops had advocated toleration, if not support, of the National Socialists. But these bishops were few in number and not particularly influential. In the main, the German Catholic leadership developed a strong resistance to Nazism in the latter years of the Weimar Republic, as Nazi political strength was growing, and it retained this view even after Hitler came to power in January 1933.

Yet by May and June of 1933, only a few months later, the general assembly of Catholic bishops, the Fulda Conference, was joining a flood tide of support for the Nazis, or at least it was proclaiming official cooperation with and implicit support for National Socialism.[4] Surely this change was due in part to direct and extreme political pressure, but it cannot be explained simply or exclusively by coercion, because German Catholicism had a substantial range of social and institutional support. As a religious institution almost equal to Protestantism in membership and organizational size, it was not some marginal or lightweight movement. We are speaking of an immense church with a highly organized and effective hierarchy and an institutional structure extending throughout the society and, in some provinces, into every town and village. How, then, is one to explain this change, in a very short period, from strong official resistance to a seemingly supportive posture? How did this radical shift in the Catholic relationship to National Socialism come about? What influences shaped this dramatic movement? These are the questions that need to be examined if we are to understand the story of Catholicism under the Third Reich, with its all-too-few moments of heroic resistance and its more common experience of compromise with and acceptance of National Socialism.

From Resistance to Capitulation

The complex story of this change has been the subject of considerable research, from the work of Guenter Lewy in the early 1960s to the more recent work of German scholars such as Klaus Scholder, Heinz Hürten, and Ludwig Volk, and from North American scholars such as John Conway and Ernst Helmreich.[5] These and other studies have together revealed four central elements in the adjustment of German Catholicism to an acceptance of National Socialism, or at least to a posture of submission, especially in the critical years of 1933–34. Only a brief and general review of these factors is possible here.

First, German Catholicism was under pressure to exhibit and encourage nationalism. The long legacy of the "cultural struggle" (*Kulturkampf*) is an essential background piece here. Beginning in 1871, Otto von Bismarck and the Prussian Protestant elite implemented a series of efforts intended to suppress the influence of Catholics and reduce their public role. Although this anti-Catholic policy gradually diminished until it was eventually overturned in the 1880s in an agreement with Pope Leo XIII, it left behind deep social wounds. Catholics emerged from this struggle with the self-perception of an embattled minority under wholly unjustified suspicion. In an effort to disprove the charge that German Catholics were somehow less than true Germans, they tended to develop an urgent patriotism. Later, in the supercharged atmosphere of post–World War I Germany—a time of extraordinary national sensitivity based upon a widespread feeling of victimization and international abuse—German Catholics were eager to demonstrate an appropriately zealous degree of patriotic fervor. As is often true of minorities out to confirm a common cause with the majority, there was a tendency to overdo it. In the Germany of the 1920s, German Catholics had just such a tendency toward hypernationalism. The more the Nazis became the chief proponents of German nationalism, especially after National Socialism took over the German state, the more difficult it became for Catholics to resist giving their approval.

Second, the Catholic Church nurtured an attitude generally adverse to Enlightenment ideas and values, including the assertion of individual rights and the ideal of shared governance. As a result of its struggle in the aftermath of the French Revolution and under the influence of a series of very conservative popes in the nineteenth century, Catholicism came to view many of the progressive developments of modern life as threats to the validity of traditional life and meaning. Catholics had become deeply suspicious of revolutionary change, including changes in the way a society governs itself. Even though Catholic political influence was a strong part of the Weimar experience through the Catholic Center Party, there was a persistent view among many Catholics that democracy was part of a modern secular conspiracy hostile to the Church. There was at the same time a tendency to identify all forms of liberalism with atheism and modern corruption.

Third, it was common at that time, on the eve of National Socialist rule, to hear fearful voices warning of Bolshevism. Catholics were not, of course, alone in their concern about the far left. Many middle- and upper-class Germans feared that communists would take over and dismantle the economic structure and then go on to throw Germany into social chaos in their effort to achieve some alien, Marxist-Leninist ideal. But Catholics had an extra and obvious religious concern, namely that Marxist atheism would overwhelm the church and the people of faith. There was, in addition, a fourth factor in the well-documented fact of Nazi force and intimidation against the Catholic church: the brutal strategies that National Socialists used against the church's youth organizations, the physical and literary attacks against its priests, the bureaucratic obstruction of the Catholic press and schools, and open harassment of Catholic political groups, especially from February 1933 until the collapse of the Center Party and the creation of a Concordat agreement in July 1933.

Each of these four factors, now widely accepted by historians, was a powerful force militating against Catholic resistance; together they spelled a devastating barrier to any effective dissent, especially if there developed at the same time an attractive, internal Catholic counterargument to the church's initial resistance to Nazism. This essay will argue that such a counterargument did develop, providing a rationale for Catholic acceptance of Nazi rule.

There is, moreover, a fifth and possibly decisive explanation for the Catholic capitulation—a factor that should be mentioned, even though it is not widely acknowledged, probably because it is so controversial and potentially intimidating. This explanation points to the apparent division in the Catholic church in Germany itself. Was the German Catholic hierarchy deeply concerned about maintaining the fabric of Catholicism in Germany? Would they be able to hold the church together if they did not come to terms with Nazism, given the strong support for the Nazi movement among rank-and-file Catholics? Such questions suggest a deep dilemma between resistance to National Socialism at the risk of schism, on the one hand, and compromise with National Socialism in order to maintain the church's national unity, on the other. Actually, since Catholic decisions in this larger political sphere were made in the Vatican, this choice fell more to the papacy than to the German bishops themselves. This explanation assumes an expectation within the Church's leadership that they would risk a substantial apostasy among German Catholics if some working relationship could not be established with the Third Reich.

Would German Catholics have defied a statement from Rome ruling that Catholics must oppose the Third Reich and work against the very state so many of them supported? Is it credible that fear of such a rejection of papal initiative was the real driving force behind the German bishops' actions? Did they fear a popular Catholic backlash? Did they fear that such a division with Rome would result in an independent national church if they and the Vatican did not come to terms with Hitler? This theory, though compelling in many respects, does not yet enjoy the documentation or the consensus accorded to the first four reasons mentioned above. However, we can safely assume that these five factors, in whole or in part, brought German Catholicism into an undeniably official and popular relationship with National Socialism.

Beyond Capitulation to Accommodation

As persuasive as this set of reasons may seem for explaining the dramatic change in the Catholic attitude toward National Socialism in 1933, it accounts for a *capitulation* more effectively than for an *accommodation*. Yet, in fact, the real change that many Catholics advocated and in large part succeeded in achieving involved an enthusiastic accommodation or affirmation of National Socialist ideals. The standard rationale tells us why the Catholic church buckled, but it does not indicate why a substantial part of the church swung so thoroughly toward National Socialism, or what historical and theological reasons they had for such an affirmation.

This is the real question, namely, the question of what convinced so many Catholics that National Socialism could be their friend and ally. If the church had been dragged to capitulation by coercion and raw Nazi power alone, there would be less suspicion about its complicity today and little need for further historical or theological analysis. Reality, however, is otherwise. The evidence demonstrates wide Catholic enthusiasm for the Nazi movement, even if it stopped short of the kind of reconciliation and endorsement seen in the Protestant German Christian Movement. Tighter organizational integration and internal controls within Catholicism made such a complete endorsement much more difficult to express; nonetheless, the evidence shows that from ordinary parish life up to the conferences of German bishops there was a growing acceptance of and, in some circles, great enthusiasm for the Nazi cause.

This shift to accommodation might have rested, to be sure, on a foundation of political calculation and perceived necessity. But this would have satisfied neither the broader Catholic mind nor the Catholic intellectuals. Such an accommodation needed a distinctively Catholic justification of National Socialism. In the dense and disciplined atmosphere of early-twentieth-century Catholicism in Germany, such a substantial shift would have to be grounded in a clear theological and historical justification. Such a shift in Catholic attitude required a persuasive theological rationale for the compatibility of Catholicism and National Socialism. This is precisely what emerged in the middle months of 1933.

A small but sophisticated group within the Catholic theological community began to work in parallel with political forces to convince both the church's episcopal leadership and lay Catholics that National Socialism was not only acceptable to Catholics but necessary. Their project was narrow in scope, and it only operated for a brief period. But it would be a mistake to see in this brief flash of attention only some marginal movement, for these individuals performed two vital functions. They built bridges between Catholicism and Nazism that made it possible for well-educated, thinking Catholics to shift from resistance to the Nazis to acceptance of Nazis, and they also effected this in an absolutely critical period, March to September of 1933. During this period, National Socialism was consolidating and cementing its social control over the German people and its political authority vis-à-vis the shattered Weimar Republic. This is also the period when much of the potentially effective institutional resistance, including that of the Catholic church in Germany, was being neutralized. It was a time when well-reasoned historical and theological bases for Catholic support of National Socialism could have an extraordinary effect, well beyond the influence and attention such theological thought would have had in normal times.

Because of their prestige and influence with both the bishops and the wider Catholic population, five Catholic theologians merit special attention, even though only one can be discussed in any detail here. Each of these theologians played an effective role in this change from resistance to accommodation. Of the five, the two most famous at that time were Karl Adam of Tübingen and Karl Eschweiler in Braunsberg. Michael Schmaus was a third, who, while growing in his influence, was then very early in his career. Theodor Brauer is almost entirely ignored today but was then a well-known professor of practical theology at Cologne, a man whose writings were widely read in Catholic lay circles. Finally, there was Joseph Lortz, who became one of the premier Catholic historians in the twentieth century and who, although he was still early in his career, had already written the most widely read church history text in Germany. Each of these men had a telling effect on the shift in the relationship between Catholicism and National

Socialism, but it is Lortz who may be seen as the most pivotal figure, both because of the scope of his argument and because of its persuasive appeal to the Catholic intellectual community.

As a prelude to a closer look at Joseph Lortz, it is helpful to understand that he had a distinctive importance in 1933. Lortz was the leader of a small academic circle in Braunsberg that took on the goal of changing German Catholic attitudes toward the Nazis. He was instrumental in starting, as part of the work of this circle, a publication series, *Reich und Kirche (Imperial State and Church)*, which argued the compatibility of Catholicism and National Socialism in that particularly critical time of mid-1933. This series of pamphlets was, in fact, the first Catholic theological promotion of an accommodation with National Socialism after the Nazi accession to power in January 1933. Lortz also developed his view of National Socialism in complete continuity with his historical-theological scholarship. Finally, in that critical summer of 1933, Lortz wrote a widely read pamphlet that, in a carefully constructed series of arguments, appealed precisely to those conservative, educated Catholics who wanted to support the National Socialist movement but had not yet found a theological and intellectual justification for doing so.

Lortz's Background and Theological Context

Joseph Lortz was born in Grevenmacher, Luxembourg, on 13 December 1887. He decided in his teenage years to prepare for the priesthood and began the study of theology and philosophy in Rome in 1907. He then continued his education in Fribourg, Switzerland, from 1911 to 1913 and was ordained in Luxembourg in 1913. After doctoral studies in Bonn, where he completed a dissertation on Tertullian in 1920, Lortz went to Würzburg to study under the well-known church historian Sebastian Merkle and to assist him in research. While in Würzburg, from 1923 to 1929, Lortz completed his postdoctoral studies and at the same time served as an instructor and pastor to students in the university.

In 1929, he received an appointment as a professor of church history at the State Academy of Braunsberg in East Prussia. Here Lortz gained his initial prominence as the author of a textbook widely used in university and seminary curricula: *The History of the Church from the Standpoint of the History of Ideas*. This text became not only the foundation for his scholarly career but also a key presuppositional piece to his understanding of the church's positive relationship to the National Socialist movement. Although Lortz wanted to become Merkle's successor at Würzburg, this opportunity did not open to him, and in 1935, he accepted an appointment to the Catholic Faculty at the University of Münster, a position that he held until the end of the war.

After the war, Lortz was barred from continuing as a professor in a state university. He had joined the Nazi Party in 1933 and he was unsuccessful in clearing himself of this tainted political record before the Allied tribunals, despite his protestations that he had abandoned both the party and the Nazi cause in the mid-1930s.[6] In 1950 he was able, however, to receive an appointment as director of a new, quasi-official, scholarly institute in Mainz, the Institute for European History. Under his direction this became one of the leading centers for historical research in Germany, particularly in the field of western religious history and, most specifically, in medieval and reformation church history. While director of that institute and until his death in 1975, Lortz resumed a very active publishing career in church historical studies, especially as a pioneer in Catholic studies of Martin Luther and the Reformation. Once again he gained a position of international academic and intellectual renown.

As we look for the origins of Lortz's attraction to Nazism, it is important to note three foundational concerns that emerged early in his work. For Lortz, atheistic communism (Bolshevism), Enlightenment individualism, and a general religious-cultural fragmentation were the three disastrous elements in modern life which, he believed, led to a "postmedieval civilization." On the basis of these concerns, Lortz saw not just a compatibility between Catholicism and National Socialism but the possibility therein of religious renewal and mutual reinforcement. He saw in the Nazi movement the kind of aggressive resistance to communism that would protect the rights of the church and ensure its defense. He was also attracted to the "socialist" dimension of the movement, understood as an assertion of the priority of the community over the individual. This represented for him a reversal of the excessive focus in modernity on the autonomy of the person that developed under the influence of Enlightenment thought. Finally, and most important, Lortz wanted to affirm what he saw in the National Socialist German Workers Party (NSDAP): a force to bring back an integration of nation and church, of German culture and Christianity. This would recreate the synthesis he viewed as the genius of medieval Christendom, now lost in modernity, a loss he deeply regretted. The National Socialists, while no lovers of the church, to be sure, could nonetheless be strong agents of the church's deepest interests and simultaneously the protectors of *Germania*.

Each of these three focal points remained central in Lortz's thought. Even though he later would claim disenchantment, even rejection of Nazism, he never renounced or qualified his commitment to this threefold foundation. Any inquiry about Lortz, especially in his relation to the Nazis, must examine these three elements in some detail. It should also indicate how these affirmations related to the so-called Jewish question and how they were influential in the contest for Catholic recognition and popular acceptance of the National Socialist regime.

The key to Lortz's approach to Nazism is that he developed his historical scholarship within a theological vision. The strength of his assessment for Catholic readers arose from his attempt to integrate National Socialist ideology with his historical-theological conception of Catholicism. Lortz had come to early attention in Braunsberg because of his effort to set the history of the church within the context of intellectual history and to tie his historiography to a neoscholastic view of the nature of the Church, both of which were clearly reflected in his widely used textbook *The History of the Church from the Standpoint of the History of Ideas.*[7] He now approached National Socialism within the same intellectual framework, employing three important assumptions. First, Lortz believed history should be written in the service of theology. Both his general historical work and his special studies in the Reformation were grounded in this theological vision, which assumed God's providential role to be fundamental to history. Thus, the church established by God had to be understood as part of a theological reality beyond history, grounded in the ultimate mystery of God. Second, Lortz had an extraordinarily high view of this church as a transcendent reality. Influenced by M. J. Scheeben, Émile Mersch, Sebastian Merkle, and perhaps Romano Guardini, his description of the church as mysterium framed a view of the church as an objective, sacred entity. It was an organism of truth and holiness in history, yet paradoxically caught in sinful rebellions of political, social, intellectual, and religious dimensions. His view of God's providential will in history joined with his belief in the transcendent role of the church led to Lortz's third judgment, so provocative for many in his time. Lortz saw an inner theological necessity for spiritual renewal that had its counterpart in an outer historical necessity for political and social reform. There was for him a natural connection between the objective truth of the church and the true unity of society. More important, he came to see a logical connection between the redemptive role of Catholicism and the social and political reforms sought by National Socialism.

Lortz's Stance within the 1933 Crisis of Catholicism

Although Lortz quickly threw his support to National Socialism in the Catholic contention over relations with the Party in 1933, this was not really a new or pioneering step. In fact, it had direct continuity with his research and writing and occupied a fully integrated place within his efforts to identify the essence of ecclesiastical history. First published in 1932, his church history text illustrates a desire to move beyond the usual chronological narrative of events and catalog of traditional themes and theological terms. In the foreword, Lortz sets forth this intention: "What I am attempting to restore here is the actual history [of the church], in its diversity of structure and its complex stratification, . . . but [I want] to do so in such a way that ideas emerge as the dominating power."[8] Lortz's assessment of the history of ideas reflected his belief that the church was on a perilous course, visibly evident in modern life but rooted in a long and tragic history. He thought he saw a long-term post-medieval path toward the disintegration of church and society, resulting largely from subjectivism and a subjectivist liberalism. He detected the beginnings of this dissolution as early as the twelfth century: "Since the end of the thirteenth century, no, actually already in the middle of the twelfth century a disintegration begins to occur, which (seen as a whole) again and again misled people away from the Church. In fact, a *seven-hundred-year demolition process* lies behind us."[9]

Lortz understood this disintegration as a developing crisis already evident at the height of the Middle Ages. Even during the thirteenth century, the glorious age of scholasticism and gothic achievement, he identified the beginnings of a movement in the church away from medieval ecclesiastical universalism toward secular nationalistic thought. He found in the scholastics a nascent dissolution of the harmony between faith and reason, a manifestation of subjective criticism. He noted the roots of secularized interests, increasingly evident within the church itself and the growing penetration of a worldly spirit. He added to this litany his perception that even in the genuine elements of reform, that is, the growing conciliar movement, there was a spreading infection of nationalistic and democratic ideas regarding laicization and the distribution of authority. Thus, Lortz's study of church history, especially in his strongest area of medieval Christian thought, provided an early, framing negativism about modernity, which he maintained as a thesis right through his analysis of the nineteenth century.

Unexpectedly, however, when he arrived at his analysis of the twentieth century, still in this same original edition of the *History of the Church*, Lortz rather suddenly broke into a very different voice, speaking of a number of steps toward recovery:

> It goes without saying that an age does not end abruptly on any fixed date or in such an absolute way so as not to influence the following age. The transformation in men's minds is never entirely a constructive one and, thus, the subversive elements which characterized the nineteenth century are still at work. But insofar as [our present situation] is constructive, it is so in reaction against those spiritual factors and attitudes to life which laid the foundation of the modern age, which fashioned modern development and then dominated it until the turn of the century. The new trend is (a) *Philosophically*, a turn from doubt, hypercriticism, historicism, or subjectivism, to a form of objectivism in one form or another (with a basis in phenomenological

philosophy). (b) *Ethically,* the trend is from unrestrained freedom to authority, from the egoism of individualism to communal thinking. (c) *Politically,* the liberal and democratic idea together with its most concrete political manifestation, parliamentarianism, is yielding to the principle of leadership in the form of dictatorship, or government without parliamentary majorities, or nonparty government (Fascism, Nazism). (d) *Religiously,* there is a better understanding of the value of institutional religion, of the value of a church as such, and an appreciation also of the unique character of religion and its special claims.[10]

When one reads Lortz's sentiments from 1933 in the context of his ideas on postmedieval history, there is no surprise in finding that he welcomed the Nazi seizure of power as a "turning point" of major significance for the cultural and religious history of the German people. He spoke of the "fundamental kinship" between the church and National Socialism, the shared antipathy toward the erosion of morality, the common respect for law, and the protection of communal values. He saw in the National Socialist accent on national unity prospects for a deeper religious unity within the German church.

Lortz had a growing conviction that only a dramatic political change, one with great unifying force, could overcome the deep legacy of division and disintegration. In "National Socialism and the Church," the textual supplement from 1933, Lortz envisioned that National Socialism would prove the occasion for "nothing less than the crowning achievement of the church's developmental direction throughout the whole of the nineteenth century."[11] At last, the church would be in a position to reassert itself religiously and spiritually, because of a compatible political environment, because of the timely rise of a new force in German life. Thus, Lortz writes: "A comparison of the conclusions of our analysis of the nineteenth century until our time with the fundamental thought and emphases of National Socialism shows to what an extraordinary degree and sense the Nazi movement has become the *fulfillment of our time.*"[12] Lortz had found the renewed vision that had been lost at the very height of the Middle Ages. He saw the recipe for reform in a return to the medieval synthesis of Christianity and culture.

Nonetheless, Lortz still had not specified how this connection between the church and National Socialism could be concretely interpreted, especially in light of the strong hostility that characterized so much of the Catholic attitude toward the Nazis. This was the project to which he turned in the summer of 1933 in Königsberg. As the Nazi Party continued to consolidate its control of German society and as Lortz continued to recognize the possibilities and advantages of a close relationship, he decided to use the occasion of an academic lecture to formulate these views more thoroughly. From this lecture emerged the central piece that brought Lortz into the Nazi Party and into the forefront of the Catholic reconciliation with the Nazi effort.

The Catholic Approach to National Socialism

Lortz appears to have started work on a lecture, which he had been invited to give to Königsberg students, very soon after Hitler came to power. He probably began this work in February 1933, well before the demise of the Center Party and before the public became aware of negotiations toward a Concordat. He later claimed that this lecture reflected a continuity between his thinking on National Socialism and revisions in his church history text in the early months of 1933, and there is no reason to doubt him. Although Lortz was clearly not in the center of Catholic discussion in those days—actually he was tucked away in the marginal intellectual arena of Braunsberg—he intended this lecture for a wider audience. Subsequently published as the first pamphlet in the series *Reich und Kirche,* this lecture emerged as probably the first public theological assessment of the new Nazi regime by a major Catholic figure. It became a significant part of the controversy over how Catholics were to relate to National Socialism, and it propelled Lortz into the forefront of the debate, bringing him a degree of notoriety that would come back to haunt him after the war.

Under the title "The Catholic Approach to National Socialism," Lortz's Königsberg lecture caused both widespread interest and a storm of protest. It came out just at a time when many Catholics wanted to give unhindered, unrestricted support to the new regime but were burdened by continuing church strictures and by fresh memories of discrimination and persecution. At the same time, many other Catholics were shocked by its attempt to bridge what they had assumed for so long were unbridgeable differences. It was not a long piece, less than thirty pages, and intended to be a popular and readable tract for Catholic laity. Each of its three sections can be reviewed quite briefly.

In the first section, Lortz reflected upon the persistent political tension and strife between the various organizations of the Catholic church and the National Socialist movement. He recognized that this history had been more than difficult, filled as it was with mutual hostility, recrimination, even violence. Yet he appealed to Catholics to recognize that the political reality of their situation forced an acceptance of National Socialism not only as the dominant political power in Germany but as the very state itself. Instead of bemoaning this fact, Lortz recalled the twin political threats of recent times: the communist menace and the threat of national dissolution through parliamentary chaos. Although National Socialism clearly promised to remove these two most disastrous threats, Catholics have persisted, according to Lortz's claim, in a failure to see the inherent value that Nazism possessed and presented politically. "There was especially a genuine, even tragic ignorance of the forceful, positive power, ideas, and plans of National Socialism, as they had been authentically set down in Hitler's book, *Mein Kampf*, and had been generally available as early as 1925. For this omission, we all bear our part of the guilt. We [Catholics] openly take it upon ourselves in the sense of the concept of sacrifice for the sake of the whole people for whom we have given so much in so many ways."[13]

Catholicism had been wrong in its judgments, blinded by partisan political loyalties and the distracting misunderstandings that some leaders used to avoid a confrontation with the true enemies. Moreover, National Socialism was no longer merely a political movement, it was now the actual basis for national unity and stability: "National Socialism today is not only the legitimate holder of state power in Germany. It is, only a few short months after the succession of power, the German state itself. This state stands in a truly decisive battle for the rescue of the entire people in this present circumstance. It has made its peace with the Church. . . . It is striving in an effort heretofore unknown in Germany for the realization of an inner unity of all the common people. In an obviously urgent way, such an exercise is producing in German Catholicism, out of the most diverse regions, an agreement with National Socialism which comes from within. This task will be decisive for the Church in Germany and no less so for National Socialism."[14] Thus, Catholics cannot realistically continue to think in terms of a separate political destiny. If Catholics give up such a hope, they would enjoy the prospect of cultural and communal influence and join the larger social unity so indispensable for German salvation.

In the second section of his lecture, Lortz went to the heart of the matter by listing specific ways that Catholicism and National Socialism are compatible. He returned to the phrase he had used earlier in the supplement to his church history text, recalling Catholics to certain points of "fundamental kinship." First among these is the common opposition to communism (Bolshevism), liberalism, and relativism. Actually, in Lortz's wider historical perspective of the roots of the modern era and the history of the church since the sixteenth century, the principle threats were liberalism and relativism, in which communism represented the central demonic example. The deeper intellectual and theological issue, however, was subjectivism, which has already been noted as Lortz's main culprit in the erosion of western thought and life or, perhaps more to his thinking, in the dissolution of Christian civilization. The intellectual and social movements that centered on the individual person as subject had become for Lortz the root of modernist problems.

Here Lortz remained in complete continuity with his writings in ecclesiastical history, especially his *History of the Church*. This disaster of subjectivism became, as noted above, the key to his understanding of the failure of later medieval Christendom and the heart of his conception of the fateful ambiguity in Luther and the Reformation. National Socialism, in his view, was compatible with Catholicism in its attack on both liberal principles and subjective relativism, and it was an ally in the restoration of a social framework more conducive to the work of the church.

A second kinship between Catholicism and National Socialism for Lortz is the common effort against permissiveness and immorality, against a flawed understanding of society characterized by the loose contemporary norms of social behavior leading to the degeneration of society. But now, he claimed, there was hope for a common effort of regeneration: "National Socialism is an outspoken opponent of godlessness and public immorality, as it has dominated modern civilization in the increasing effect of liberal permissiveness and turning society toward an unchristian life. We Catholics have protested tirelessly in countless press campaigns, pamphlets, sermons, conference resolutions and parliamentary proposals against trash and filth [*Schund und Schmutz*]. But this effort remained mainly in the theoretical realm, because we were not the state. But now, because of National Socialism, the power exists to be independently effective and in its attack upon the cesspool of the capital [Berlin] we already see the result."[15]

Lortz described this kinship as well in a common rejection of the general liberal tendency to accent personal pleasure. There is a false sense of freedom and equality in liberal society that, in its celebration of the individual, ignores God's own created arrangement in the natural order of things. It also contravenes directly the Catholic understanding that God's grace and design operate within the diverse and unequal realities of nature.[16]

Again and again in Lortz, the seeds of disintegration in liberalism and subjectivism were matched against decisive resolution in the combined commitment of church and National Socialist state. Perhaps of equal importance to Lortz, however, was that this partnership afforded the church the opportunity to return to its primary spiritual task. National Socialism provided a renewed chance to recover the essence of the church's strength in explicit creed and emphasis on faith:

> Perhaps what is most important is this: "Catholic" signifies *a basic religious creed*. We have just come through a period which threatened, through its [intellectual] relativism as well as through the vast actual relativizing of life, to exterminate any genuine strength in every area of life. It is now extremely valuable for the Catholic understanding of religion as revelation that through National Socialism the formal attitude of a creedal standard [*Bekenntnismässig*],

which had almost completely dropped out of circulation, is once again in place in the widest ranks of society as a valuable attitude. In fact, this is true with an unexpected intensity. "Faith" no longer appears as something of lesser worth or weak, but rather as momentous and heroic, through which humanity realizes the best dimension of itself.[17]

Lortz went on to point to a kinship with the Nazis in a reemphasis upon the genius of German culture, a "renaissance" in which the integral role of the church will be further recognized. He asserted a strong connection between National Socialist views of social unity and equality and the corporatist principles of Pius XI's 1931 encyclical, *Quadragesimo anno*. He pointed to a concurrence between National Socialist recoveries of concepts of noble sacrifice and strength and the accent in Catholicism on a resurgence of strong faith that realizes itself in social commitment. Ridiculing a kind of arid Catholic intellectualism, he looked with idealistic hope to a partnership with the Nazis that could lead to the recovery of a Catholic spirituality of "the concrete and the whole of being human and even the whole of nature."[18]

His final point, however, is especially characteristic of Lortz. Here he concluded that National Socialism meant the unity of the German people and, for Lortz, that was a Christian unity. The political unity of the Volk was but a reflection of a deeper spiritual unity that framed the elliptical poles of church and state. This unity meant a return to perhaps the greatest vision of the grand medieval achievement. It promised a return to Christendom. Further, echoing his pioneering ecumenical work in the Catholic analysis of the Reformation, Lortz saw this unity as a step toward overcoming the western schism of Christianity. Lortz saw in National Socialism not only an avenue out of the modern social and moral morass, but he saw as well the theological vision he wanted to see: western cultural and spiritual integration. At the very end of the treatise, he wrote a fateful warning: "Either this movement rips through to the rescue or we land in chaos. No one can deny any longer the inexorable result. Such chaos, however, would be the destruction of the nation and the ruin of the German church. And that closes the discussion."[19] It was clear for Lortz that the essential connection of Catholicism and National Socialism was key, not only to the stability and continued viability of the German nation and culture, but also to any continuing prospect for Germany as a Christian society.

Even from this brief review of Lortz's Königsberg lecture, themes emerge that would have profound consequences in the thinking of German Catholics. Lortz taught them how to reconcile Catholicism with Nazism. Furthermore, beyond the power of these ideas to bind Catholics to National Socialism, there was considerable potential in this treatise for the Nazis themselves. As they pursued policies that suppressed individual rights, victimized the Jews,

---

Michael B. Lukens

forced social conformity, and criminalized deviance, they had this Catholic theologian on their side.

Lortz's emphasis on the kinship between Catholic and Nazi ideals recalls a common concept in practical politics, namely, the old conviction that "the enemy of my enemy is my friend." That can be seen in the anticommunist and antiliberal convergence he emphasized. But Lortz was not willing to see this convergence merely as mundane politics. Rather, he saw the rise of National Socialism as a *providential* act, pitting a powerful political movement against the faithless compromises and moral erosion of modern liberalism and its communist offspring:

> The deeper nature of National Socialism first became partially evident to broader acknowledgement through its strong and vigorous opposition to Bolshevism. Bolshevism is the radicalization of the Marxist program through the revision of social democratic liberalism into a despotic dogmatism under the leadership of dictatorial power. It intentionally seeks the expansion of its materialistic domination over the whole world. Germany, as the center of Europe, is the most important country for the accomplishment of this plan. It has to be seen as providential that just at this moment there has arisen over against Bolshevism a victorious opponent in the NSDAP, which is just as far from the weakness of liberalism as Bolshevism but at the same time with a bitter hatred of Bolshevistic materialism.[20]

Lortz also accepted a necessary use of force, in his scorn for the weakness of Weimar liberalism and praise for the toughness of the Nazis:

> The secret of [National Socialist] success is in the nature of its attack against [communism] and in a more constructive way than simply providing a better substitute for fallen idols. It proves the softness of the legitimate, established powers in old Europe, which have prospered to death, that National Socialism is still so little thanked for this simple life-saving act. The complete inner overthrow of communism, admittedly, cannot be achieved by power alone. However, the fact that terror is to be broken only through force is a forgotten truism and one which usually demands employment in life. This fact Hitler has rightly rediscovered. So, for the present, his emergence has meant the salvation of Germany, and Europe with it, from the chaos of Bolshevism, i.e., from the destruction of Christian Europe.[21]

This was certainly the kind of ammunition welcomed by some Catholics in their effort to legitimize and affirm an aggressive police policy against those opponents who were perceived as a chaotic threat to the social and religious harmony of the nation's majority.

Another theme that emerged in Lortz's work in 1933 is the assertion of the priority of the community over the rights and place of the individual. Lortz repeatedly accented a Nazi password, *Totalitätsanspruch*, meaning the "claim of the Whole." This is a claim that differed dramatically from the Enlightenment tradition of the preeminence of the individual, and Lortz not only understood but explicitly affirmed the difficulty of this value: "One ought not to diminish or disguise this claim of the Whole. It is by no means generally comfortable. Were it so, it would fit poorly with the great decisions which it has to carry out. Life-changing decisions always mean struggle. Only in the recognition of that claim of the Whole and at the same time of its positive mastery, through the cooperation of the Church and Catholics, is there for both nation and Church an acceptable and worthy resolution [of our situation], namely, our common fulfillment."[22]

Both the common assault of National Socialism and the church against communism and their common reassertion of the "claim of the Whole" brought Lortz to emphasize a theme with potentially the most damaging significance for German Catholicism. Lortz saw in National Socialism the renewed possibility for a cultural and religious synthesis, a unity of state and church that would return *Germania* to the supposed glories of the High Middle Ages and restored Christendom that had been long lost. For Lortz this would not only provide a social consensus essential for a moral and stable society; it would also presuppose social integration on the basis of a common religion, which, of course, would be Christianity understood in Catholic terms.

The common foundation in Catholic Christianity thus became the basis for both consensus in moral values and for unifying state policy. The place and role of non-Christians, even minority Christian expressions, was clearly problematic in such a view. These people, most notably in 1933 the Jews, lay outside the synthesis, incompatible with majority values and might. They became liabilities to social unity and harmony, yet this is the very social unity that Lortz perceived as essential to the church. In fact, this social-religious unity was, for Lortz, at the core of the church's mission of promoting the gospel and fulfilling the will of Christ:

> [T]he newly emphasized national life of Germany could serve the Church as a blessing instead of being harmful, as feared by all too many people of little faith. For a thorough consideration of the nearly two-thousand-year history of the Church shows in the basic teaching from the sacred realm that the growth of the Church is tightly bound to the cultural community [*Volkstum*] of those ethnic groups [*Stämme*] and peoples in which the Church to a singular degree performs its work. This cultural entity [*Volkstum*] operates as the mother-source of the Church's growth. Indeed, in it we can perceive with the greatest certainty the governance of providence, which has enabled the fulfillment of the gospel in particular times and among a particular people and thereby enhanced its growth.[23]

This is not pure racism. The ground for Lortz's synthesis of Catholic Christianity and national culture is found in his neoscholastic theology, with its consistent claim of the inseparability of nature and grace. It rests in the understanding that God is revealed not simply in Scripture but through interventions in history and nature as well, in the naturally designed realities of our community and cultural experience as well as in the course of historical events. There is an "inner correlation" between God's design in nature and history and the particular characteristics of distinctive communities and cultures. Thus, it is an axiom of such a theology of grace that faithfulness requires support and enhancement of whatever is naturally distinctive in the peculiar strength and talent of a particular group, for example, ethnic German culture.[24]

This is not an explicit claim of superiority or an appeal for uniformity, but rather a complex theological basis for seeing God's will in the pursuance of particularity, in the very integrity of a "special culture." Yet, at the same time, it is easy to realize how potentially damaging this could be in any association with the Nazis, which, intentionally or not, would be an association with Nazi racism. When Lortz used words like *Volkstum* and *Stämme*, he was attaching his neoscholastic arguments to the Nazi catchwords of the day. Thus, the argument for a correlation of grace and nature could be perceived as an argument for exclusion of alien characteristics, namely, Jews, from such a distinctive culture. The elimination of any threats or distractions to the divinely ordered German culture could be perceived as a measure of Catholic faithfulness.

Lortz never dealt directly with the question of minority religious expression or the "problem" of other religious groups, except perhaps in his discussion of the division between Protestants and Catholics, which he also expected to be overcome in the unifying incentives of National Socialism. Yet it is quite clear that there was no integrated place in such a renewed German culture for those who were outside the Christian community. Lortz did not deal explicitly in this treatise or elsewhere with Jews or Judaism in his contemporary situation, but it is fair to say that he did not need to do so; his concept spoke loudly and clearly to his contemporaries. One cannot leap thereby to any certainty that Lortz, therefore, also explicitly supported the suppression of Jews or the Aryan legislation in the period from 1933 to 1937. But it is nevertheless obvious that his language and thinking lent support, at least in the minds of some, to policies of "political coordination" [*Gleichschaltung*] and comprehensive harmonization, that is, to the Nazi policies of racial exclusion.

This call to a higher, destined unity was for Lortz nothing less than a divine mission. It was a call to a grand and great cause, and he sought to inspire Catholics to see in National Socialism a divinely appointed moment for restoration and renewal. They needed only to achieve the necessary attitude of commitment and sacrifice that he already saw in the Nazis themselves: "We know only too well that for a great many National Socialists the state creed and the readiness to sacrifice for it completely surpasses the commitment of those in the Church for its mission. Yet it still remains the case that National Socialism in a most profound sense prepares the way to faithfulness and even encourages the concept of the Church to live anew."[25]

Conclusion

From this brief examination of Joseph Lortz's work, several conclusions seem quite clear. First, the unifying element in his thought was the development of a political theology based on mainstream, normative Catholic theological viewpoints. No innovative theological construction was introduced here; rather it was an appeal to elements common to a German Catholic consensus. Lortz attempted to create a distinctively Catholic alternative to the kind of partisan political response that Catholics had used since the cultural conflicts of the late nineteenth century, in particular, an alternative to support for a Catholic political party such as the Center Party. Lortz saw in true Catholicism a spiritual-religious emphasis that in an ideal way complements the political dimension of the state. Thus, he argued for a Catholic acceptance of the Nazis because he thought their aims compatible with Catholic aims. Although he saw this political-religious conjunction as a rejection of "political theology," in the sense of formal political participation, his whole effort was an exercise in the development of a very political theology, based on the assumption of Church and Party correlation, rooted in a synthesis of intellectual orientation and social purpose.

This revised political theology, it can be shown, was directly exploited by the Nazis in achieving an even greater hold on German society. Lortz gave German Catholics a respectable, traditional theological rationale for participation in or at least acquiescence toward National Socialism. He related this to the mission of the whole church, a view that could be especially appealing to the priests and bishops. The leadership was under enormous pressure in the critical middle months of 1933, both from the Nazi party and from lay Catholics, to sanction a more positive attitude toward the Nazis. The teaching offices of the church could make convenient and widespread use of Lortz's views and his stature.

Catholic theologians such as Lortz gave a theological and intellectual legitimacy to National Socialism precisely at a time when the question of popular acceptance of the Nazis hung in delicate balance. In making a case for the compatibility of Catholicism with National Socialism, these theologians built upon the prestige and intellectual authority that Church academic figures had in the minds of Catholic laity. They thereby played an influential role in creating total political control for the Nazis and a total social and spiritual disaster for the church.

Post-Holocaust Theology

German Theological Responses since 1945

Micha Brumlik

In few countries has the relationship of Christian churches to Judaism been transformed so radically as in Germany after the Second World War, particularly in the West. There the increased willingness of Christians, especially Protestants, to deal with their traditional anti-Judaism has resulted from shock at their human and moral failure toward Jews under National Socialism. Yet it would be a profound misunderstanding to see these transformed attitudes as only one possible expression of Christian belief, as several Third World churches have done in the ecumenical context. By attributing these altered attitudes merely to a sense of guilt, outsiders have diminished the theological significance of these changes for Christian faith as a whole. Even if some of the denominations involved, such as the German Lutherans, were specific to Germany, the reality is that the Christian churches in National Socialist Germany failed the Jews because of a tradition they shared, to a great extent, with all churches everywhere.

Appreciation for the altered Christian perspective toward Judaism must not be naive. Changes in academic theology and in attitudes found among the more educated, activist laity are not the same as widespread changes in thinking among churchgoers. There is no proof that these changes—as expressed in revised Protestant church regulations and Catholic bishops' declarations—have become an accepted part of the beliefs held by the majority. In addition, it should be noted that the theologians whose work is outlined here remain a minority, still outnumbered by their conventionally minded colleagues. Furthermore, a distinct new form of anti-Judaism has developed within progressive church circles and on the margins of the political left.

This essay will trace these developments and related changes within the institutional church. It will focus on the thinking of prominent individual theologians in order to highlight key political and theological conflicts. The rela-

169

tionship between Jews and Christians in postwar Germany will be described, mainly from the perspective of the Christian churches. Since the focus will be upon development in church attitudes, the contributions of Jewish thinkers such as Ernst Ludwig Ehrlich, Robert Raphael Geiss, Pinchas Lapide, Bernd Günter Ginzel, Peter Levinson, and Pnina Naveh Levinson will be mentioned only in passing.[1]

This emphasis reflects also the diminished Jewish presence in postwar Germany, comprising now approximately sixty thousand people in contrast to the half million residents there prior to 1933. With a few exceptions, rabbis in Germany tend to be uninterested in this debate, some due to their Orthodox perspective, others because their education and background (mainly Israeli) do not provide the necessary impulse. The attitude of most rabbis only mirrors that of their congregants, the vast majority of whom lack interest in or understanding of Christian-Jewish activities. This, too, is a consequence of the Holocaust. Members of the Societies for Christian-Jewish Cooperation (*Gesellschaften für christlich-jüdische Zusammenarbeit*), which were initiated after the war by groups from the United States, can often count on more mockery than supportive cooperation.

The Confessing Church and Its Legacy

After World War II, the apparent triumph of the Confessing Church provided the theological starting point for an examination of the Holocaust in the Evangelical Church of Germany (EKD). Early resistance by the Pastors' Emergency League, based upon Barthian theology, was seen to have preserved the character of Protestant faith, preventing its appropriation by the state. Likewise, the Confessing Church and its Councils of Brethren, in a position based upon the Barmen Declaration, had opposed the *völkisch* transformation of the gospel attempted by the German Christian Movement. Following good Lutheran tradition, however, this church resistance had not challenged the right of the National Socialist state to exercise authority in its own sphere. The resulting limits on the church's position became evident in the Confessing Church's attitude toward the Jews. Even today, assumptions about this issue are shaped more by myth than by objective knowledge of the facts.

We can begin with the debate about implementing the Aryan Paragraph in the church, a debate instigated by enthusiastically cooperative church leaders, not the Nazi state. Dialectical and liberal theologians from Marburg, including Rudolf Bultmann and Hans von Soden, cited Pauline theology and the work of Karl Barth to oppose the Aryan Paragraph, arguing that people who had been born Jewish and baptized into Christianity should not be excluded from the ministry, nor should there be mandatory establishment of separate parishes for Christians of Jewish descent. These Marburgers were opposed by theologians at Erlangen, especially Paul Althaus and Werner Elert, who referred to the Old Testament "orders of creation" as natural arrangements for human societies, established for all time according to God's will. The German Volk must be considered one such order of creation. In an unconventional interpretation of Lutheran theology, they then claimed that this concept allowed the formation of a specifically German, *völkisch* Christianity in which Christians of Jewish descent had no claim to an equal place.

The dialectical theology that opposed such interpretations found its clearest articulation in the Barmen Declaration, inspired by Barth. The main theme of the Barmen Declaration emphasized the exclusive role of Christ as God's Word. This Christomonic and Christocentric theology insisted upon the Johannine assumption that belief in Jesus as the Christ is the only way to God and provides the only true knowledge about God. Thus, Barmen sharply rejected all other sources of religious experience and knowledge, including the cultural or historical.

On the one hand, such a narrow interpretation effectively ruled out all *völkisch* interpretations of Christianity from the standpoint of German history. On the other hand, however, it prevented any positive reference to Jews and their faith. Bultmann's dialectical theology, based upon Paul and Luther, did not distance him very far from the theology of Emanuel Hirsch and the German Christians, rooted in German idealism. They shared a basic premise: the insistence on the conflict, overshadowing all else, between law and gospel. In exegesis and sermons about the Old and the New Testaments, this premise allowed for no other conclusion than to attribute to Jews a legalism inimical to freedom and subjectivity. Such an emphasis reserved the message of liberation for the Christian point of view alone.

Thus, the focal point of the debate was the singularly Christian concept of freedom, a theme put on the agenda in the early modern era by Martin Luther, who drew upon the tradition of Paul. The subsequent philosophy of German idealism and, ultimately, the emergence of the linguistic humanities offered a theoretical extension of this perspective. This debate pinpoints an allegedly substantial difference between Judaism and Christianity. In the ancient church, with its apologetics and scholasticism, Christians had insisted that their New Testament, added to the Old, gave them an advantage over the Jews. Now Christians began to argue that they possessed not only an advantage but something essentially different: a New Testament that does not so much fulfill the Hebrew Bible as supersede it and, perhaps, contradict it. This perspective tests the relationship between the two Testaments as well as the relationship of Jesus to Judaism. Even the ancient church had assumed a radical discontinuity between Jesus and the Judaism of his time. This new direction, however, assumed a radical discontinuity between the Old and New Testaments. Such an approach can hardly avoid being anti-Jewish and anti-semitic, and it united both the Confessing Church and the German Christian side of the theological debate in Germany.

Clearly there were no thoughts of Christian theological solidarity with Judaism during the Third Reich. An additional factor in the church's indifference was the prevalence of an antiliberal political attitude. In the decades before Hitler came to power, the great majority of educated Germans (including Protestant theologians) held little regard for the values of democracy, including cultural pluralism, and they viewed modern Jews as the advocates and representatives of an uprooted, disconnected *Zeitgeist* in the service of mammon.[2] Whatever the achievements of the Confessing Church, almost no one fought on behalf of practicing Jews (exceptions include Dietrich Bonhoeffer and Barth's theoretical reflections). Anti-Jewish preconceptions continued to shape judgments about mass murder even after the war, but gradually recognition of the horrors inflicted upon Jews forced a debate about Christian failure and its theological roots. That in turn led to a renewal of the relationship between Christians and Jews in postwar Germany.

Theologically, the revision of Christian attitudes toward Judaism had several stages, moving from the wartime theorems of the German Christians to the central principles of Confessing Church theology. Barthian theology initially formed the basis for this rethinking process, which was increasingly fueled by the arguments of liberal theology and, finally, by new concepts that emerged from the encounter with Judaism itself. In the process, Christian theologians dissolved the purported singularity and uniqueness of Christianity from within, leading it back into Judaism, but this proved to be a process that many other Christians perceived as threatening.

Postwar Systematic and Institutional Developments

There are four systematic stages of renewal in the postwar Jewish-Christian relationship, which arose in response to the four central arguments of the German Christians. The latter had distinguished themselves from Judaism, first, in the separation between law and gospel. Second, this separation was impelled by a concept of religious history that made the Israelite and Jewish religion contingent, above all, upon the Old Testament. Third, this historiography became tied to systematic arguments based upon modern subjective philosophy, arguments which, fourth, otherwise agreed with socially conservative, nationalistic, and *völkisch* goals.

In response to these German Christian claims, the critique based upon Barthian theology first underscored the *unity* of law and gospel. Second, it emphasized the irrevocable unity of New and Old Testament, and third, it thereby introduced a purely biblical exegesis no longer dependent upon outside philosophies or sources of knowledge. Fourth, without actually approaching a liberal understanding of politics, this critique replaced the old *völkisch* and nationalist content with socially progressive, leftist ideals. Finally, it also became self-evident that the unbiblical myths most closely tied to antisemitism had to be eradicated, exegetically and systematically. These included the belief in an "Aryan" Jesus, the claim that Jews were Christ-killers, and the notion that Jews lost their role in salvation history because they were blind and bedazzled deniers of the Messiah.

These clarifications produced a Christian theology of Judaism in which the Old Testament had been systematically rehabilitated; in particular, the relationship between law and gospel was no longer divided between the New and the Old Testaments. Although still historically critical, exegesis now dealt with the question of Judaism's continuity in Christianity. At the same time, the hypothesis of the Aryan Jesus disappeared, as did the thesis of the Christ-killers. However, this removed primarily the excesses of the German Christians. The classic theological ideas about the newness of Jesus' message, the blindness of the Jews as witnesses, and therefore, the Christian church as the new Israel were retained. Liberal theology already had taken these positions during the period between the wars, and they remained consistent with the dialectical theology of the Bultmann school. In fact, it can be said that early postwar Christian theology had returned to where Pauline-oriented dialectical theology had been in the era between the wars. Although explicitly opposed to antisemitism, this theology contained a systematic anti-Judaism, even though that stance was neither inspired by race nor expressed in antisemitic terms. Theologians now acknowledged that the historical splitting off of the Old Testament had been an error and that the resultant allocation of law to the Old and gospel to the New Testament contradicted the spirit of Jesus and the apostolic Scriptures themselves; but the Protestant churches would not give up their emphasis on the distinction between law and gospel or their claim that the theme of love in Jesus' life and preaching had overcome Jewish legalism. Only when Protestant piety confronted the historical reality of industrial mass murder did there emerge a new impulse in theological thought.

Consider the Confessing Church Council of Brethren's 1949 Darmstadt Declaration. Despite its explicit repentance and its rejection of German Christian doctrine, this statement interpreted the Holocaust as an expression of God's wrath against Jewish disobedience, thereby reinforcing the anti-Jewish element within Christian doctrine. Darmstadt expressed nothing less than a sweeping historical-philosophical thesis that attributed the deaths in the gas chambers to God, thereby validating the supremacy of the new, "true" Israel of Christian faith and implying, by logical necessity, that the murderous deeds of the SS had invalidated the Jewish faith.

In fact, in an earlier "Statement on the Jewish Question" from April 1948, the Reich Council of Brethren of the Evangelical Church of Germany had already asserted that Israel, since it crucified the Messiah, had counteracted its election and rejected salvation. The death and resurrection of Christ was said to be the sole hope for Israel, and the statement added, "that God will not be mocked is the silent sermon of the Jewish faith, a warning to us, a reminder to the Jews about whether or not they want to convert to Him in whom alone their salvation stands."[3]

These offensive and absurd theses, with their recurrent demand that a God of love be transformed into a God of revenge, were crassly naturalistic in their method of argument and could not be sustained. A theological interpretation of the Holocaust was needed, as was a reevaluation of Judaism in its own right, no longer as merely an aspect of Christianity. The offensiveness of the anti-Judaic interpretation of the Shoah, blaming Jews for their own murder, left no other option than the revision of all assumptions about Jews in the modern Christianity shaped by Luther. These assumptions held that God's wrath had been provoked because Jews were unwilling to accept Jesus' gospel of love and freedom and preferred to continue to submit to the fatal and pharisaic law, but precisely these assumptions had allowed Christian hostility to Jews and helped make their massacre possible. Therefore, theologians began to consider counterassumptions—that the genocide was not God's punishment, that Jews were not guilty, and that, despite their rejection of the message of Jesus, they remain God's chosen people, retaining divine loyalty and love. This thesis led to a reconsideration of the doctrine of law and gospel and to the acknowledgment that the Jewish religion, not just the Old Testament, is also gospel.

Here the question of the role and person of Jesus arises anew. If Judaism is equal to Christianity as a religion based upon the Bible, then what, one might ask, is the need for Christianity? Of what does the belief in Jesus as Messiah consist, if not the belief in his newness? In the end, is Jesus only one path by which people find their way to the God of Israel, in accordance with the prophetic promises? In fact, the debate has now reached a point, in some circles, where Christian identity is in question and where it can seem as though the Jewish people have taken Jesus' place.

Steps toward a Revision

Early postwar confessions of guilt came from individual regional churches as well as from joint meetings at Stuttgart and Darmstadt. Furthermore, after the war the famous Martin Niemöller, a former German nationalist turned early adherent of the Confessing Church, lectured across Germany on questions of guilt. (Partly because of his concentration camp imprisonment as a personal prisoner of the Führer, which lasted from 1937 to1945, during the Nazi regime he had never made a statement about the relationship of the Confessing Church to Jews and Judaism.) But only in 1950 at the EKD synod in Berlin-Weissensee did the first theologically sophisticated declaration emerge on the issue of Christians and Jews. It expressed guilt and called for change, but it also reflected the difficulty inherent in rethinking long-held doctrine:

> We believe in the Lord and Savior who came as man out of the people of Israel. We confess a church, which out of Jews and Gentile Christians is joined together into one body, and whose peace is Jesus Christ.
> We believe that God's covenant with his chosen people of Israel also remains in effect after the crucifixion of Jesus Christ.
> We acknowledge that, through neglect and silence before the God of compassion, we too are guilty of the crimes committed against the Jews by members of our people.
> We warn all Christians against the wish to offset that which has come upon us Germans as the judgment of God against that which we have done to the Jews; for in judgment, God's mercy seeks those who are contrite.
> We ask all Christians to renounce all antisemitism and, where it rises anew, to resist it vigorously, and to encounter Jews and Jewish Christians in the spirit of brotherhood.
> We ask Christian congregations to protect the Jewish graveyards in their areas, insofar as they are untended.
> We ask the God of compassion to bring about the day of fulfillment, when we, with the rescued Israel, will sing the praises of the victory of Jesus Christ.[4]

This document, quoted here in its entirety because of its subsequent importance, expressed arguments that were theologically central to the official church but that could not be easily found in earlier teachings. These include the emphasis on Jesus' descent from Israel and Israel's continued election. Today we cannot tell whether new, deeply felt convictions were being articulated here, or whether this statement was simply a political expedient. In fact, the main topic of the Weissensee synod was not the relationship of Christians to Jews, but the future of peace in Europe. During the meetings, participants quickly concluded that without an initial statement about the Jews, no subsequent declarations would be credible, particularly to the foreign community.

In this declaration, only the affirmation of God's ongoing promise to Israel was truly new and dynamic. To acknowledge that Jesus was born a Jew simply reflected a core element of Christian belief. However, what had not been common in the Christian tradition was the self-evident conclusion—that anti-semitism, with respect either to Jews or to Christians of Jewish descent, had to be rejected. Barth contributed to this postwar reassessment, as did his student, Hans Joachim Iwand. In a 1967 letter to Eberhard Bethge, Bonhoeffer's biographer, Barth asked the following questions with regard to the National Socialist era: "Was it basically correct that the church, as the Confessing Church, mind you—the official church applauded, as is known—was silent about the Nuremberg laws? Was it right, as happened at the time, to say: the granting and denial of civil rights is a matter for the people and the state alone, and does not concern the church? Was it right that in 1938 the persecuted Jews were not at all or hardly prayed for?"[5] The implicit criticism in this series of questions was already apparent in the Weissensee statement of 1950.

In the Catholic Church, comparable statements came considerably later, beginning with Vatican II in the 1960s and this passage from "Nostra Aetate": "Although the Jewish authorities . . . together with their followers demanded the death of Christ, nonetheless, one can neither place this burden without differentiation upon all the Jews who lived at that time nor upon the Jews today. The Church is certainly the new people of God. Still, the Jews may not be portrayed as rejected or cursed by God."[6]

This Vatican declaration is remarkable for its relatively late date and the fact that its appearance was probably connected to continued pressure on the Catholic Church to address Pius XII's action or inaction in response to National Socialism. In addition, placement of this statement under the title "Relationship of the Church to Non-Christian Religions" undercuts the idea of a special relationship between Judaism and Christianity, even though a special relationship was conceded as historical fact.

In November 1975 the collective synods of the dioceses in the Federal Republic of Germany produced a declaration that built upon "Nostra Aetate." It is quoted here in its entirety because of its significance:

> We are the land whose most recent political history is darkened by the attempt to eradicate the Jewish people. And, as a whole during this period of National Socialism, despite the exemplary behavior of individuals and groups, we were a church community which continued to live too much with its back turned to the fate of this persecuted Jewish people, with gaze fixed too strongly upon the threat to its own institutions, and which remained silent about the crimes done to the Jews and Judaism. Many became guilty through sheer fear for their lives. It weighs especially upon us that even Christians participated in this persecution. The practical honesty of our willingness for renewal depends upon the admission of this guilt and

the readiness to learn from our nation's painful history and our church's guilt as well. It requires a particular alertness from our German church against all tendencies to reduce human rights and misuse political power, a special readiness to help all who today are persecuted for racist or other ideological motives, and, above all, the assumption of particular obligations for the burdened relation of the entire church to the Jewish people and their religion. We Germans in particular are not permitted to deny or play down the connection between the salvation of God's people of the old and the new covenants, a connection the Apostle Paul himself saw and acknowledged. For in this sense, too, we in our country have become indebted to the Jewish people. Ultimately, in light of a hopeless horror like that of Auschwitz, the credibility of our talk about the "God of hope" rests upon the fact that there were countless people, Jews and Christians, who repeatedly named and called upon this God, even in such a hell. Herein rests a task for our people, also with respect to attitudes toward the Jewish people among other peoples and in the world community. We see the German churches as having a special obligation within the universal church precisely to bring about a new Christian relation to the Jewish people and its religious history.[7]

This statement is well-meaning and it shows a great self-assurance within the Catholic church. The bishops assume German responsibility for the National Socialist crimes much more clearly than in the Vatican declaration, and they address the co-responsibility of German Catholicism without further elaboration. At the same time, however, there is a hint of ambiguity. Why does the statement emphasize that *German* Catholics may not deny or play down the theme of salvation in its relationship to the Old and the New Covenants [*sic!*]? Are non-German Catholics given an implicit freedom to remain hostile to Jews, to "play down" the connection between Jews and salvation? Admittedly, the statement does end with a reference to German Catholics teaching the universal church on this issue.

If one compares the official Catholic and Protestant declarations, it is striking that Catholicism seems more concerned with correcting the theory that substitutes the New for the Old Israel, that is, the theory that replaces the synagogue with the church. On the Protestant side, the focus is more upon retracting the anti-Judaic theme of God's condemnation of Jews. Both approaches have the same basic goal: a strict adherence by the church to the Apostle Paul's regulations about the relationship between the Jewish and Christian congregations. It appears, however, that the Catholic approach is more fully accepting of the Old Testament and the unity of both Testaments than is the strongly Lutheran-influenced Protestantism of Germany, with its greater emphasis on and contrast between law and gospel and its aversion to "works" in response to the law.

In 1975, the same year as the declaration of the German Catholic bishops, thirty years after the end of the Second World War, the Council of the EKD published a study that provided a strong orientation for the Christian-Jewish relationship, even if it made no theological or liturgical commitments. As members of the "Evangelical Church of Germany's Study Commission on Church and Judaism," a number of renowned scholars worked on the document, including Helmut Gollwitzer, Martin Hengel, Peter von der Osten-Sacken, Martin Stöhr, and Rolf Rentdorff.[8] Citing Paul's words in the Letter to the Romans—"Remember it is not you who support the root, but the root that supports you"—this study, written between 1973 and 1975, took positions on a number of matters. It addressed the common roots of Christianity and Judaism, the one God, the holy Scripture, the people of God; it also reflected upon the divergent attitudes of the two religions toward history and fulfillment, the relation of the Christian congregation to the people of God, the different forms of Jewish experience in Israel and the Diaspora, the state of Israel, and theologically problematic areas such as encounter and witness. The study traced the division of the Jewish and Christian congregations in a historically sensitive way, noting in particular the problematic nature of the Christian mission to Jews. At no point does it ignore the history of anti-Judaism and antisemitism or, in particular, the issue of the National Socialist mass murder. Still, the complicity of the Protestant churches under National Socialism—especially of the Confessing Church—is not acknowledged, at least not with the same clarity as in the Catholic bishops' declaration.

At the same time, there emerged in Protestant thought an odd historical and philosophical judgment: "The catastrophe of genocide and annihilation [Holocaust] is, for the Jewish people in Israel and in the Diaspora, bound to the name of Auschwitz in Poland, the largest extermination camp. Like Hiroshima, Auschwitz became a symbol for the experience of the horror of annihilation and a turning point in historical and theological thought, especially within Judaism."[9]

This statement accurately reflects attitudes during the early 1970s. As an antisemitic, racist, self-contained means of murder, Auschwitz was compared with the wartime use of the atomic bomb over Japan, a morally questionable act but not one that challenges the heart of Christian doctrine. Furthermore, Auschwitz was viewed primarily as a theme of Jewish existence, and not as the central challenge to Christianity that brings everything into question. This was also true of the first German responses to so-called Jewish post-Holocaust theology, which appeared in a 1982 German anthology.[10] Only in light of this still relatively naïve point of departure can we understand how the Study Commission on Church and Judaism pondered Christianity's future attitude toward Jews:

> After all that has happened, there is great diversity of opinion today about how Christian witness toward Jews can be formed in the right fashion. In past years, discussion about this revolved mainly around the two terms *mission*

and *dialogue.* Often, these were understood as opposites that ruled each other out. In the meantime, however, the insight has grown that mission and dialogue are two dimensions of the one Christian witness. . . . Not only the term *mission* but also the term *dialogue,* as a description of Christian witness, is a loaded term for Jews. Because of this, Christians today face the task of reflecting anew, with regard to the Jews, about how they are to understand their conviction that Jesus Christ means salvation for all people, how they name it and what shape they want to give it.[11]

The grammatical logic of the last sentence, which speaks explicitly of "all people," permits no other conclusion than that, according to the convictions of the authors of the study, salvation through Jesus alone holds "objectively" for Jews as well as Christians. The only perceived difficulty appears to be a subjective one, based upon the lost credibility of Christians after the Holocaust: How can more authenticity be won? The possibility that the real problem of Christian witness to Jews is an objective one is not even considered. Since the mid-1970s, then, theological work on this problem represents the essential, original achievement of a Christian post-Holocaust theology in Germany and, with that, the most important contribution of German theologians to a new understanding of Christianity in principle.

Auschwitz and the Crisis of Christian Theology

In a 1977 essay that remains groundbreaking, Catholic theologian Johann Baptist Metz found the decisive words. Here Christian theology was no longer directed solely at what theologians had done or left undone, but at the substance and transmission of the Christian faith: "The question as to whether there will be a Reformation, a return to shared roots in the relationship between Christians and Jews, will always be decided ultimately, at least in this country, on how we Christians stand on Auschwitz, how we Christians assess it for ourselves. Whether we allow it to be truly the end, . . . the catastrophe of our history from which one finds his way out only through a radical change, with new standards, or whether for us it is only a monstrous accident in our history that does not affect its course."[12]

Metz demands, as a consequence of Auschwitz, a new orientation for Christian theology, a renunciation of the role of 'victor' that Christianity had taken on to hide its own messianic weakness. In addition, this reorientation must recall the drastic deficiencies in the Christian record of political resistance, and, finally, it must welcome the practical consequences of true Christianity—consequences that would lead to the end of Christianity as a bourgeois religion. All this leads to an unequivocal demand that must apply to all future Christian theology—and for the systematician Metz, historical and exegetical questions play a secondary role—namely: "to do no more theology that is formulated in a way that remains or could remain untouched by Auschwitz."[13]

During the same period, Metz's challenge was not only supported —as, for example, in the collection edited by Martin Stöhr[14]—but it was deepened systematically by Protestant and Catholic theologians alike. Here the fields of New Testament exegesis, the history of Old and New Testament exegesis and, finally, systematic theology have proven especially fruitful. A reformulated New Testament exegesis wrestled with whether certain New Testament Scriptures are truly critical of Judaism, as those with an anti-Judaic interpretation claimed, or whether they in fact primarily represent a debate within Judaism at the time of Jesus. The historical study of Old Testament exegesis questioned the extent to which German Old Testament scholarship, greatly influenced by Julius Wellhausen, had promoted anti-Jewish clichés. In particular, to what extent had Protestant theology used anti-Jewish presuppositions in its emphasis on the contrast between law and gospel, its accusations about Jewish legalism, and its denial of the connection between the two Testaments? Systematic theology turned to a renewed reading of Paul's Letter to the Romans from a historical perspective. This made it possible to interpret the catastrophe of Auschwitz as a result of Christian indifference to Judaism and the people of Israel, thus bringing the Christian faith to its senses by recalling its Jewish roots.

Thus, a renewed biblical theology arose that has approached the Hebrew Bible in its own context—where possible, by reaching back to the Talmudic and rabbinic sources, without reverting to New Testament interpretation. This approach has included New Testament exegesis as well, by offering a New Testament reading that takes into consideration Jewish interpretations. Such a reading regards the two Testaments together; it refuses to view the New as the fulfillment of the Old, and it attempts to read the Old Testament in such a way that it does not amount to an expropriation of Jewish faith.

If this truly is to be a revision of Christian theology, based upon its own sources —and not a revision introduced externally from a humanistic point of view—then what matters most of all is finding a central point within the New Testament Scriptures. Here, attention has been directed primarily to the one author in the New Testament canon who wrestled explicitly with the relationship of Judaism to Christianity, namely Paul, particularly in his Letter to the Romans. Osten-Sacken provides an example. In a convergence with much of the Scandinavian and North American scholarship on Paul (that by Krister Stendahl, for example), he has emphasized the Jewish context of Paul's questions. He has also examined more closely the meaning of Paul's unwavering affirmation of God's promise to the Jews. The focus is on the central confrontation between law and gospel and the central role of the Jews in salvation history:

> Since the days of Paul, the existence of Abraham, as he depicts it in Romans 4, is not only lived out under eschatological circumstances in the connection to Jesus Christ, but also—and, indeed, to a far greater degree—in the Jewish people. If one holds before one's eyes the history of Jewish suffering, brought about to a great extent by Christians, it is for long stretches a singularly lived hope "in the God who awakens the dead," "hope against hope," so that its motto could be what Paul said of Abraham: "No distrust made him waver concerning the promise of God, but he grew strong in his faith as he gave glory to God, fully convinced that God was able to do what he had promised" (Romans 4:20-21). A theological reception of Paul that includes Israel alone in the category of "works of law" in the Pauline sense, is incapable of recognizing the existence of this faith and hope among the Jewish people. Still less is it capable of recognizing that it is the Torah, the holy law, which brought Israel to such an existence in faith and hope. A reception of the kind implied [i.e., equating Judaism with law] must therefore ask itself whether in teaching the word of God it does not pose an obstacle to the power of this word and its freedom more than it promotes it.[15]

The exegetical result makes clear that all talk of Judaism and the Jews must begin with their ongoing election, because of which the Christian's relationship to Jews alive today has a central theological and not just an ethical-moral significance. This in turn intensifies the problematic nature of theodicy in light of Auschwitz.

Berlin theology professor Friedrich W. Marquardt is the most radical representative of a renewal of Christianity based on its Jewish roots. His main theme involves the relationship, not only of the historical Jesus, but of the resurrected and proclaimed Christ to the Jews, who have been affirmed in their ongoing election. For if it is correct—as both Paul and the other New Testament Scriptures report—that Jesus was a Jew and only a Jew, then it must be asked to which tradition the essential characteristics of the resurrected Christ belong. For Marquardt, who began the revision of his thinking with a "dogmatic experiment,"[16] along with a study of the land of Israel, there is no doubt that the essential characteristic of Jesus for the redemptive God was his Jewishness. Because of this, the resurrected Christ, too, achieves his messianic power exclusively from God's commitment to the Jews. From this emphasis on covenant thinking and its corresponding promises, the subsequent anchoring of the living and the dead Jesus in the Jewish people and its language leads Marquardt to two conclusions about Christology. First, he develops a sharp critique of all attempts to elucidate the significance of Jesus by interpreting him outside the Judaic context and, thereby, falsely universalizing him. Second, he rejects all systematic attempts to assign Jesus significance through trinitarian doctrine gained from the patterns of Greek ontology. He then adds,

> But as a consequence this means that, biblically, the thought cannot be avoided: the "true people" are primarily the Jews elected by God and called to his service. They learn what it means to be human in their service—and others learn it from them. It is indeed important to the Bible that the "true people" understand themselves as coming from "Adam," that is, from all people; they are not only with them, but called upon their behalf and for this reason "present." But all people, in turn, must understand: the history of their descent from God boils down to their part in the history of Israel. Only thus do they become "true people." The *"vere homo"* is a Jew. The church's christology has not seen or has been unable to see this biblical fact. Established in mission, in its struggle for the broadest common ground, [the church] did not want to see [this point] in its unfounded pursuit of being understood and comprehended by everyone; and for that reason it chose an a-Jewish form. The Jewishness of Jesus did not speak to it, possessed no content of proclamation, and for that reason was simply not "worth naming." In this, clearly, [the church] at its core was unbiblical, because, considering the biblical scriptures, the Jewishness of Jesus is not only worth mentioning but worthy of notice in the sense of an arbitrary message. The scriptures about Jesus proclaim Jesus particularly as a Jew, summon him as a Jew before the forum of the peoples. In our opinion, this is even the elementary proclamation of Jesus Christ through the New Testament.[17]

Even if the messianic power of Jesus can still be spoken of, it refers to descent: it is through covenant, land, and language—the relation of the God of Jesus to the Jewish people—that the Gentiles may partake through the person of Jesus. This circumstance alone has saving power. The experience of Auschwitz forbids us, nonetheless, from speaking of Jesus himself as the Messiah of the Jews. As a result, the belief in him as the Messiah of the Gentiles becomes questionable.

The historical examination of the physical catastrophe of the Jewish people and the moral crisis of a Christianity that, actively or passively, was part of the worst crimes in human history have thereby thoroughly discredited the message of Jesus. The extent of the evil prohibits all talk of historical messianism and salvation, and this can lead only to a reevaluation of the Jewish rejection of Jesus. This rejection, as is known, referred to the messiahship sworn to by the disciples. For this reason, on the basis of historical experience and for the sake of a new dialogue with the Jews, Osten-Sacken speaks of a necessary "renunciation of theological absolutism" by the church.[18] With that, he has discovered the most succinct and at the same time extensive formula in the renewed Christian theology; to what extent this can be maintained is another question. Osten-Sacken's liberal theology, with its accent on the hope-giving power of the Torah and its theory of a renunciation of absolutist

Christology, has left the area of Jewish-Christian conflict over promise and fulfillment behind. This makes possible a central role for the present in light of hope for the future.

The crimes committed against the Jewish people in Auschwitz made it inevitable that the Holocaust would have an impact on theology on historical and ethical grounds. Systematic theology has also been affected. Berthold Klappert, in particular, has dedicated himself to this task of rethinking. The goal of Klappert's reflections is a special Christian solidarity with Jews and an attempt to move the extermination camps into a systematic context. As Klappert himself knows, these reflections are not immune from the danger of consecrating senseless, gruesome crimes by giving them theological significance, for example, equating Jewish suffering with the cross of Christian theology. There is an uncomfortable irony here: It is instinctive and virtually unavoidable to believe that the crimes of the Holocaust should never have occurred, yet that might have left Christian theology in its state of blindness. Klappert ties the fate of Jesus on the cross and the suffering of the Jewish people under National Socialism closely together, so closely that the idea already raised by John XXIII—that Israel, in a certain sense, is the Christ of humanity—is not far-fetched. The result, however, poses the acute problem of a Christian theology that plunders the Jewish fate, a practice Elie Wiesel commented on in *A Beggar in Jerusalem,* where he wrote that Christianity always occupied itself with the Jews when it became bored: "they call that theology."[19]

It becomes clear that the different subdisciplines of a renewed Christian theology collide with each other. While Old Testament scholars like Rentdorff[20] and New Testament scholars like Osten-Sacken attempt to allow Judaism to speak for itself by emphasizing Jesus in his Jewishness, it is apparently impossible for systematic theology to do anything but place Judaism on the margin of Christian salvation history or proclamation:

> In the experience of Auschwitz and the remembrance of Auschwitz, the messianic hope of Judaism and its anticipated confirmation in the story of Jesus led to the question that Elie Wiesel articulated in this way: "Why does the messiah not come when the world is so evil?" . . . And if we assume that he were to come after Auschwitz, after these six million Jewish dead, would it not be too late, in particular too late for him, as the representative of the messianic and redemptive hope of Israel and the world? But does not the Jewish posing of this question have its Christian counterpart? If the history of Jesus is a unique anticipation and confirmation of the messianic hope of Israel, how then can the world be so devilish and evil as it was in Auschwitz and apparently still is? . . . We have hardly begun to contemplate seriously the connection between the annihilation of God in Auschwitz, on the one hand, and the deprivation of God's rights in the crucified one, on the other.[21]

With this, the Jewish people become the star witness, even martyr, for the truth of the Christian message, providing an antidote for a Christianity that has been poisoned by Auschwitz: "For me, the fundamental dependence of the Christian church and theology upon the Jewish witnesses of the experience of God in Auschwitz is the distressing product of a theology after Auschwitz. Auschwitz is the most Job-like experience after the cross. The experience of the absence and presence of God there, the Jewish tale of the silence of God, from the terror of God up to the hanging and burning of God—which was only witnessed by Jews and can only be told by them, listened to in humiliation by us Christians—renders us dependent upon Judaism. Its storytellers and witnesses in Auschwitz reveal, as a fact, the eternal communion of the crucified with his suffering people."[22]

In contrast to Klappert, Marquardt escapes this danger because, along with historically oriented exegetes like Osten-Sacken, he concentrates totally upon the historical Jesus. Like Klappert, Marquardt and Osten-Sacken almost equate Jesus with the Jewish people, but—with the Jewish experience of Auschwitz in mind—they renounce a pervasive Christology. It can be said that the more Jesus is placed into the milieu from which he came, the more he loses his christological characteristics, and with that, his suitability as the object of a systematic theology. In fact, Marquardt understands himself more as a dogmatist interested in the correct reading of the confessions than as a systematic theologian who wants to speculate, beyond the transmitted texts and their instructions for faith, about the being of God and world history.

Anti-Jewish Reactions

Unfortunately, the positions delineated here represent anything but a majority view. In fact, at all levels of academic theology opponents have arisen who, with varying degrees of thoroughness, defend the traditional stance, both in the academic arena and in church politics. Someone like Ulrich Wilckens, who has written a thorough commentary of the Letter to the Romans,[23] represents the usual thesis that a certain degree of anti-Judaism necessarily exists in Christianity. The late Göttingen New Testament scholar Georg Strecker insisted upon the unbridgeable gap between Torah and Gospel, citing Paul and Bultmann, and lamented the degree to which Christianity had given way to Jewish reproaches. In addition, proponents of a somewhat apologetic systematic theology, confronted by Emanuel Hirsch's position on the Old Testament, want to differentiate strictly between his "National Socialist mistakes" and the theological cause he represented. As recently as 1993, this author heard the systematic theologian Joachim Ringleben express the opinion that Judaism had been superseded by Jesus himself and that this, in turn, constituted a lasting wound on the body of Judaism.

Similar positions can be found in academia among those who oppose the renewal of the Christian-Jewish relationship that began in a number of regional Protestant churches after the Rhineland synod resolution of 1980. This resolution, with its renunciation of the proclamation of Christian belief among nonbelievers, particularly its renunciation of the traditional mission to the Jews, appears to question the core belief in the universality of the Christian message. The explicit renunciation of an absolutist Christology means more than an acknowledgment of Christian guilt toward Jews; it recognizes Judaism's own integrity of faith. The implications of this proposition can be found already in an interconfessional dialogue from before the First World War, specifically in Franz Rosenzweig's debate with his cousin Rudolf Ehrenberg.[24] Rosenzweig wrote that no one comes to the Father except through the Son, unless they are already with the Father, as are the Jews.

We can only speculate on the motive behind the systematic and political resistance to a post-Auschwitz Christian theology. Is it fear of the fact that the Christian proclamation loses its core and its identity when it acknowledges Jewish doubts about Jesus? Is it that Christians, who secure their Christianity primarily through the Old Covenant, become painfully aware that they must live their faith not in its own right, but as participants on the periphery of Judaism—that they are in essence some kind of incomplete Jews? Or is it—as Strecker occasionally implied—that Protestant Christians surrendering their christological center also abandon their national identity as Germans at the same time? Is it possible that through this reorientation, Christians and Christianity would become so insecure that a new form of anti-Judaism could arise, as the expression of anxious self-assertion? Cannot an objective dialogue proceed more fruitfully when the partners can relate to one another on equal terms—eye to eye—and without a sense of guilt, particularly on one side?

Several unusual examples illustrate the problems of an insistence upon Christian opprobrium. In fact, the heftiest protest against Judaism has not come from the realm of more conservative circles, but primarily from the progressive fringes of the Protestant church in Germany: from the spheres of feminism and pacifism, which in all other questions are in energetic conflict with the other critics named above. In fact, classic anti-Judaism has became articulated most clearly in these highly explosive and socially sensitive realms involving gender and international peace efforts. Ironically, although their ideas about Christianity seem radical, secular, and universal, these progressive spheres produced the clearest protest against taking the new Christian theology seriously. In the universal insistence upon the rights of women and the struggle for peace, Judaism once again appeared to these circles—at least for a time—as a particular troublemaker.[25]

This was especially true for the first wave of feminist theology, which in its early stages was primarily done on the popular level, not the academic. This movement raised questions about the Old and New Testaments and about systematic theology. At the end of the 1970s, books by Pastor Elga Sorge and by the religious educators Gerda Weiler and Christa Mulack criticized Judaism in a manner that seems not only anti-Judaic but antisemitic. In a work based upon the Old Testament, Weiler argued that tolerant matriarchal fertility religions in Canaan had been annihilated by patriarchal Hebrews. Incited by fanatic Levites from the south, whose monotheism made the humane belief in a holy marriage of the mother goddess and her young bridegroom impossible, the Hebrews had promoted a warlike society that was marked, above all, by the oppression of women. Such oppression was even described in terminological allusions to the Holocaust, as in the term *Ausmordungen* (a "murdering out"). These massacres are always identified as the deeds of Hebrews.[26] Sorge, at the time a pastor, also became interested in a matriarchal religion, specifically the rediscovery of the goddess at the heart of Christianity. In this exploration, she proposed that the Ten Commandments in the book of Exodus be transformed into ten permissions. Repeatedly, Sorge offered the Jewish basis of the established Christian churches, especially its contemporary embodiment, orthodox Judaism, as proof of Christianity's animosity toward people and, above all, women.

The same tendency continues in its most extreme form in the books of Christa Mulack. Making use of the religious psychology of C. G. Jung, she has postulated a concept of God that includes feminine characteristics, commensurate with and inspired by the cabala. This she contrasts with what she calls the Yahwistic picture of God, which, in its patriarchalism, animosity to nature, and belligerence, she sees as the ultimate basis for the general crisis of ecology and civilization in the modern world. She argues that the hatred of women in the Hebrew Bible points to structural similarities between women's path of sacrifice through world history and Jesus' path of sacrifice through the streets of Jerusalem. Jesus himself, who had proved to be an "arrogant Jew" in his encounter with the Canaanite woman, needed the instruction of women to "come to the essence of his teachings. In retrospect, it turns out that the annihilation of the Jewish people in the Holocaust was nothing other than a delayed consequence of the "Yahwistic system of death."[27]

These opinions, advocated by popular academic authors, have been disseminated on a far greater scale by Franz Alt, a well-known journalist who joined the peace movement from the wing of the Christian Democratic Union (CDU) concerned with traditional values. His bestseller, *Jesus: Der erste neue*

Man (Jesus: The First New Man), strengthens the stereotype of a Jewish religion founded upon violence. Alt bases his case upon the writings of a renowned religious psychologist, Hanna Wolff, who in numerous books contended that Jesus archetypically embodied the principles of modern tolerance and individuation. For Christians, the consequence of this had to be the rejection of Old Testament scriptures, among other things.[28]

This Jungian tradition also marks the Old and New Testament exegeses of Eugen Drewermann, a Paderborn college professor and Catholic priest barred from duty, whose unusually prolific production of lengthy books has amazed the public for years. Against his professed intentions, Drewermann's psychological reading of the Bible disseminates anti-Judaism. He tries to emphasize that the Jews are to be protected from antisemitism. On the basis of his historically uncritical exegesis grounded in narrative archetypes, however, he necessarily arrives at the conclusion that the Pharisees so frequently libeled in the Gospels do, in fact, embody the neurotic, petty, dark side of human existence.[29] A recent careful analysis of his entire oeuvre shows that Drewermann's controversial work is indeed essentially anti-Judaic.[30]

Of the authors cited above, Drewermann can best claim to be an academically trained theologian. But it is remarkable how, almost without exception, all these authors rely upon dated exegetical and historical analysis—literature that often enough originated in that era when erudite Christians submitted to the National Socialist state, willingly or at least without protest. It is surely not so much a matter of bad will as insufficient sensitivity to the history of German theology when feminist authors indiscriminately adopt the positions of men like the orientalist Hartmut Schmökel or the New Testament scholar Leonard Goppelt,[31] or when a progressive author like Drewermann cites the former SS man Ethelbert Stauffer, of all people. Though purportedly guided by historical and philosophical principles of analysis, the massive critique of Christianity and Christian-Jewish monotheism undertaken by Drewermann and others has developed a momentum that obstructed their ability to critique their own theological tools.

Admittedly, it would be unfair to attribute these erroneous positions solely to insufficient theological training. Because of its critical Christian consciousness, academic feminist theology also stirred up anti-Jewish prejudice. In particular, the Tübingen theologian Elisabeth Moltmann-Wendel is unrestrainedly eager in this respect. But it should also be noted that, more recently, serious academic feminist theologians have worked more carefully on these issues; in particular, Katharina Kellenbach, Marie Therese Wacker, and Leonore Siegele-Wenschkewitz should be mentioned.[32]

Finally, heated debates about pacifism and Israel during and after the Persian Gulf War should be mentioned. In particular, such debates disrupted the "Arbeitsgemeinschaft Juden und Christen" task force at the German Evangelical *Kirchentag*—a controversy that found literary expression in a sharp polemical exchange between the Jewish theologian Edna Brocke and the leftist Protestant Jürgen Moltmann.[33] Here Moltmann opines that nothing justified the military crushing of Iraq, he questions the justification of a universal concern for the particular existence of Israel, and, finally, he claims that justice must not be sacrificed to partisanship for Israel. Clearly, this prominent leftist Protestant theologian has not grasped the renewal of Christian theology. His conclusion that he is only able to read the Tenach (the Hebrew Bible) and its texts (described as "texts of terror") in the light of the gospel—"as the early in the light of the later . . . in this redemptive light they seem shocking to me"—is sheer, classic anti-Judaism, resting upon the substitution theory.[34]

The Outlook

This conflict shows that the renewal of Christian theology in Germany, particularly Protestant theology, is only in its beginning stages, despite decades of preliminary work by a few. The second EKD study in 1991, "Christen und Juden II," goes further than the first in many respects; it insists energetically that the points of difference may not be repressed and otherwise wrestles with the problems of solidarity with the state of Israel.[35] In Catholicism, whose official pronouncements are less pluralistic, the gradual rethinking process was accompanied primarily by Old Testament exegetical and historical works—works that are equally as thorough as Protestant works, but less radical in their revision of fundamentals.[36]

As both its adherents and opponents have discovered, the renewal of Christian theology in its relation to Judaism involves nothing less than a fundamental revision of Christianity itself and the revision of directions that, in the course of almost two millennia, have led to catastrophic results. Today, at the end of the Christian era, this revision also offers a path of reorientation: the way back to the roots. The other path, primarily advocated by ecumenical theologians, strives for an openness to all religions—from the far eastern systems of belief to the African or Oceanic natural religions. It cannot be said whether a Christianity that has reconsidered its Judaism will have anything in common with a Christianity for whom the Hebrew Bible is neither more nor less significant than the Bhagavad-Gita or the holy book of Maya. It can be predicted, though, that a Christianity that reaches out to all the religions of the world will hardly be in a position to preserve its Jewish roots. Under the banner of National Socialism in Germany, one sector of the church made such an attempt at synthesis. Ultimately, the failure of this approach led to the gradual theological rethinking I have described here.

NOTES

Chapter 1: Robert P. Ericksen and Susannah Heschel

1. Gitta Sereny, *Into That Darkness: From Mercy Killing to Mass Murder* (New York: Vintage Books, 1974), 58.

2. Christopher R. Browning, *Ordinary Men: Reserve Police Battalion 101 and the Final Solution in Poland* (New York: Harper Collins, 1992).

3. Daniel Jonah Goldhagen, *Hitler's Willing Executioners: Ordinary Germans and the Holocaust* (New York: Alfred Knopf, 1996).

4. Götz Aly, Peter Chroust, Christian Pross, *Cleansing the Fatherland: Nazi Medicine and Racial Hygiene,* trans. Belinda Cooper (Baltimore: Johns Hopkins University Press, 1994); Ernst Klee, *"Euthanasie" im NS-Staat: Die "Vernichtung lebensunwerten Lebens"* (Frankfurt am Main: S. Fischer, 1983).

5. Hereafter we will delete quotation marks around "Aryan." Readers should note, however, that it is a racist term, a hypothetical construct with no identifiable relation to reality.

6. For a discussion of these events, see Michael Burleigh and Wolfgang Wippermann, *The Racial State: Germany 1933–1945* (Cambridge: Cambridge University Press, 1991). See also Henry Friedlander, *The Origins of Nazi Genocide: From Euthanasia to the Final Solution* (Chapel Hill, N.C.: University of North Carolina Press, 1995).

7. Philip P. Hallie, *Lest Innocent Blood be Shed: The Story of the Village of Le Chambon, and How Goodness Happened There* (New York: Harper & Row, 1979).

8. Saul Friedländer, *Kurt Gerstein: The Ambiguity of Good,* trans. Charles Fullman (New York: Alfred Knopf, 1969).

9. Karl A. Schleunes, *The Twisted Road to Auschwitz: Nazi Policy Toward German Jews 1933–1939* (Urbana, Ill.: University of Illinois Press, 1970).

10. Robert Gellately, *The Gestapo and German Society: Enforcing Racial Policy 1933–1945* (Oxford: Clarendon Press, 1990), 61.

11. David Bankier, *The Germans and the Final Solution: Public Opinion Under Nazism* (New York: Oxford University Press, 1992), 73.

12. Ibid., 122.

13. Ibid., 127, 142.

14. Ian Kershaw, *The "Hitler Myth": Image and Reality in the Third Reich* (New York: Oxford University Press, 1987); Bankier, *The Germans and the Final Solution,* 145; and Martin Broszat, *Hitler and the Collapse of Weimar Germany,* trans. Volker R. Berghahn (New York: Berg, 1987).

15. Bankier, *The Germans and the Final Solution,* 120–21, 133–34, 146.

16. Ibid., 147.

17. Ibid., 146.

18. Ibid.

19. See, for example, Robert P. Ericksen and Susannah Heschel, "The German Churches Face Hitler: An Assessment of the Historiography," *Tel Aviver Jahrbuch für Deutsche Geschichte 1994* (Tel Aviv, 1994), 433–59.

20. See Clemens Vollnhals, *Evangelische Kirche und Entnazifizierung 1945–1949: Die Last der nationalsozialistischen Vergangenheit* (Munich: R. Oldenbourg, 1989).

21. Peter Mathesen, *The Third Reich and the Christian Churches* (Grand Rapids, Mich.: W. B. Eerdmans, 1981), 100.

22. Susannah Heschel, "Church Protests During the Third Reich: A Report on Two Cases," *Kirchliche Zeitgeschichte* 10, no. 2 (1997): 377–88. See, for example, the letter written by Walther Schultz protesting the Nazi Party order that the swastika be used only in official party contexts and be removed from church institutions. Undated correspondence, Berlin Document Center, Schumacher Collection on Church Affairs, T580, R. 42; also in Bundesarchiv Koblenz, BA R43II/150, fiche no. 3.

23. Carl Amery, *Die Kapitulation; oder, Der real existierende Katholizismus* (Hamburg: Rowohlt, 1963, 1988); translation published as *Capitulation: An Analysis of Contemporary Catholicism*, trans. Edward Quinn (London: Melbourne, Sheed and Ward, 1967).

24. Jehovah's Witnesses were referred to in Nazi Germany as *Bibelforscher* (Bible Students), based on their earlier official name, International Bible Students Association.

25. See, for example, Christine King, *The Nazi State and the New Religions: Five Case Studies in Non-Conformity* (New York: Edwin Mellon Press, 1982); and also Brian R. Dunn, "The Death's Head and the Watchtower: Jehovah's Witnesses in the Holocaust Kingdom," Jack Fischel and Sanford Pinsker, eds., *The Churches' Response to the Holocaust, Holocaust Studies Annual*, II (Greenwood, Fla.: The Penkevill Publishing Company, 1986).

26. Martin Luther, *On the Jews and their Crimes* (1543).

27. Susannah Heschel, *Abraham Geiger and the Jewish Jesus* (Chicago: University of Chicago Press, 1998).

28. Abraham Geiger, *Das Judentum und seine Geschichte* (Breslau, 1865), 117–18.

29. Ernest Renan, *Life of Jesus*, trans. Charles Edwin Wilbour (New York: Carleton, 1864), 300.

30. Ibid., 325.

31. Ibid., 224–25.

32. Geiger, *Das Judentum und seine Geschichte*, 198.

33. Theodor Keim, *Geschichte Jesu nach den Ergebnissen heutiger Wissenschaft* (Zurich: Orell Füssli, 1875); Adolf Hausrath, *Neutestamentliche Zeitgeschichte. Erster Teil: Die Zeit Jesu* (Heidelberg: Bassermann, 1868); Emil Schürer, *Lehrbuch der neutestamentlichen Zeitgeschichte* (Leipzig: J. C. Hinrichs'sche Buchhandlung, 1874); second edition published as *Geschichte des jüdischen Volkes im Zeitalter Jesu Christi* (Leipzig: J. C. Hinrichs'sche Buchhandlung, 1886–1887); 3rd edition published in 1898.

34. Adolf von Harnack, *What Is Christianity?* trans. Thomas Bailey Saunders (New York: Harper & Brothers, 1957), 47–48; originally published as *Das Wesen des Christentums* (Berlin, 1900), 30–31.

35. Leo Baeck, "Romantic Religion," in *Judaism and Christianity: Essays by Leo Baeck*, trans. and ed. by Walter Kaufmann (Philadelphia , 1958), 192, 189–292; originally published as "Romantische Religion," *Festschrift zum 50 jährigen Bestehen der Hochschule für die Wissenschaft des Judentums* (Berlin, 1922), 1–48.

36. Rudolf Bultmann, *Primitive Christianity in Its Contemporary Setting*, trans. by R. H. Fuller (New York: Meridian Books, 1956), 66, 68, 79.

37. Ibid., 72, 77, 78.

38. Ernst Käsemann, "Protest!" *Evangelische Theologie* 52, no. 2 (1992): 177–78.

39. Theophil Wurm, Letter to Bruderrat, 17 January 1949, Landeskirchlichesarchiv Darmstadt, Bestand 36/73, cited in Christoph Raisig, *Die kirchliche Schuld—das verhinderte Gespräch* (Duisburg: Ludwig Steinheim Institut für deutsch-jüdische Geschichte, forthcoming). All translations are our own unless otherwise indicated.

40. *Berlin 1960: Bericht über die vierte Tagung der zweiten Synode der Evangelischen Kirche in Deutschland vom 21. bis 26. Februar 1960,* published by Auftrag des Rates von der Kirchenkanzlei der EKD, 257; cited by Raisig, *Die kirchliche Schuld*, 81.

41. Friedrich Wilhelm Marquardt, *Von Elend und Heimsuchung der Theologie: Prolegomena zur Dogmatik* (Munich: Kaiser, 1988), 138.

42. Jörg Zink, *Neue Zehn Gebote* (Stuttgart: Kreuz Verlag, 1995).

43. Christa Mulack, *Jesus: Der Gesalbte der Frauen* (Stuttgart: Kreuz, 1987), 155–56.

44. Jürgen Moltmann, *Experiences of God*, trans. Margaret Kohl (Philadelphia: Fortress Press, 1980), 22.

Chapter 2: Robert P. Ericksen

1. The issue of willing participation in brutality toward Jews is discussed in Christopher R. Browning, *Ordinary Men: Reserve Police Battalion 101 and the Final Solution in Poland* (New York: Harper Collins, 1992); and also in Daniel Jonah Goldhagen, *Hitler's Willing Executioners: Ordinary Germans and the Holocaust* (New York: Alfred Knopf, 1996). Robert Gellately, *The Gestapo and German Society: Enforcing Racial Policy 1933–1945* (Oxford: Clarendon Press, 1990), highlights the surprisingly small number of Gestapo agents in Nazi Germany and the large percentage of indictments and prosecutions initiated on the basis of denunciation by private citizens.

2. Paul Althaus, *Die deutsche Stunde der Kirche*, 3rd ed. (Göttingen: Vandenhoek & Ruprecht, 1934), 5. All translations are my own unless otherwise indicated.

3. Ibid., 19.

4. Ibid., 7.

5. Paul Althaus, "Kirche, Volk und Staat," in *Kirche, Volk und Staat*, ed. Eugen Gerstenmeier (Berlin, 1937), 30.

6. Paul Althaus, *Kirche und Staat nach lutherische Lehre* (Leipzig: A. Deichert, 1935), 29.

7. See relevant citations in Robert P. Ericksen, *Theologians under Hitler: Gerhard Kittel, Paul Althaus and Emanuel Hirsch* (New Haven: Yale University Press, 1985), 108.

8. Please note that the terms "Aryan" and "non-Aryan" are controversial. They do not represent historical reality, but rather the dreams of antisemites who want to believe in their own racial purity.

9. Paul Althaus and Werner Elert, "Theologische Gutachten über die Zulassung von Christen jüdischer Herkunft zu den Ämtern der deutschen evangelischen Kirche," *Theologische Blätter* 12, no. 11 (Nov. 1933): 321ff. The statement signed by Bultmann and the Marburg faculty is found in *Theologische Blätter* 12, no. 10 (Oct. 1933): 289ff.

10. Paul Althaus, "Kirche, Volk und Staat," 18.

11. Paul Althaus, *Kirche und Volkstum: Der völkische Wille im Lichte des Evangeliums* (Gütersloh, 1928), 34. Note that this statement precedes the National Socialist regime by five years.

12. Gerhard Althaus, interview by author, 30 September 1982.

13. See, for example, Ericksen, *Theologians under Hitler*, 142–43.

14. Emanuel Hirsch, "Ich werde Hitler wählen!" *Göttinger Tageblatt*, 9–10 April 1932. Hirsch signed this letter on 8 April 1932.

15. Emanuel Hirsch, *Das kirchliche Wollen der deutsche Christen* (Berlin: Max Grevemeyer, 1933), 7.

16. Hirsch's NSDAP membership number was 5,076,856 and his supporting member of the SS number was 216,529. Berlin Document Center, Partei Kanzlei Korrespondenz file.

17. See Ericksen, *Theologians under Hitler*, 167–77.

18. Interviews with Professors Hermann Dörries (14 October 1972), Götz Harbsmeier (13 October 1972), Joachim Jeremias (14 October 1972), and Wolfgang Trillhaas (2 November 1982).

19. See my discussion of these events in Ericksen, *Theologians under Hitler*, 191–93.

20. Hans Martin Müller is one of those advocating a rehabilitation of Hirsch's work. See *Christliche Wahrheit und neuzeitliches Denken: Zu Emanuel Hirschs Leben und Werk* (Tübingen: Katzmann, 1984). Müller also edited and introduced the fiftieth anniversary edition of Hirsch's work, *Das Alte Testament und die Predigt des Evangeliums* (Tübingen: Katzmann, 1986).

21. Emanuel Hirsch, *Die gegenwärtige geistige Lage im Spiegel philosophischer und theologischer Besinnung* (Göttingen: Vandenhoek & Ruprecht, 1934), 114.

22. Ibid., 161–62.

23. See Wolfgang Tilgner, *Volksnomostheologie und Schöpfungsglaube: Ein Beitrag zur Geschichte des Kirchenkampfes* (Göttingen: Vandenhoeck & Ruprecht, 1966).

24. Emanuel Hirsch, *Deutschlands Schicksal*, 2nd ed. (Göttingen: Vandenhoek & Ruprecht, 1922), 142–43.

25. Emanuel Hirsch, "Theologisches Gutachten in der Nichtarierfrage," *Deutsche Theologie*, 5 (May 1934), 182–92.

26. Emanuel Hirsch, *Das Wesen des Christentums* (Weimar, 1939), 158–65.

27. See chapter 4 below for a further discussion of the "Aryan Jesus."

28. Emanuel Hirsch, *Das Alte Testament*, 36.

29. Ibid., 49.

30. Ibid., 169. This statement comes from an article that originally appeared as "Jesus und das Alte Testament," *Deutsche Theologie* 8 (November 1937), 836–45.

31. Ibid., 46.

32. Ibid.

33. Hans Martin Müller, "Das Wort vom Kreuz und das Alte Testament: Zur Einführung," in Hirsch, *Das Alte Testament*, 7.

34. Ibid., 12.

35. Ibid., 11.

36. Ibid., 12 n. 10.

37. Charlotte Klein, *Anti-Judaism in Christian Theology* (Philadelphia: Fortress Press, 1978), 6.

38. Ibid., 7.

39. Ibid., 39.

40. Emanuel Hirsch, quoted in Willy Schottroff, *Das Reich Gottes und der Menschen: Studien über das Verhältnis der christlichen Theologie zum Judentum* (Munich: Chr. Kaiser, 1991), 188.

41. Ibid., 189.

42. Hirsch, "Nachwort zu meinem Buche über das Alte Testament," in *Das Alte Testament*, 132–33. This "Afterword" was written in 1937 but not accepted for publication by *Deutsche Theologie* and the time. See *Das Alte Testament*, 127, n 1.

43. Ibid., 133.

44. Ibid., 135.

45. Compare Carsten Nicolaisen, "Die Stellung der 'Deutschen Christen' zum Alten Testament," in *Zur Geschichte des Kirchenkampfes: Gesammelte Aufsätze*, ed. H. Brunotte (Göttingen: Vandenhoeck & Ruprecht, 1971), 2:206.

46. Schottroff, *Das Reich Gottes und der Menschen*, 189 ff.

47. Ibid., 184–85.

48. Hirsch, *Das Alte Testament*, 33.

49. Schottroff, *Das Reich Gottes und der Menschen*, 192.

50. Gerhard Kittel, *Die Probleme des palästinischen Spätjudentums und das Urchristentum* (Stuttgart: W. Kohlhammer, 1926), 125 n. 3.

51. Gerhard Kittel, *Die Judenfrage* (Stuttgart: W. Kohlhammer, 1933), 61–62.

52. Ibid., 39.

53. These letters from Herbert Loewe to Gerhard Kittel, 11 August 1933, and Kittel's response to Loewe are found in the Kittel personality file, Wiener Library, London.

54. Gerhard Kittel and Eugen Fischer, "Das antike Weltjudentum. Tatsachen, Texte, Bilder," *Forschungen zur Judenfrage* 7 (Hamburg, 1943): 10–11. See a description and citations for Kittel's other work in this journal in Ericksen, *Theologians under Hitler*, 61–66.

55. Gerhard Kittel, "Die ältesten Judenkarikaturen. Die 'Trierer Terrakotten,'" *Forschungen zur Judenfrage* 4 (Hamburg, 1940): 259. This article represents Kittel's first attempt to

deal with the caricatures (which were apparently forgeries, it turns out). Then in volume 7 of the journal Eugen Fischer joined him in a more extensive effort.

56. Gerhard Kittel, "Die Behandlung des Nichtjuden nach dem Talmud," *Archiv für Judenfragen*, vol. 1, Group A1 (Berlin, 1943), 7.

57. Ibid., 15–16.

58. Gerhard Kittel, *Meine Verteidigung*, 27. I am indebted to the late Dr. Herman Preus of Luther Theological Seminary, St. Paul, MN, for access to this document, a defense statement written by Kittel in June 1945 after his arrest by French occupation forces and circulated among his friends. A second, longer version dated November/December 1946 can be found in the Tübingen University Archive. The French incarcerated Kittel for seventeen months and he never returned to his university position. He died at the age of 59 in 1948. See Ericksen, *Theologians under Hitler*, 28 ff.

59. Gerhard Kittel, "Das Rassenproblem der Spätantike und das Frühchristentum," lecture, 15 June 1944, University of Vienna. I found this typescript in the Theological Library, Tübingen University, along with another Vienna lecture delivered 22 March 1943, "Die Entstehung des Judentums."

60. Kittel, *Meine Verteidigung*, 33.

61. Ibid.

62. Kittel, *Meine Verteidigung*, Tübingen University Archive, second version (Nov./Dec. 1946), 58.

63. Ibid., 7.

64. It is interesting to compare in this regard Wolfgang Gerlach's study, *Als die Zeugen schwiegen: Bekennende Kirche und die Juden* (Berlin: Institute Kirche und Judentum, 1987), in which he finds antisemitism rife even within the Confessing Church.

Chapter 3: Doris L. Bergen

Some of the material in this essay appears in a different, expanded form in my book, *Twisted Cross: The German Christian Movement in the Third Reich* (Chapel Hill: University of North Carolina Press, 1996).

1. Quoted in "Propaganda an der Chaussee," in *Schnellbrief für Glieder der Bekennenden Kirche*, no. 31 (2 Oct. 1935): 120, LKA Bielefeld, Wilhelm Kirchenkampf (hereafter 5,1) folder number 555, 1.

2. See data from Ministry of Church Affairs, "Zusammenstellung über Kirchenaustritte und Kirchenrücktritte bezw: Übertritte, ermittelt nach den von den Kirchen veröffentlichten Zusammenstellungen," [1940], BA Koblenz, R 79/19.

3. Because of fragmentation within the Movement and missing or inaccessible membership files, it is difficult to gauge the number of German Christians at any given time. However, German Christians and their opponents generally accepted the figure of six hundred thousand as a reasonable estimate of the Movement's numerical strength in the mid-1930s, arguably its weakest phase. See, for example, a circular from the German Christian regional office in Dresden, signed Martin Beier, 9 July 1934, "An alle Mitarbeiter der DC!," including reference by German Christian Reich Leader Christian Kinder to the six hundred thousand members of his organization. LKA Bielefeld, 5,1/290,2.

4. The German term *evangelisch* is used as a general label to include Lutheran, Reformed, and United churches. Because the English "evangelical" has very different connotations than the German *evangelisch*, I have translated *evangelisch* in its broad usage as *Protestant*. All translations are mine unless otherwise specified.

5. Donald Niewyk, "Solving the 'Jewish Problem'—Continuity and Change in German Antisemitism, 1871–1945," *Leo Baeck Yearbook* (1990): 369.

6. Guida Diehl, "Grundsätze für die Glaubenserneuerung," in *Was ist der Eisenacher Arbeitsring?*, flier of the New Land Movement (Eisenach, 1934), p. 2, KAG Minden, file

Neulandbewegung. I am grateful to the Kommunalarchiv in Minden for permitting me to use this collection.

7. "Gespräche mit Katholiken: Nationalkirche auch in anderen Ländern?" in *Die Nationalkirche—Briefe an Deutsche Christen*, no. 28/29 (9 July 1939), 311.

8. Raul Hilberg discusses the development of a definition of "Jews" in Nazi Germany in *The Destruction of the European Jews*, rev. ed. (New York: Holmes & Meier, 1985), 1, 65–80.

9. On the church elections see John S. Conway, *The Nazi Persecution of the Churches, 1933–45* (New York: Basic Books, 1968), 41; Kurt Meier, *Der Evangelische Kirchenkampf*, vol. 1, *Der Kampf um die "Reichskirche"* (Göttingen:Vandenhoeck & Ruprecht, 1976), 103–9; and Shelley Baranowski, "The German Protestant Church Elections: *Machtpolitik* or Accommodation?" *Church History* 49 (1980): 298–315.

10. The text of Hitler's radio address before the church election of July 1933 appears in *Dokumente zur Kirchenpolitik des Dritten Reiches*, ed. Carsten Nicolaisen, vol. 1, *Das Jahr 1933* (Munich: Christian Kaiser, 1971), 119–22.

11. On Müller and his career, see Thomas Martin Schneider, *Reichsbischof Ludwig Müller: Eine Untersuchung zu Leben, Werk und Persönlichkeit* (Göttingen:Vandenhoeck & Ruprecht, 1993).

12. For extensive coverage of the German Christian movement in 1933, see Günther van Norden, *Der deutsche Protestantismus im Jahr der nationalsozialistischen Machtergreifung* (Gütersloh: Gütersloher Verlagshaus Mohn, 1979).

13. On Hess's statement and its background, see Klaus Scholder, *Die Kirchen und das Dritte Reich*, vol. 1, *Vorgeschichte und Zeit der Illusionen, 1918–1934* (Frankfurt: Ullstein, 1977); English edition published as *The Churches and the Third Reich*, vol. 1, *Preliminary History and the Time of Illusions, 1918–1934*, trans. John Bowden (Philadelphia: Fortress, 1987), 572.

14. Reinhold Krause, "Rede des Gauobmannes der Glaubensbewegung 'Deutsche Christen' im Groß-Berlin," held in the Sports Palace, 13 November 1933, reproduced for publication from a stenographical record, pamphlet in LKA Bielefeld, 5,1/289,2.

15. Exact figures for the number of German Christians who left the Movement after the Sports Palace Affair are unavailable. A Security Service report claimed 250 pastors quit the movement in Württemberg alone. See "Lagebericht Mai/Juni 1934," T-175, 415/2940753. See also "Sonderbericht: Die Lage in der protestantischen Kirche und in den verschiedenen Sekten und deren staatsfeindliche Auswirkung," Feb./March 1935, T-175, 409/2932647; and "Gegnerbekämpfung," 25 June 1942, T-175, 285/2780127.

16. A former German Christian called the mid-1930s the most vicious period of the church struggle. See Friedrich Kessel to Heinrich Stüven, 6 November 1953, Osterode/Harz, KAG Minden, file Freie Volkskirche 2.

17. On Kerrl and his appointment, see Meier, *Der Evangelische Kirchenkampf*, 2:66–78; and Leonore Siegele-Wenschkewitz, *Nationalsozialismus und Kirche: Religionspolitik von Partei und Staat bis 1935* (Düsseldorf: Droste, 1974).

18. In 1936, the process of reuniting German Christian splinter groups began in earnest with creation of the League of German Christians (Bund der Deutschen Christen). See unpublished manuscript by the German Christian chronicler, Friedrich Wieneke, "Zehn Jahre Deutsche Christen," (Berlin, 1942), 15, KAG Minden; and Kurt Meier, *Die Deutschen Christen: Das Bild einer Bewegung im Kirchenkampf des Dritten Reiches* (Göttingen: Vandenhoeck & Ruprecht, 1964), 147–51.

19. Already by April 1939 representatives of German Christian groups and individuals of non-German, Christian orientation had pledged cooperation in the so-called Godesberg Declaration (Godesberger Erklärung). See Meier, *Die Deutsche Christen*, 267–78. The Godesberg Declaration, a response to the Archbishop of Canterbury's condemnation of National Socialist aggression against Czechoslovakia, repudiated ecumenism and "World Protestantism" and presented Christianity as the irreconcilable religious foe of Judaism. See

Armin Boyens, *Kirchenkampf und Ökumene, 1933–1939: Darstellung und Dokumentation* (Munich: Christian Kaiser, 1969), 256–57.

20. Literature on the German church in wartime is scantier than for the other periods of the Third Reich. Useful exceptions are Helmut Baier, *Kirche in Not: Die bayerische Landeskirchen im Zweiten Weltkrieg* (Neustadt a. d. Aisch: Verein für bayerische Kirchengeschichte, 1979); Meier, *Der Evangelische Kirchenkampf*, vol. 3; and Günter Brakelmann, ed., *Kirche im Krieg: Der deutsche Protestantismus am Beginn des II Weltkriegs* (Munich: Christian Kaiser, 1979).

21. On developments in the Protestant Church and, to a lesser degree, on the fate of the German Christian movement after the collapse of the National Socialist regime, see Armin Boyens, Martin Greschat, Rudolf von Thadden, and Paolo Pombeni, *Kirchen in der Nachkriegszeit: Vier zeitgeschichtliche Beiträge* (Göttingen: Vandenhoeck & Ruprecht, 1979); Gerhard Besier, *"Selbstreinigung" unter britischer Besatzungsherrschaft: Die Evangelisch-lutherische Landeskirche Hannovers und ihr Landesbischof Marahrens, 1945–1947* (Göttingen Vandenhoeck & Ruprecht, 1986); Clemens Vollnhalls, *Evangelische Kirche und Entnazifizierung, 1945–1949: Die Last der nationalsozialistischen Vergangenheit* (Munich: R. Oldenbourg, 1989).

22. The naming of the German Christian Movement is described by an adherent, Arnold Dannenmann, in *Kirche im Dritten Reich: Die Geschichte der Glaubensbewegung "Deutsche Christen"* (Dresden: Oskar Günther, 1933), 10, 48. See also Wieneke, "Zehn Jahre Deutsche Christen," 5.

23. An overview of the early work of Leffler and Leutheuser and their involvement with the Berlin circle of German Christians is provided in Meier, *Die Deutschen Christen*, 1–16.

24. For an outside view of the relationship between the German Christian movement and *völkisch* predecessor groups, see Chef des Sicherheitsamtes, "Lagebericht, Mai/Juni 1934," T-175, 415/2940752. A German Christian view of precursors is found in Constantin Grossmann, *Deutsche Christen: Ein Volksbuch: Wegweiser durch die Glaubensbewegung unserer Zeit* (Dresden: Eam Ende, 1934), 17–25.

25. "Austritte bei den Deutschen Christen," *Der Montag*, no. 46 (27 Nov. 1933), clipping in BA Potsdam, DC-I, 1933–35, p. 125.

26. Manuscript by Eleanor Liebe-Harkort, "Aus meinen Lebenserinnerungen (1884–1936)," pp. 1–4, KAG Minden, Liebe-Harkort folder.

27. For a thoughtful assessment of the concept of the church struggle, see Georg Kretschmar, "Die Auseinandersetzung der Bekennenden Kirche mit den Deutschen Christen," in Paul Rieger and Johannes Strauss, eds., *Kirche und Nationalsozialismus: Zur Geschichte des Kirchenkampfes* (Munich: Claudius, 1969), 117–21. Criticism of the misuse of the notion of the church struggle is offered by Friedrich Baumgärtel, *Wider die Kirchenkampf-Legenden* (Neudettelsau: Freimund, 1959).

28. It is easy to forget that most Protestants allied themselves neither with the German Christians nor with the Confessing Church, although this point is made in numerous places. See, for example, Kurt Meier, *Volkskirche 1918–1945. Ekklesiologie und Zeitgeschichte*, no. 213, *Theologische Existenz Heute* (Munich: Christian Kaiser, 1982), 61.

29. See "Kanzelabkundigung Wilhelm Niemöller in Bielefeld—Jakobuskirche, 2.7.1933," LKA Bielefeld, 5,1/358,2. Wilhelm Niemöller's colleague in Bielefeld, the pastor Friedrich Buschtöns, moved in exactly the opposite direction, from the Pastors' Emergency League to ardent support of the German Christian cause. See Friedrich Buschtöns to Karl Wentz, 10 November 1958, 26 January 1959, and 31 January 1959, KAG Minden, file no. 15, Schriftwechsel Prof. Wentz-F. Buschtöns.

30. Bonhoeffer to Erwin Sutz, 18 April 1934, in Dietrich Bonhoeffer, *Gesammelte Schriften*, 6 vols., ed. Eberhard Bethge (Munich: Christian Kaiser, 1958), 1:339–40.

31. An overview of neopagan groups is available in Hubert Cancik, "'Neuheiden' und totaler Staat: Völkische Religion am Ende der Weimarer Republik," in *Religions- und*

Geistesgeschichte der Weimarer Republik, ed. Hubert Cancik (Düsseldorf: Patmos, 1982), 176–212.

32. On Hauer see Margarete Dierks, *Jakob Wilhelm Hauer, 1881–1962: Leben, Werk, Wirkung* (Heidelberg: L. Schneider, 1986). Dierks devotes only passing attention to Hauer's activities in the German Faith Movement.

33. But even the German Faith Movement never came close to rivaling German Christian membership numbers. In 1937, a representative reported to the Ministry of Church Affairs that the group included "40,000 full members who have left the church, and about another 30,000 sympathizers who have not yet done so." "Vermerk," signed Haugg, 18 January 1937, BA Potsdam, DG-II, 1936–37, 415.

34. "Luther's 'deutsches Christentum,'" in *Glaube und Tat: Religionsbuch für deutsche Jungen und Mädel,* ed. Friedrich Fliedner (Bielefeld: Velhagen & Klasing, 1940), 122.

35. [Unknown first name] Schenke, "Luther: *Wider die Jüden und ihre Lügen,*" in DC-Nationalkirchliche Einung, *Informationsdienst,* no. 2/43 (25 Jan. 1943), 4–5, EZA Berlin, 1/A4/565.

36. See [unknown first name] Franzen, "Protesterklärung des Bundes für Deutsche Kirche gegen den Erlaß des Landeskirchenausschusses in Schleswig-Holstein an die Geistlichen der Landeskirche vom 11. März 1936," Kiel, 7 May 1936, EZA Berlin, 1/C3/307.

37. E. Petri, *Zu Jesu Füßen: Wegweiser für deutsche Christen* (Berlin: Verlag der Deutschkirche, im Auftrage des Bundes für deutsche Kirche, 1927), 19. Thanks to Professor Rudolf Fischer, Bielefeld, for making this and other pamphlets available to me.

38. [Unknown first name] Ankermann, "Der deutsche Christ und die Heidenmission," *Mitteilungen der Glaubensgemeinschaft Deutsche Christen,* no. 21 (21 May 1933), 2, LKA Bielefeld, 5,1/289,2.

39. *Die angebliche Irrlehre der "Deutschen Christen,"* circular issued by the leadership of the Reich Movement of German Christians (31 May 1935), LKA Bielefeld, 5,1/290,1.

40. "Fragekasten," *Evangelium im Dritten Reich,* no. 1 (16 Oct. 1932), 7.

41. Siegfried Knak, *Kirchenstreit und Kirchenfriede beleuchtet von den Erfahrungen der Mission aus,* 2nd ed. (Berlin: Heimatdienst, 1934), 22.

42. Ludwig Müller, *Der deutsche Volkssoldat* (Berlin: Tempelhof, 1939), 56.

43. Wilhelm Stapel, "Kampf um die evangelische Kirche," in *Deutsches Volkstum,* reprinted as "Worum kämpft der Pfarrer'not'bund," in *Evangelium im Dritten Reich,* no. 2 (14 Jan.1934), 20, LKA Bielefeld, 5,1/289,1. The biblical reference to women speaking in the church is found in I Corinthians 14:34.

44. *Die angebliche Irrlehre der "Deutschen Christen",* 1.

45. Manfred Klüppel, in his study of euthanasia policies in two Hessian institutions, points out that the Jewish patients were the first to be removed and murdered. See *"Euthanasie" und Lebensvernichtung am Beispiel der Landesheilanstalten Haina und Merxhausen* (Kassel: Gesamthochschule Kassel, 1985), 15. See also Henry Friedlander, *The Origins of Nazi Genocide: From Euthanasia to the Final Solution* (Chapel Hill: University of North Carolina Press, 1995).

46. See Ernst Klee, *"Euthanasie" im NS-Staat: Die "Vernichtung lebensunwerten Lebens"* (Frankfurt am Main: S. Fischer, 1983), 36–38.

47. For reactions of the Protestant and Catholic churches with regard to Nazi initiatives in this area, see Kurt Nowak, *"Euthanasie" und Sterilisierung im "Dritten Reich": Die Konfrontation der evangelischen und katholischen Kirchen mit dem "Gesetz zur Verhütung erbkranken Nachwuchses" und der "Euthanasie-Aktion"* (Göttingen: Vandenhoeck & Ruprecht, 1978). German Christians receive little attention in Nowak's book.

48. O. Kleinschmidt, "Der Deutsche Christ und die Rassenfrage," in *Die Deutschen Christen Reichs-Kalender 1935,* ed. Christian Kinder (Meissen: Schlimpert & Püschel, 1935), 44–45.

49. Wolfgang Stroothenke, *Erbpflege und Christentum: Fragen der Sterilisation, Aufordnung, Euthanasie, Ehe* (Leipzig: Leopold Klotz, 1940), 26.

50. See Klee, *"Euthanasie" im NS-Staat,* 280.

51. Martin Niemöller, "Sätze zur Arierfrage in der Kirche," *Deutsches Pfarrerblatt,* no. 4 (23 Jan. 1934), 46, clipping in LKA Bielefeld, 5,1/289,1.

52. See 1936 correspondence regarding Pastor Goosmann in Berlin-Adlershof, in EZA Berlin, 50/210/II and EZA Berlin, 50/4, especially Alfried Bobsin to Chair of Provincial Church Committee, Berlin, 6 July 1936, EZA Berlin, 50/4, item 52; and Goosmann to unknown, 21 September 1936, EZA Berlin, 50/4, item 33.

53. Order signed Dr. Werner, Protestant Upper Consistory, to Protestant Consistories in the internal area of jurisdiction, 4 July 1939, EZA Berlin, 7/1960.

54. The Upper Consistory explicitly patterned its relaxation of proof of Aryanism requirements on measures adopted by the Ministry of the Interior on 20 September 1943, (RM Bl IV. 1943, sp. 1505).

55. For example, the outspoken and energetic non-Aryan pastor from Bochum, Hans Ehrenberg, was incarcerated in Sachsenhausen in 1938; his wife managed to secure his release and the family moved to England. Ehrenberg had been active in the Confessing Church but was urged to restrain himself by elements in the organization that regarded his non-Aryan status as something of an embarrassment. See Wilhelm Niemöller, *Wort und Tat im Kirchenkampf* (Munich: Christian Kaiser, 1969), 363.

56. "Thüringens evangelische Kirche schließt Juden aus," in *Deutsche Allgemeine Zeitung,* no. 100 (28 Feb. 1939), BA Potsdam, Reichlandbund clippings (RLB), 1864, 145.

57. See reference to these pieces of church legislation in untitled Confessing Church response to the Godesberg Declaration (May 1939), EZA Berlin, 50/600, 30.

58. For a brief summary of these measures against Jews in Germany, see Lucy S. Dawidowicz, *The War Against the Jews, 1933–1945,* 10th anniversary ed. (New York: Bantam Books, 1986), 375.

59. "Bekanntmachung über die kirchliche Stellung der evangelischen Juden vom 17 Dez. 1941," in *Kirchliches Gesetz- und Verordnungsblatt,* no. 17 (29 Dec. 1941), 117–18, EZA Berlin, 50/576, 40.

60. "Wesen und Entstehung der Judenfrage—Auszug aus einem Vortrag von K. F. Euler," Deutsche Christen Nationalkirchliche Einung, *Informationsdienst,* no. 4 (29 April 1944), p. 6, EZA Berlin, 1/A4/566.

61. "Das Alte Testament im Unterricht," unlabeled clipping (4 Nov. 1933), in LKA Bielefeld, 5,1/289,1.

62. Reinhold Krause, "Rede des Gauobmannes," pp. 6–7, LKA Bielefeld, 5,1/289,2.

63. Report signed "Evang.-Luth. Stadtpfarramt, St. Mang.-Kempten" (20 Sept. 1935), p. 2, LKA Nuremberg, KKU 6/IV. The reference is to "the Cushite woman" whom Moses had married and who was the subject of strife between Moses and his siblings. God punished Miriam for her rebellion by striking her with leprosy (Numbers 12:1 ff).

64. Excerpts from [unknown first name] Loy to Johannes Pack, 9 November 1936, Duisburg-Hamborn, AEKR Düsseldorf, NL Schmidt, no. 17, 68–69.

65. [Unknown] Weber to President and Members of the Berlin Fraternal Council (*Bruderrat*), 9 November 1936, Berlin, reproduced in *Beschwerden persönlicher Anliegen und Mitteilungen seitens des Berliner Bruderrates und seiner Mitglieder, Jan. 1936–Dez. 1936,* p. 8, EZA Berlin, 50/4.

66. Julius Leutheuser, "Liebe Kameraden in der Heimat und im Felde!," 20 December 1941, Russia, Deutsche Christen Nationalkirchliche Einung, *Informationsdienst,* LKA Bielefeld, 5,1,293.

67. German Christian Pastors' Association, Bielefeld, "Die Trauung," in *Theologischer Arbeitsbrief* (1 May 1942), p. 2, LKA Bielefeld, 5,1/295,1.

68. Hans Schmidt, *Die Nationalkirche als religiöse Erbe und überkommene Verpflichtung für die nach uns Kommenden,* circular of the DC Nationalkirchliche Einung Theol. Arbeitskreis (Saarburg/Trier, 20 Jan. 1943), p. 17, EZA Berlin, 1/A4/565.

69. Wilhelm Schielmeyer to Ludwig Müller, 1 December 1933, EZA Berlin, 1/C4/17. Schielmeyer referred to Luke 17:20-21, John 18:36-37, and John 8:44.

70. H. Vogel, untitled piece beginning, "Du Mutter heranwachsender Kinder," in *Die deutsche Mutter*, (Potsdam: Reich Office for Women's Service n.d.), p. 7, KAG Minden, loose materials.

71. "Bericht über eine 'Konfirmandenprüfung' der Thüringer Deutsche Christen in Berlin-Siemensstadt am 22. III. 1939," LKA Bielefeld, 5,1/588.

72. Krause, "Rede des Gauobmannes."

73. Report signed "Evang.-Luth. Stadtpfarramt, St. Mang.-Kempten," 20 September 1935, p. 2, LKA Nuremberg, KKU 6/IV.

74. Excerpt from presentation by Hans Hermenau, "Unsere Seelsorge am deutschen Volke," in "Bericht über die Tagung des Frauendienstes Gr. Berlin in Spandau am 27. II. 1942," EZA Berlin, 50/600, p. 2.

75. Werner Wein, *Das Evangelium jenseits der Konfessionen* (Stuttgart: [publisher unknown], 1939), 228.

76. See announcement regarding Kapferer's *Die Bergpredigt als Kampfansage gegen das Judentum*, in Karl Dungs, ed., *Nationalkirchliche Einung Deutsche Christen, Fachabteilung Kirchenpolitik*, no. 4 (Essen-Kupferdreh: 13 Jan. 1944), EZA Berlin, 1/A4/566.

77. See Heinz Weidemann, "Mein Kampf um die Erneuerung des religiösen Lebens in der Kirche: ein Rechenschaftsbericht," (1942), pp. 4–5, BA Koblenz, R 43 II/165, fiche 4:322–23.

78. Heinz Weidemann to Franz Ritter von Epp, December 1936, BHStA Munich, Reichstatthalter (RSth) 636/7.

79. Weidemann, "Mein Kampf," 4–5.

80. *Das Evangelium Johannes deutsch*, forward by Heinz Weidemann (Bremen: H. M. Hauschild, 1936), for example, pages 5, 12, and 29; passages from John 1:40, John 3:31 ff., and John 7:1.

81. There is some uncertainty about the fate of the other projected segments of the *Volkstestament*. Some accounts refer to an edition of the New Testament called the *Volkstestament*, but presumably they were using the collective title for the first part only; in any case, I could locate no copies of anything but *Die Botschaft Gottes*.

82. Karl Eichenberg, "Sie waren anders als ihr Ruf: Die Deutschen Christen," unpublished manuscript, (1970s), 22, KAG Minden, no. 6410.

83. See *Die Botschaft Gottes*, ed. Institute for Study and Elimination of Jewish Influence in German Church Life (Weimar,1940), 95–96.

84. "Ein feste Burg ist unser Gott," and "Du meine Seele singe." See program titled "Wach auf, wach auf, du deutsches Land, du hast genug geschlafen," for meeting of the German Christian Faith Movement in Dortmund, 22–24 June 1933, LKA Bielefeld, 5,1/294,3.

85. Krause, "Rede des Gauobmannes."

86. Friedrich Tausch, "Entwurf zu einem Propagandadienst der Reichskirchenregierung" (8 May 1935), pp. 1, 3, EZA Berlin, 1/A4/93.

87. Wilhelm Bauer, *Feierstunden Deutscher Christen* (Weimar: Verlag Deutsche Christen, 1935), 47–48.

88. Bauer, *Feierstunden Deutscher Christen*, 44.

89. *Lieder der kommenden Kirche*, forward by Heinz Weidemann (Bremen: Verlag "Kommende Kirche," 1939), contains 112 hymns. An expanded version with 186 hymns appeared subsequently: *Gesangbuch der kommenden Kirche* (Bremen: Verlag "Kommende Kirche," n.d.).

90. Advertisement from *Evangelische Nachrichten* (23 April 1939) for "*Die Lieder der kommenden Kirche*, hrsg. von Landesbischof Lic. Dr. Weidemann," including quotations from Weidemann's forward, LKA Bielefeld, 5,1/293.

91. *Großer Gott, Wir loben Dich!* (Weimar: Der neue Dom, 1941).

92. Fritz Loerzer to Otto Dibelius, 31 July 1948, p. 7, KAG Minden, file Loerzer.

93. [Unknown first name] Heilsbronn to Protestant Lutheran Regional Church Council, Nasbach, 1 June 1945, LKA Nuremberg, LKR II 246, Bd. IX.

94. See complaints by Lieutenant-Colonel Marshall M. Knappen, head of the Religious Affairs Section in the Office of Military Government for Germany, United States (OMGUS), about reluctance on the part of Protestant organizations to denazify adequately, in report from Knappen to Lucius Clay, "Stewart W. Herman: Interview with Major-General Clay at Berlin on December 5th, 1945," in *Die evangelische Kirche nach dem Zusammenbruch: Berichte ausländischer Beobachter aus dem Jahre 1945,* ed. Clemens Vollnhalls (Göttingen: Vandenhoeck & Ruprecht, 1988), 305.

95. See, for example, "Marshall M. Knappen. Report on Interview with Bishop Wurm of Württemberg (leading Protestant ecclesiastic of Germany), 22 June 1945," and Martin Niemöller to Karl Barth, 15 June 1946, both in Vollnhalls, *Die evangelische Kirche nach dem Zusammenbruch,* 26, 135–36.

96. See English translation of the Stuttgart Declaration and discussion of its reception in Germany and abroad in Stewart W. Herman, *The Rebirth of the German Church* (New York: Harper & Brothers, 1946), 140–46.

97. See Stewart W. Hermann, "Report on German Reactions to the Stuttgart Declaration [14 Dec. 1945]," in Vollnhalls, *Die evangelische Kirche nach dem Zusammenbruch,* 309–14.

98. "Personnel Questionnaire" (English version), in Wolfgang Friedmann, *The Allied Military Government of Germany* (London: Stevens, 1947), 326–31.

99. Gotthardt Goertz's figures are included in a report commissioned by the Religious Affairs Branch of the British Occupation Authority, in Besier, *"Selbstreinigung" unter britischer Besatzungsherrschaft,* 61.

100. "Ordnung für das Verfahren bei Verletzung von Amtspflichten der Geistlichen," signed by the leadership of the Protestant Church of Westphalia and by the leadership of the Protestant Church of the Rhine Province, 1 September 1945, LKA Bielefeld, 4,55/B/26,6.

101. "Neue Wirksamkeit der früheren DC," in a circular from the Chancellery of the Protestant Church in Germany, signed Asmussen, 3 December 1947, Schwäbisch Gmünd, pp. 2–3, LKA Nuremberg, LKR II 246, Bd. IX.

102. Friedrich Buschtöns to Otto Koch, 14 October 1945, Ilsenburg, pp. 4–7, KAG Minden, no. 15.

103. For a summary of the work of Hermann Diem and his "Ecclesiastical-theological society" see Karl Haldenwang, "Die württ. evangelische Kirche und der Nazismus: Die kirchlich-theologische Sozietät," *Schwäbisches Tagblatt,* no. 67 (23 Aug. 1946), p. 6, LKA Bielefeld, 5,1/686,1.

104. Mainstream German Protestants attacked Diem for using "German Christian methods" and publishing in "Communist" papers. See Georg Schmidgall to Karl Haldenwang, 26 August 1946, Tübingen, pp. 1–4, and Hanns Rückert to Hermann Diem, 26 August 1946, Tübingen, both in LKA Bielefeld, 5,1/686,1.

105. See "Stewart W. Herman: General German Church Situation [September 1945]," in Vollnhalls, *Die evangelische Kirche nach dem Zusammenbruch,* especially pages 160–61 on the purge of "Nazi church governments."

106. See Friedrich Buschtöns to Karl Wentz, 15 July 1950, Klein-Machnow, KAG Minden, no. 15; also duplicated letter by Wilhelm Oberlies, beginning "Liebe Freunde und Kameraden," November 1949, KAG Minden, no. 17.

107. Gustav Endler to all Protestant Regional and Provincial Churches in the Federal Republic of Germany, 5 May 1953, Berlin-Hermsdorf, KAG Minden, no. 29.

108. Gustav Endler, "Konfirmationsansprache gehalten im Kriegsjahr 1942 von Pfarrer Endler, I. Kor. 3,11," attached to Endler to Supreme Party Court (Munich), 11 March 1942, Berlin, BDC, Endler Material, Oberstes Parteigericht file.

109. Eichenberg, "Sie waren anders als ihr Ruf," 14–17.

110. Guida Diehl, *Christ sein heißt Kämpfer sein: Die Führung meines Lebens* (Giessen: Brunnen, 1959), 252–54.

111. On Diehl's postwar fate, see her newsletter, *Liebe Neuländer und Neulandfreunde* (Laurenburg an der Lahn [Hesse], 20 June 1960), KAG Minden, no. 1.

112. Siegfried Leffler to Dr. Hutten, 24 September 1947, Ludwigsburg, pp. 1–2, LKA Nuremberg, LKR II 246, Bd. IX.

113. See, for example, "Siegfried Lefflers Widerruf," in "Kirchliche Nachrichten," *Evangelisches Gemeindeblatt für Augsburg und Umgebung*, no. 5 (1 Feb. 1948), 21, KAG Minden, no. 2.

114. See Vollnhalls, *Evangelische Kirche und Entnazifizierung*, 287; also notation by Karl Wentz, dated July 1960, on copy of "Siegfried Lefflers Widerruf," KAG Minden, no. 2.

115. Ilse Werdermann to Karl Wentz, 12 March 1960, Bad Kreuznach, KAG Minden, file Werdermann. See also Ilse Werdermann to Karl Wentz, 6 May 1960, Bad Kreuznach, KAG Minden, no. 1.

116. Minutes of hearing of Hans Schmidt before justice committee, signed Consistory Councilor Rößler, 22 October 1947, Düsseldorf, pp. 2–3, AEKR Düsseldorf, Bevollmächtigteramt d. franz. Zone, Bf 10, CD-Konsistorium KL.

117. Mägerle [name unclear] to Hermann Diem, 3 March 1948, Ludwigsburg, LKA Bielefeld, 5,1/686/2.

118. Friedrich Buschtöns to Karl Wentz, 27 November 1953, KAG Minden, no. 15.

119. Walther Fiebig to Friedrich Buschtöns, 27 February 1946, Münster, KAG Minden, V, Fi. Fiebig's exact words were as follows: "Der Vorwurf, daß wir uns nicht über die Konzentrationslager geäussert hätten, wird immer wieder einmal auch hier erhoben. Sie erinnern mit Recht daran, daß wir nichts davon gewußt haben und auch nichts wissen konnten, weil die uns zugänglichen Nachrichten anders lauteten."

120. Wilhelm Staedel to Karl Heim, 17 June 1958, Holzhausen an der Porta (Westphalia), pp. 8–10, BA Koblenz, NL 252/13.

121. Scholder, *Die Kirchen und das Dritte Reich;* Conway, *The Nazi Persecution of the Churches*. See also Ernst Christian Helmreich, *The German Churches under Hitler: Background, Struggle and Epilogue* (Detroit: Wayne State University Press, 1985).

122. In addition to the literature already noted, the following titles indicate the range of works on the period that have appeared over the past five decades: Wilhelm Niemöller, *Kampf und Zeugnis der Bekennenden Kirche* (Bielefeld: Ludwig Bechauf, 1948); Walter Conrad, *Der Kampf um die Kanzeln: Erinnerungen und Dokumente aus der Hitlerzeit* (Berlin: Alfred Töpelmann, 1957); Eberhard Klügel, *Die lutherische Landeskirche Hannovers und ihr Bischof*, 2 vols. (Berlin: Lutherisches Verlagshaus, 1964–65); Franklin H. Littell and Hubert G. Locke, eds., *The German Church Struggle and the Holocaust* (Detroit: Wayne State University Press, 1974); Leonore Siegele-Wenschkewitz, *Neutestamentliche Wissenschaft vor der Judenfrage: Gerhard Kittels theologische Arbeit im Wandel deutscher Geschichte* (Munich: Christian Kaiser, 1980); Victoria Barnett, *For the Soul of the People: Protestant Protest against Hitler* (New York: Oxford University Press, 1992).

123. Diehl, *Christ sein heißt Kämpfer sein;* Christian Kinder, *Neue Beiträge zur Geschichte der evangelischen Kirchen in Schleswig-Holstein und im Reich, 1924–1945*, 2nd. ed. (Flensburg: Karfeld, 1966); and Franz Tügel, *Mein Weg, 1888–1946: Erinnerungen eines Hamburger Bischofs*, ed. Carsten Nicolaisen (Hamburg: Friedrich Wittig, 1972).

124. Hans Buchheim, *Glaubenskrise im Dritten Reich: Drei Kapitel Nationalsozialistischer Religionspolitik* (Stuttgart: Deutsche Verlagsanstalt, 1953).

125. See Karl Heinz Götte, "Die Propaganda der Glaubensbewegung 'Deutsche Christen' und ihre Beurteilung in der deutschen Tagespresse: Ein Beitrag zur Publizistik im Dritten Reich" (PhD. diss., Münster, 1957); Eugene W. Miller Jr., "National Socialism and the Glaubensbewegung 'Deutsche Christen,' 1932–1933: Analysis of a Political Relationship" (Ph.D. diss., Pennsylvania State University, 1972); James A. Zabel, *Nazism and the Pastors: A*

Study of the Ideas of Three "Deutsche Christen" Groups, American Academy of Religion Dissertation Series, ed. H. Ganse, no. 14, (Missoula, Mont.: Scholars Press, 1976).

126. Helmut Baier, *Die Deutschen Christen Bayerns im Rahmen des bayerischen Kirchenkampfes* (Nuremberg: Verein für bayerische Kirchengeschichte, 1968).

127. The self-selective tendency in the historiography of German Lutheranism under the Nazis is addressed in Hans Tiefel, "The German Lutheran Church and the Rise of National Socialism," *Church History* 41, no. 3 (Sept. 1971): 326–36.

128. The group of former German Christians who organized the Working Group for Church History in Minden in the 1950s aimed to end the silence on their movement's past. They gathered materials from former adherents and furthered research work regarding the German Christian movement. See circular from Karl Wentz, 12 November 1956, Minden, KAG Minden, file labeled Kirchengeschichtliche A.G. Wentz's files indicate that he contacted many former German Christians to solicit materials and involvement in the group. Many of those who refused explained that they were not prepared to risk their new positions in the church.

129. Conway, *The Nazi Persecution of the Churches*, xx.

130. Reijo E. Heinonen, *Anpassung und Identität: Theologie und Kirchenpolitik der Bremer Deutschen Christen 1933–1945* (Göttingen: Vandenhoeck & Ruprecht, 1978); Hans-Joachim Sonne, *Die politische Theologie der Deutschen Christen,* (Göttingen: Vandenhoeck & Ruprecht, 1982); Schneider, *Reichsbischof Ludwig Müller.*

131. Uriel Tal, "On Modern Lutheranism and the Jews," *Leo Baeck Yearbook* (1985); Detlef Minkner, *Christuskreuz und Hakenkreuz. Kirche in Wedding 1933–1945* (Berlin: Institut Kirche und Judentum, 1986); Wolfgang Gerlach, *Als die Zeugen Schwiegen: Bekennende Kirche und die Juden* (Berlin: Institut Kirche und Judentum, 1987); Hans Prolingheuer, *Wir sind in die Irre gegangen: Die Schuld der Kirche unterm Hakenkreuz* (Cologne: Pahl-Rugenstein, 1987).

132. Some church archives, such as those in Bielefeld and Berlin, prepared special displays on the subject. The Regional Church Archive in Nuremberg produced a major exhibit to be taken on tour.

133. Susannah Heschel, "Nazifying Christian Theology: Walter Grundmann and the Institute for the Study and Eradication of Jewish Influence on German Church Life," *Church History* 63 (1994): 587–605.

134. Robert P. Ericksen, *Theologians under Hitler: Gerhard Kittel, Paul Althaus and Emanuel Hirsch* (New Haven: Yale University Press, 1985).

135. Rainer Hering, *Theologische Wissenschaft und "Drittes Reich"* (Pfaffenweiler: Centaurus-Verlagsgesellschaft, 1990).

136. Sheila Briggs, "Images of Women and Jews in Nineteenth- and Twentieth-Century German Theology," in Clarissa W. Atkinson, Constance H. Buchanan, and Margaret R. Miles, eds., *Immaculate and Powerful: The Female in Sacred Image and Social Reality* (Boston: Beacon Press, 1985), 226–59; Jochen-Christoph Kaiser, *Frauen in der Kirche: Evangelische Frauenverbände im Spannungsfeld von Kirche und Gesellschaft, 1890–1945: Quellen und Materialien* (Düsseldorf: Schwann, 1985).

137. Shelley Baranowski, *The Confessing Church, Conservative Elites, and the Nazi State* (Lewiston, N.Y.: Edwin Mellen Press, 1986). See also her article "Consent and Dissent: The Confessing Church and Conservative Opposition to National Socialism," *Journal of Modern History* 59, no. 1 (March 1987): 53–78.

138. See working paper by Manfred Gailus, "Protestantismus und Nationalsozialismus: Eine vergleichende Untersuchung über Berliner Kirchengemeinden in der Spätphase der Weimarer Republik und im Nationalsozialismus (1930–1945)," presented at the Technical University of Berlin, 1989. I am grateful to Anja Baumhoff for drawing my attention to this project.

139. Rainer Lächele, *Ein Volk, ein Reich, ein Glaube: Die "Deutschen Christen" in Württemberg 1925–1960* (Stuttgart: Calwer, 1994).

140. Doris L. Bergen, *Twisted Cross: The German Christian Movement in the Third Reich* (Chapel Hill: University of North Carolina Press, 1996).

Chapter 4: Susannah Heschel

1. Saul Friedländer, *Nazi Germany and the Jews* (New York: HarperCollins, 1997), 87.

2. "Das Heil Kommt von den Juden: Eine Schicksalsfrage an die Christen deutscher Nation," *Deutsche Frömmigkeit* 9 (September 1938): 1. All translations are my own unless otherwise indicated.

3. Walter Grundmann and Karl Friedrich Euler, foreword to *Das religiöse Gesicht des Judentums: Entstehung und Art* (Leipzig: Verlag Georg Wigand, 1942).

4. Uriel Tal, *Christians and Jews in Germany*, trans. by Noah Jacobs (Ithaca: Cornell University Press, 1975).

5. BDC, Sasse materials.

6. Kurt Meier, *Kreuz und Hakenkreuz: Die evangelische Kirche im Dritten Reich* (Munich: Deutscher Taschenbuch Verlag, 1992); John S. Conway, *The Nazi Persecution of the Churches, 1933–1945* (New York: Basic Books, 1968); Trutz Rendtorff, "Das Wissenschaftsverständnis der protestantischen Universitätstheologie im Dritten Reich," in *Theologische Fakultäten im Nationalsozialismus*, ed. Leonore Siegele-Wenschkewitz and Carsten Nicolaisen (Göttingen: Vandenhoeck and Ruprecht, 1993), 19–44.

7. University of Giessen Archives, Theologische Fakultäten B6, Band 1.

8. BA Koblenz, R43 II/150, fiche no. 3.

9. Walter Grundmann from Herbert Propp, 5 February 1938; LKA Eisenach, Grundmann correspondence.

10. LKA Eisenach, A921, Document 8.

11. Hugo Pich, Superintendent in Schneidemühl, "Entjudung von Kirche und Christentum: Die praktische Durchführung." LKA Eisenach, A921.

12. ZAK, fols 7/4166 and 7/4167. The Godesberg Declaration was printed in the *Gesetzblatt der deutschen evangelischen Kirche* 5 (6 April 1939): 1.

13. Other provisions of the addendum, including founding a central office in the church to fight against the misuse of religion for political goals, were not carried through.

14. Sasse joined the NSDAP on 1 March 1930 and received membership number 204,010. BDC, Sasse materials.

15. Telegram from Julius Streicher, "Verspreche mir von Ihrer Arbeit viel Gutes für unser Feld." Nordelbisches Kirchenarchiv, Kiel. Repertorium des Archivs der Bekennenden Kirche Schleswig-Holstein, Signatur 51, Neue Nummer 292.

16. ZAK, 7/4166. Werner joined the NSDAP on 1 January 1931; membership number 411,184. See BDC, Werner materials.

17. Walter Grundmann, *Die Entjudung des religiösen Lebens als Aufgabe deutscher Theologie und Kirche* (Weimar, 1939), 9, 10.

18. ZAK, 7/4166.

19. Wilhelm Brauer to Finanzabteilung bei der Deutschen evangelischen Kirche, 19 May 1942, ZAK, 1/C3/174.

20. "Überwachung von Arbeitstagungen der Arbeitsgemeinschaft 'Germanentum und Christentum' und ihrer Leiter Professor Wolf Meyer-Erlach und Professor Grundmann, Verweigerung von Reisesichtvermerken, 1942–1944," Archiv des Auswärtiges Amt Bestand Inland, I-D 3/4, Signatur R98796.

21. *Deutsche mit Gott: Ein deutsches Glaubensbuch* (Weimar: Verlag Deutsche Christen, 1941), 46. The foreword was signed by Grundmann, Wilhelm Buechner, Paul Gimpel, Hans Pribnow, Kurt Thieme, Max Adolf Wagenführer, Heinrich Weinmann, and Hermann Werdermann.

22. Reijo E. Heinonen, *Anpassung und Identität: Theologie und Kirchenpolitik der Bremer Deutschen Christen 1933–1945* (Göttingen: Vandenhoeck & Ruprecht, 1978).

23. Ludwig Müller, *Deutsches Gotteswort* (Weimar: Verlag Deutsche Christen, 1936). See also Müller's defense of the project, "Warum ich die Bergpredigt 'verdeutschte,'" *Briefe an Deutsche Christen* 5, no. 8 (15 April 1936): 82.

24. LKA Eisenach, C VI 2.

25. LKA Eisenach, DC III 2a.

26. In some cases the church of Thuringia reimbursed such expenses; for example, for five pastors from Austria. LKA Eisenach, DC III 2a.

27. ZAK, 7/4166.

28. During the summer of 1940, Meyer-Erlach's lectures were titled "Ist Gott Engländer?" later reprinted as a small book, which sold fifteen thousand copies. In 1941 his trip promoted lectures under the title "Das englische Christentum ohne Maske." A subsequent lecture tour was titled "Der Einfluss der Juden auf das englische Christentum." The Foreign Ministry distributed the text of one lecture, "Irland und das englishe Volk," as a pamphlet. Archiv des Auswärtiges Amt, Abteilung Inland I-D, 3/4, Signatur R98796, Number 1949.

29. Heinz Eisenhuth, Report of Tagung held 6–7 July 1939, LKA Eisenach, DC III 2a; ZAK, 1/C3/174.

30. Martin Redeker, ZAK, 1/C3/174.

31. Wilhelm Kotzde-Kottenrodt, "Eine deutsche Gottes- und Lebenskunde," lecture delivered at Institute-sponsored conference on the Wartburg, 19 July 1941. Text in LKA Eisenach, DC III 2a.

32. Walter Grundmann, *Gestalt und Sinn der Bergrede Jesu*, Schriften zur Nationalkirche Nr. 10 (Weimar: Verlag Deutsche Christen, 1939).

33. Georg Bertram, "Philo und die jüdische Propaganda in der antiken Welt," in *Christentum und Judentum: Studien zur Erforschung ihres gegenseitigen Verhältnisses. Report of the First Working Conference of the Institute for the Study of Jewish Influence on German Religious Life vols. 1–3. March 1940 in Wittenberg* hrsg. Walter Grundmann (Leipzig: Verlag Georg Wigand, 1940), 79–106.

34. Reports by Friedrich Wieneke, dated 12 July 1939, on Tagung in Eisenach July 6–7; ZAK, 7/4167.

35. Grundmann, *Die Entjudung des religiösen Lebens*, 17.

36. Grundmann, *Gestalt und Sinn der Bergrede Jesu*, 16.

37. Walter Grundmann, *Der Gott Jesu Christi* (Weimar: Verlag Deutsche Christen, n.d.). Delivered at conference in 1936.

38. Walter Grundmann, *Die Gotteskindschaft in der Geschichte Jesu und ihre religions-geschichtlichen Voraussetzungen* (Weimar: Verlag Deutsche Christen, 1938).

39. Walter Grundmann, *Jesus der Galiläer und das Judentum* (Leipzig: Verlag Georg Wigand, 1940), 143.

40. Grundmann, *Die Gotteskindschaft in der Geschichte Jesu*, 162.

41. Walter Grundmann, "Das Messiasproblem," in *Germanentum, Christentum und Judentum: Report of the Second Working Conference of the Institute for the Study of Jewish Influence on German Religious Life vols. 3–5. March 1941 in Eisenach*, hrsg. Walter Grundmann (Leipzig: Verlag Georg Wigand, 1942), 381.

42. Grundmann, *Jesus der Galiläer*.

43. "Es bleibt auch bei diesem Evangelisten immer zweifelhaft, ob Jesus aus jüdischem Stamme sei, oder, falls er es doch etwa wäre, wie es mit seiner Abstammung sich eigentlich verhalte," in *J. G. Fichte Werke*, ed. Fritz Medicus, vol. 4 (Leipzig: Verlag von Felix Meiner), 105; see also *Addresses to the German Nation*, R. F. Jones and G. H. Turnbull, trans. (Chicago: Open Court, 1922), 68–69.

44. Ernest Renan, *Essai psychologique sur Jesus Christ* (Paris: La Connaissance, 1921), 55–57.

45. Ernest Renan, *La Vie de Jesus* (Paris: Calman-Levy, 1863).

46. See, for example, Theodor Keim, *Geschichte Jesu von Nazara* (Zurich: Orell, Füßli & Co., 1867).

47. Friedrich Delitzsch, *Die grosse Täusching: Kritische Betrachtungen zu den alttestamentlichen Berichten über Israels Eindringen in Kanaan, die Gottesoffenbarung vom Sinai und die Wirksamkeit der Propheten* (Stuttgart: Deutsche Verlagsanstalt, 1920).

48. Fritz Stern, *The Politics of Cultural Despair* (Berkeley: University of California Press, 1961), 41. See also Paul de Lagarde, "Die Religion der Zukunft," *Deutsche Schriften*, vol. 1 (Munich: J. F. Lehmanns Verlag, 1934), 262; here Lagarde is cited by Alan T. Davies, "The Aryan Christ: A Motif in Christian Anti-Semitism," *Journal of Ecumenical Studies* 12 (Fall, 1975): 569–79.

49. Edmond Picard, *L'Aryano-sémitisme* (Brussels: P. Lacomblez, 1899).

50. Houston Stewart Chamberlain, *Die Grundlagen des neunzehnten Jahrhunderts* (Munich: F. Bruckmann, 1902).

51. Ernst Lohmeyer, *Galiläa und Jerusalem* (Göttingen: Vandenhoeck & Ruprecht, 1936).

52. Rudolf Otto, *Reich Gottes und Menschensohn: Ein religionsgeschichtlicher Versuch* (Munich: Beck, 1940).

53. Walter Grundmann, "Das Problem des hellenistischen Christentums innerhalb der Jerusalemer Urgemeinde," *Zeitschrift für neutestamentliche Wissenschaft* 38 (1939): 26.

54. Grundmann, *Jesus der Galiläer*, 57–58.

55. Johannes Hempel, "Der synoptische Jesus und das Alte Testament," *Zeitschrift für alttestamentliche Wissenschaft* 56 (1938): 1–34.

56. Walter Grundmann, *Der Gott Jesu Christi*, p. 7 and passim.

57. Wolf Meyer-Erlach to TMV, 6 March 1937, re: Eisenhuth's appointment, Akten: Heinz Erich Eisenhuth, UA Jena, Bestand D, No. 603.

58. Memorandum dated May 1938 to Reichsministerium für die kirchliche Angelegenheiten, Akten betreff. DC, Hochschulangelegenheiten, 1937–1940, LKA Eisenach.

59. Wolf Meyer-Erlach to TMV, 6 March 1937, Die Anstellung ordentlicher Professoren, 1936–38, UA Jena, vol. VII/910.

60. Letter from Meyer-Erlach to TMV, 23 October 1937, Die Anstellung ordentlicher Professoren, 1936–38, UA Jena, vol. VII/910.

61. Promotionsakten der Theologischen Fakultät, 1939–1941, UA Jena, Bestand J, No. 90.

62. Ibid.

63. Ibid.

64. Meier, *Kreuz und Hakenkreuz*, 164.

65. Walter Grundmann to H. J. Thilo, LKA Eisenach, Nachlass Grundmann, NG 44, vol. 2; *Briefe*, August 1942–April 1943, dated 18 November 1942.

66. Walter Grundmann to Gerhard Delling, 5 November 1942, LKA Eisenach, NG 44, vol. 2.

67. Report, signed by Georg Bertram, on the March 1944 Tagung held in the Predigerseminar in Thüringen, Akten des Landeskirchenrats der Evangelisch-Lutherischen Kirche in Thüringen über Entjudung der Kirche, 1939–47, LKA Eisenach, A 921.

68. Sievers to Pich, 15 August 1944, regarding "Der Weg zur entjudeten deutschen Reichskirche in der Glaubensgefolgschaft Jesu." Sievers writes, ". . . nachdem der totale Krieg in schärfster Form eingesetzt hat, wir nur einen Gedanken haben dürfen, wie wir unserem Vaterland in diesem Schicksalskampf dienen und helfen können. Ich muss es sowohl persönlich, als auch als Vorsitzender der Arbeitsgemeinschaft evangelischer Kirchenleiter und als stellvertretender Leiter des Instituts zur Eforschung . . . ablehnen, mich jetzt mit der Neugestaltung der Kirche zu befassen und ich möchte auch Ihnen dringend empfehlen, diese Sache jetzt ruhen zu lassen."

69. Bishop Schultz to President Rönck, 2 August 1944. LKA Eisenach, A921.

70. Georg Bertram, *Denkschrift: betr. Aufgaben eines theologischen Forschungs-Instituts zu Eisenach 6 May 1945*, p. 1, Bestand A921: Akten des Landeskirchenrats der Evangelisch-Lutherischen Kirche in Thüringen über Entjudung der Kirche, 1939–47, LKA Eisenach.

71. LKA Eisenach, A921.

72. The University of Giessen was closed by American military forces in 1945 because of its Nazi sympathies. In 1955 Bertram was reinstated as instructor in Old Testament. He was also given an instructorship in Hebrew at the University of Frankfurt. Bertram died in 1979.

73. Walter Grundmann to Thuringian church officials, 12 December 1945, LKA Eisenach, DC III 2a.

74. Ibid.

75. Erich Hertzsch to Grundmann, 14 January 1946, LKA Eisenach, DC III 2a.

76. Letter from Thüringen Landesamt für Volksbildung, 13 September 1945, signed Wolf, Landesdirektor: "Wir entlassen Sie daher auf Grund #2 der Verordnung über die Reinigung der öffentlichen Verwaltung von Nazi-Elementen mit sofortiger Wirkung aus dem öffentlichen Dienst," LKA Eisenach, DC III 2a.

77. Personalakte Walter Grundmann, Thüringisches Hauptstaatsarchiv, Weimar.

78. Gerhard Besier and Stephan Wolf, eds., *Pfarrer, Christen und Katholiken: Das Ministerium für Staatssicherheit der ehemaligen DDR und die Kirchen,* 2nd ed. (Neukirchen-Vluyn: Neukirchener Verlag, 1992), Document 133, p. 653.

79. Wolf Meyer-Erlach, "Verfolgung durch die Partei," 12 June 1945, Promotionsakten, 1941–47, UA Jena, Bestand J, No. 92. Regarding his name, see Gaudozentenbundsführer to Reichsamtsleitung des NSD-Dozentenbundes, Dr. Redenz, Munich, 8 August 1938, Wolf Meyer-Erlach Akten, UA Jena Bestand D, No. 2031 An unsigned report to the Gestapo describes Meyer-Erlach's attendance at the synagogue and refers to him as "der Synagoge-Meyer." "Meyer-Erlach: Berüchtigt durch seine Einweihungsrede der Synagoge der jüdischen Gemeinde Heidingsfeld bei Würzburg 1929, führender Kopf der Deutschen-Christen. Poseur- und Schauspieler-natur mit starkem hysterischen Einschlag. Sehr starkes Geltungsbedürfnis."

80. Walter Grundmann, *Erkenntnis und Wahrheit: Aus meinem Leben, unveröffentlichte Selbstbiographie aus dem Jahre 1969,* pp. 44f, LKA Eisenach.

81. Bundespräsidialamt Bonn, Ordenskanzlei, personal correspondence, Az: OK 123-032-05 (H 89/61). The commendation mentions Meyer-Erlach's establishment of a home in 1952 for East European refugee girls and his organization since 1956 of five thousand Christmas and Easter packages for shipment to Germans living in the Soviet zone.

82. Wolfgang Gerlach, *Als die Zeugen Schwiegen: Bekennende Kirche und die Juden* (Berlin: Institut Kirche und Judentum, 1987).

83. ZAK, 1/A4/170.

84. Together with his colleague Rudolf Bultmann, von Soden was active in formulating the "Marburg Report" of September 1933, which opposed application of the Aryan Paragraph in the realm of the Church. See Erich Dinkler and Erika Dinkler-von Schubert, eds., *Theologie und Kirche im Wirken Hans von Sodens: Briefe und Dokumente aus der Zeit des Kirchenkampfes, 1933–1945,* vol. 2 (Göttingen: Vandenhoeck & Ruprecht, 1984).

85. Hans von Soden, review of *Jesus der Galiläer und das Judentum,* by Walter Grundmann. *Deutsches Pfarrerblatt: Bundesblatt der deutschevangelischen Pfarrervereine und des Bundes der preussischen Pfarrervereine* 46 (5 April 1942): 49.

86. Hans Freiherr von Soden, "Die Godesberger Erklärung," n.d., [anonymous private archive], University of Marburg.

87. For a discussion of comparable developments within the field of Indology, see Sheldon Pollock, "Deep Orientalism? Notes on Sanskrit and Power Beyond the Raj," in: *Orientalism and the Postcolonial Predicament: Perspectives on South Asia,* ed. Carol A. Breckenridge and Peter van der Veer (Philadelphia: University of Pennsylvania Press), 76–133.

88. Friedrich Wilhelm Marquardt, *Von Elend und Heimsuchung der Theologie: Prolegomena zur Dogmatik* (Munich, 1992), 91–99.

Chapter 5: Shelley Baranowski

1. I prefer to use the term *"Evangelical"* rather than *"Protestant"* in this context (unless doing so results in an inappropriate meaning in English) because *"Evangelical"* refers to the Reformation's emphasis on preaching the Word *(Evangelium)*.

During the Weimar Republic, there were twenty-eight *Landeskirchen*. These comprised Lutheran, Reformed, and United churches, by virtue of administrative unions between Lutheran and Reformed congregations that took place under royal supervision during the nineteenth century. In 1919, the *Landeskirchen* established the German Evangelical Church Federation *(Deutsche Evangelische Kirchenbund)*.

2. See Shelley Baranowski, *The Confessing Church, Conservative Elites, and the Nazi State* (Lewiston, N.Y.: Edwin Mellen Press, 1986), 62–63.

3. Ibid., especially 66–88. Kurt Nowak's new synthesis reinforces this point: Kurt Nowak, *Geschichte des Christentums in Deutschland:. Religion, Politik und Gesellschaft vom Ende der Aufkärung bis zur Mitte des 20. Jahrhunderts* (Munich: C. H. Beck, 1995), 285.

4. See Kurt Meier, *Kreuz und Hakenkreuz: Die evangelische Kirche im Dritten Reich* (Munich: Deutscher Taschenbuch Verlag, 1992), 225–36.

5. Nuanced discussions on the conservatism of church leaders characterize recent scholarship on Weimar church history. The newer work suggests that the church leaderships developed a flexible attitude toward the Republic, rather than adhering to a rigid monarchicalism. See especially Daniel R. Borg, *The Old-Prussian Union Church and the Weimar Republic: A Study in Political Adjustment, 1917–1927* (Hanover: University Press of New England, 1984); David J. Diephouse, *Pastors and Pluralism in Württemberg 1918–1933* (Princeton: Princeton University Press, 1987); Kurt Nowak, *Evangelische Kirche und Weimarer Republik:. Zum politischen Weg des deutschen Protestantismus zwischen 1918 und 1932* (Göttingen: Vandenhoeck & Ruprecht, 1981); and J. R. C. Wright, *"Above Parties:" The Political Attitudes of the German Protestant Church Leadership* (Oxford: Oxford University Press, 1974).

6. See Shelley Baranowski, *The Sanctity of Rural Life: Nobility, Protestantism and Nazism in Weimar Prussia* (New York: Oxford University Press, 1995), 95–97, 171–76.

7. For a discussion of Protestant moral and cultural fixations, see Baranowski, *The Sanctity of Rural Life*, 102–14 as well as Borg, *The Old-Prussian Union Church*, 168–212, and Diephouse, *Pastors and Pluralism in Württemberg*, 209–257.

8. On the status of Jews during the interwar period, see Donald Niewyk, *The Jews in Weimar Germany* (Baton Rouge: Louisiana State University Press, 1980); and Sarah Ann Gordon, *Hitler, Germans, and the "Jewish Question"* (Princeton: Princeton University Press, 1984). For a longer view, see Werner Eugen Mosse, *The German-Jewish Economic Elite, 1820–1935: A Socio-Cultural Profile* (Oxford: Clarendon Press, 1989). According to Mosse, Jews were still unable to establish themselves in public affairs, despite their place in the liberal professions.

9. "Die 'ernsten Bibelforscher' und das Judentum," *Bote von Pommernstrand: Sontagsblatt der Synode Rügenwalde*, 16, no. 11 (15 March 1925). Consult also Borg, *The Old-Prussian Union Church*, 195–202.

10. The Old Prussian Union consisted of the provincial churches of Prussia as it existed between the Napoleonic wars and unification. After Bismarck's unification, six *Landeskirchen*, including Hannover and Saxony, retained their independent identities, although their states were now incorporated within Prussia. See Borg, *The Old Prussian Union Church*, xii.

11. Works on the "church struggle" *(Kirchenkampf)* that are usually consulted include John S. Conway, *The Nazi Persecution of the Churches* (London: Weidenfeld and Nicolsen, 1968); Georg Denzler and Volker Fabricius, eds., *Die Kirchen im Dritten Reich:. Christen und Nazis Hand in Hand?* 2 vols. (Frankfurt am Main: Fischer, 1984); Kurt Meier, *Der evangelische Kirchenkampf: Gesamtdarstellung in drei Bände* (Göttingen: Vandenhoeck & Ruprecht, 1977–84); and Klaus Scholder, *Die Kirchen und das Dritte Reich*, vol. 1, *Vorgeschichte und Zeit*

der Illusionen 1918–1934 (Frankfurt: Ullstein, 1977), vol. 2, *Das Jahr der Ernüchterung 1934* (Berlin: Ullstein, 1985). In recent years, scholarship on the church struggle has turned to the experiences of less well-known pastors and laypeople. See, for example, *Subjekt und Milieu in NS-Staat:. Die Tagebücher des Pfarrers Hermann Klugkist Hesse 1936–1939,* ed. Gottfried Abrath (Göttingen: Vandenhoeck & Ruprecht, 1994).

12. Although it revises earlier assumptions about the social composition of Nazi voters, the newest research continues to emphasize the Protestantism of the Nazi electorate. See especially Jürgen Falter, *Hitlers Wähler* (Munich: C. H. Beck, 1991), 179–86.

13. "Nicht Reaktion, sondern Reformation," *Junge Kirche* 19 (7 December 1933): 365–68.

14. Reinhold von Thadden-Trieglaff, "Laienkriche oder Lebendige Gemeinde?" *Junge Kirche* 18 (16 November 1933): 298.

15. Because the Old Prussian Union combined Lutheran and Reformed churches under a common administrative structure, the regional Lutheran churches considered it lacking in confessional integrity.

16. Robert P. Ericksen, "The Barmen Synod and Its Declaration: A Historical Synopsis," in *The Church Confronts the Nazis: Barmen Then and Now,* ed. Hubert Locke (New York: Edwin Mellen Press, 1984), 70.

17. Heinrich Vogel, "Christ the Center of the Declaration of Barmen," in *The Barmen Confession: Papers from the Seattle Assembly* (Lewiston, N.Y.: Edwin Mellen Press, 1986), 11–12.

18. The Dahlem Synod established a "provisional administration" to take the place of the church administration that the German Christians had corrupted.

19. Of the three bishops of the intact churches, Marahrens was the most thoroughly discredited after the war by the new church leadership, which included many prominent figures from the Confessing Church. Eberhard Klügel's biography, *Die lutherische Landeskirche Hannovers und ihr Bischof, 1933–1945* (Berlin: Lutherisches Verlagshaus, 1964) is a highly apologetic, and therefore revealing, defense of the bishop's career.

20. For a full, if somewhat undigested, discussion of the church committees, see Meier, *Der evangelische Kirchenkampf,* vol. 2.

21. See Baranowski, *Confessing Church,* 66–75, and Ian Kershaw, *Popular Opinion and Political Dissent,* (Oxford: Clarendon Press, 1983), 156–84.

22. This is becoming a prominent theme in newer scholarship on the German Christians. See Susannah Heschel, "Nazifying Christian Theology: Walter Grundmann and the Institute for the Study and Eradication of Jewish Influence on German Church Life," *Church History* 63, no. 4 (1994): 587–605; and Doris L. Bergen, *Twisted Cross: The German Christian Movement in the Third Reich* (Chapel Hill: North Carolina University Press, 1996).

23. The most thoroughgoing critique of ecclesiastical antisemitism is that of Wolfgang Gerlach, *Als die Zeugen schwiegen: Die Bekennende Kirche und das Judentum* (Berlin: Institut Kirche und Judentum, 1987), soon to appear in English translation. See also Victoria Barnett, *For the Soul of the People: Protestant Protest against Hitler* (New York: Oxford University Press, 1992), 122–28.

24. See Robert P. Ericksen's introductory discussion in *Theologians under Hitler: Gerhard Kittel, Paul Althaus and Emanuel Hirsch* (New Haven: Yale University Press, 1985), 1–27.

25. The already intense discussion regarding the antisemitism in early Christianity has likely accelerated as a result of Elaine Pagels' book, *The Origin of Satan* (New York: Random House, 1995). See also Paula Fredriksen, *From Jesus to Christ: The Origins of the New Testament Images of Jesus* (New Haven: and London: Yale University Press, 1988), and John G. Gager Jr. *The Origins of Antisemitism: Attitudes toward Judaism in Pagan Antiquity* (New York: Oxford University Press, 1983).

26. For other studies of the German Christians in addition to Bergen's, see James A. Zabel, *Nazism and the Pastors: A Study of the Ideas of Three Deutsche Christen Groups* (Missoula, Mont.: Scholars' Press, 1976), Kurt Meier, *Die Deutschen Christen:. Das Bild einer Bewegung im Kirchenkampf des Dritten Reiches* (Göttingen: Vandenhoeck & Ruprecht, 1964), and Hans-Joachim Sonne, *Die politische Theologie der Deutschen Christen: Einheit und Vielfalt*

Deutsch-Christlichen Denkens, dargestellt anhand des Bundes für Deutsche Kirche, der Thüringer Kirchenbewegung "Deutsche Christen" und der Christlich-Deutschen Bewegung (Göttingen: Vandenhoeck & Ruprecht, 1982).

27. For the complete text, see Conway, *The Nazi Persecution of the Churches*, 342–44.

28. James Bentley, *Martin Niemöller 1892–1984* (New York: Free Press, 1984), 45; Leo Stein, *I Was in Hell with Niemöller* (New York: Fleming H. Revell Co., 1942), 120.

29. Dietrich Bonhoeffer, "Die Kirche vor der Judenfrage," in *Gesammelte Schriften*, ed. Eberhard Bethge, vol. 2 (Munich: Christian Kaiser Verlag, 1959), 44–53, esp. 45.

30. Gerlach, *Als die Zeugen schwiegen*, 83–88.

31. Ernst Helmreich, *The German Churches under Hitler: Background, Struggle, and Epilogue* (Detroit: Wayne State University Press, 1979), 149–50.

32. Gerlach, *Als die Zeugen schwiegen*, 122.

33. Ibid., 54–60. See also Bonhoeffer, "Die Kirche vor der Judenfrage."

34. Out of approximately eighteen thousand pastors, only thirty were "non-Aryan," according to Meier, *Kreuz und Hakenkreuz*, 157.

35. See Gerlach, *Als die Zeugen schwiegen*, 83–88; and Barnett, *For the Soul of the People*, 128–30.

36. Gerlach, *Als die Zeugen schwiegen*, 122. The use of antisemitic discourse to attack ecclesiastical opponents was quite common in both the Evangelical and Catholic churches. See Doris L. Bergen, "Catholics, Protestants, and Christian Antisemitism in Nazi Germany," *Central European History* 27, no. 3 (1994): 329–48, especially 335.

37. Gerlach, argues that had Bonhoeffer stayed, his influence on Martin Niemöller would have prevailed. Instead, Niemöller worked closely with Karl Barth in defining the opposition's position toward the German Christians, and in Gerlach's view, Barth was considerably less attentive to the significance of the Aryan Paragraph. Gerlach, *Als die Zeugen schwiegen*, 86.

38. Baranowski, *Confessing Church*, 59–62.

39. The entire text of the Barmen Declaration can be found in Arthur C. Cochrane, *The Church's Confession under Hitler* (Philadelphia: Westminster Press, 1962), 238–47.

40. Eberhard Busch, *Karl Barth: His Life from Letters and Autobiographical Texts*, trans. John Bowden (Philadelphia: Fortress Press, 1976), 245–55.

41. For the relationship between theology and politics in Barth, see George Hunsinger ed., *Karl Barth and Radical Politics* (Philadelphia: Westminster Press, 1976). The forthcoming translation of Gerlach's, *Als die Zeugen schwiegen* will include a new epilogue on Barth's attitude toward Judaism.

42. Baranowski, *Confessing Church*, 83–85; Gerlach, *Als die Zeugen schwiegen*, 152–59.

43. Otto Dibelius, *In the Service of the Lord: The Autobiography of Bishop Otto Dibelius* (New York: Holt, Rinehart and Winston, 1964), 95.

44. Barnett, *For the Soul of the People*, 144–54; Michael Phayer, *Protestant and Catholic Women in Nazi Germany* (Detroit: Wayne State University Press, 1990), 197–203.

45. See Nowak, *Geschichte des Christentums in Deutschland*, 259–68.

46. Heschel, "Nazifying Christian Theology, " 603–4.

47. Michael Burleigh, *Death and Deliverance: "Euthanasia" in Germany 1900–1945* (Cambridge: Cambridge University Press, 1994), 166.

48. For works that deal with Protestantism and eugenics, see Jochen-Christoph Kaiser, *Sozialer Protestantismus im 20. Jahrhundert:. Beiträge zur Geschichte der Inneren Mission 1914–1945* (Munich: Oldenbourg, 1989); Burleigh, *Death and Deliverance*, esp. 167, 178–80, Kurt Nowak, *Euthanasie und Sterilisierung im Dritten Reich:. Die Konfrontation der evangelischen und katholischen Kirche mit dem "Gesetz zur Verhütung Erbkranken Nachwuchses" und der "Euthanasie-Aktion,"* 2nd ed. (Göttingen: Vandenhoeck & Ruprecht, 1984); and Claudia Koonz, "Eugenics, Gender, and Ethics in Nazi Germany: The Debate about Involuntary Sterilization 1933–1936," in *Reevaluating the Third Reich*, eds. *Thomas Childers and Jane Caplan (New York: Holmes and Meier, 1993)*, 66–85.

49. Kaiser, *Sozialer Protestantismus*, 449.

50. See especially Omer Bartov, *Hitler's Army: Soldiers, Nazis, and War in the Third Reich* (New York: Oxford University Press, 1991); and Raul Hilberg's classic work, *The Destruction of the European Jews* (Chicago: Quadrangle Books, 1967).

51. Meier, *Kreuz und Hakenkreuz*, 171–72.

52. Ibid., 173. Meier notes that although the churches succeeded in derailing the euthanasia project for a time, they could do little to stop the Holocaust. Even works that have been critical of the churches, like John Conway's *The Nazi Persecution of the Churches*, tend to argue that Nazi repression mitigates ecclesiastical sins.

53. See especially, Robert Gellately, *The Gestapo and German Society* (Oxford: Clarendon Press, 1990).

54. My comparative observations are drawn from Tim Mason, "Whatever Happened to 'Fascism?'" in *Reevaluating the Third Reich*, 253–62, esp. 259; Jonathan Steinberg, *All or Nothing: The Axis and the Holocaust 1941–1943* (London: Routledge, 1990); and Susan Zuccotti, *The Italians and the Holocaust: Persecution, Rescue, and Survival* (New York: Basic Books, 1987).

55. Kershaw, *Popular Opinion and Political Dissent*, 331–40.

56. Ibid., 340–57.

57. For Hitler's personal popularity, see Ian Kershaw, *The "Hitler Myth": Image and Reality in the Third Reich* (Oxford: Clarendon Press, 1987).

58. Kaiser, *Sozialer Protestantismus*, 387. The apologetic potential of "secularization" as an explanation for the rise of National Socialism and the lack of resistance became a staple in postwar West Germany. For a sharp assessment of the Federal Republic's attempt to come to terms with Nazism, see Richard J. Evans, *In Hitler's Shadow: West German Historians and the Attempt to Escape from the Nazi Past* (New York: Pantheon, 1989).

59. Kershaw, *Popular Opinion and Political Dissent*, 336–37.

60. Gellately, *The Gestapo and German Society*, 179–84.

61. See the synthesis of Hugh McLeod, *Religion and the People in Western Europe, 1789–1970* (Oxford: Oxford University Press, 1981). Secularization did take hold from the 1960s on, even in West Germany, where the major churches remained state supported. See Nowak, *Geschichte des Christentums in Deutschland*, 291–322.

Chapter 6: Kenneth C. Barnes

1. Goldberg's comment may be found in "Bonhoeffer and the Limits of Jewish-Christian Dialogue," *Books and Religion* 14 (March 1986): 3. Eberhard Bethge's biography of Bonhoeffer was first published in Germany in 1967 and in English translation in 1970. This chapter will refer to the English paperback edition, *Dietrich Bonhoeffer: Man of Vision, Man of Courage*, translated by Eric Mosbacher, et al. (New York: Harper & Row, 1977). The collected works, *Gesammelte Schriften*, under Bethge's editorship were published in six volumes from 1958–1974 by Chr. Kaiser Verlag of Munich. In addition to Bonhoeffer's major theological works, portions of the collected works have been translated into English in three volumes. I will cite English translations when they are available. One of the most recent long works praising Bonhoeffer for an unwavering strong stand against Nazi persecution of the Jews is Christine-Ruth Müller's *Dietrich Bonhoeffers Kampf gegen die nationalsozialistische Verfolgung und Vernichtung der Juden* (Munich: Chr. Kaiser Verlag, 1990).

2. The criticisms began with William Jay Peck, "From Cain to the Death Camps: Bonhoeffer and Judaism," *Union Seminary Quarterly Review* 28 (Winter 1973): 158–76. While Peck repudiated the young Bonhoeffer, he remained enamored with the man of the Resistance movement and Tegel prison. The criticism continued with Ruth Zerner, "Dietrich Bonhoeffer and the Jews: Thoughts and Actions, 1933–1945," *Jewish Social Studies* 37 (1975): 235–50; and Stanley N. Rosenbaum, "Dietrich Bonhoeffer: A Jewish View," *Journal of Ecumenical Studies* 18 (Spring 1981): 301–7.

3. The most complete biography of Bonhoeffer is Eberhard Bethge's *Dietrich Bonhoeffer.* For more readable accounts of Bonhoeffer's life, see Edwin Robertson, *The Shame and the Sacrifice: The Life and Martyrdom of Dietrich Bonhoeffer* (New York: Macmillan, 1988); and Mary Bosanquet, *The Life and Death of Dietrich Bonhoeffer* (New York: Harper & Row, 1968).

4. The residents of the Grunewald neighborhood were 13.54 percent Jewish, while Berlin was 4.3 percent and Germany was 0.9 percent Jewish. Figures are from Müller, *Dietrich Bonhoeffers Kampf gegen die nationalsozialistische Verfolgung und Vernichtung der Juden,* 321.

5. See Eberhard Bethge, "Dietrich Bonhoeffer and the Jews," in John D. Godsey and Geoffrey B. Kelly, eds., *Ethical Responsibility: Bonhoeffer's Legacy to the Churches* (New York and Toronto: Edwin Mellen Press, 1981), 50–52.

6. Bethge, *Dietrich Bonhoeffer,* 110, 124.

7. Ibid., 211.

8. Wolfgang Gerlach, *Als die Zeugen schwiegen: Bekennende Kirche und die Juden* (Berlin: Institut Kirche und Judentum, 1987), 416.

9. Bethge, *Dietrich Bonhoeffer,* 198–99.

10. Ibid., 209.

11. For a discussion of the political machinations within the German church struggle in 1933, see Klaus Scholder, *The Churches and the Third Reich,* trans. John Bowden (Philadelphia: Fortress Press, 1988), 280–357; and Ernst Helmreich, *The German Churches Under Hitler: Background, Struggle, and Epilogue* (Detroit: Wayne State University Press, 1979), 133–46.

12. For the context and a textual history of Bonhoeffer's essay, see chapter 7 of Marikje Smid, *Deutscher Protestantismus und Judentum 1932/1933* (Munich: Chr. Kaiser, 1990), 415–47. The essay is published in English as "The Church and the Jewish Question," in Dietrich Bonhoeffer, *No Rusty Swords: Letters, Lectures and Notes 1928–1936* (New York: Harper & Row, 1965), 221–29. For the original German text of the essay see Bonhoeffer, *Gesammelte Schriften,* 2: 44–53.

13. Bonhoeffer, *No Rusty Swords,* 227–29.

14. Ibid., 223. For a discussion of conservative Lutheran political theology of the 1920s and early 1930s, see Wolfgang Tilgner, *Volksnomostheologie und Schöpfungsglaube* (Göttingen: Vandenhoeck & Ruprecht, 1966); and Robert P. Ericksen, *Theologians Under Hitler: Gerhard Kittel, Paul Althaus, and Emanuel Hirsch* (New Haven: Yale University Press, 1985).

15. Bonhoeffer, "The Church and the Jewish Question," 226–27. For a discussion of the survival in American Christianity of the punishing curse theory of Jewish suffering, see Charles Y. Glock and Rodney Stark, *Christian Belief and Anti-Semitism* (New York: Harper & Row 1961).

16. Bonhoeffer, *No Rusty Swords,* 221–22, 225.

17. Ibid., 225–26.

18. Gerlach, *Als die Zeugen schwiegen,* 56–57.

19. Robertson, *The Shame and the Sacrifice,* 96.

20. For the text of the pamphlet, see Bonhoeffer, *Gesammelte Schriften,* 2: 62–69. For Bethge's discussion, see Bethge, *Dietrich Bonhoeffer,* 235–36.

21. Bonhoeffer, quoted in Bethge, *Dietrich Bonhoeffer,* 231.

22. Gerlach, *Als die Zeugen schwiegen,* 57–58; Bethge, *Dietrich Bonhoeffer,* 231–33.

23. Bethge, *Dietrich Bonhoeffer,* 237–46.

24. Ibid., 247–50.

25. Bonhoeffer, *No Rusty Swords,* 235.

26. Ibid.

27. Bethge, *Dietrich Bonhoeffer,* 403–7; Müller, *Dietrich Bonhoeffers Kampf gegen die nationalsozialistische Verfolgung und Vernichtung der Juden,* 210–11.

28. Bethge had originally dated this statement in 1938, around the time of *Kristallnacht.* By the early 1980s he decided that Bonhoeffer said this in 1935 while at Finkenwalde, for at the time, the communal life of the seminary centered around a rediscovery and application

of Roman Catholic monastic traditions. See Bethge, "Dietrich Bonhoeffer and the Jews," 71–72.

29. Dietrich Bonhoeffer, *The Cost of Discipleship*, translated by R. H. Fuller, with some revision by Irmgard Booth (New York: Macmillan, 1963).

30. See Richard Gutteridge's comments in *The German Evangelical Church and the Jews 1879–1950* (Oxford: Basil Blackwell, 1976), 278, 287; and Bethge, *Dietrich Bonhoeffer*, 505.

31. Bethge, *Dietrich Bonhoeffer*, 536–37.

32. Bethge, "Dietrich Bonhoeffer and the Jews," 74–75.

33. See Bethge's discussion of these events in *Dietrich Bonhoeffer*, 555–65. For the text of the letter see Bonhoeffer, *Gesammelte Schriften*, 1:320.

34. Visser't Hooft recounted that during the war he carried a briefcase containing sensitive material with him at all times so that he could burn it on the spot should the Germans invade Switzerland. Willem Visser't Hooft, interview with author, July 1981. Visser't Hooft also recorded that Bonhoeffer had reported to him about the continued practice of euthanasia by the Nazi regime. Bonhoeffer, *Gesammelte Schriften*, 4:534.

35. For Bell's report to Sir Anthony Eden about this meeting with Bonhoeffer, see Bonhoeffer, *Gesammelte Schriften*, 1: 372–77.

36. Bethge, *Dietrich Bonhoeffer*, 649–51. For the text of the report about Jewish deportations, see *Gesammelte Schriften*, 2: 640–43.

37. The most detailed accounting of Operation 7 is in Müller, *Dietrich Bonhoeffers Kampf gegen die nationalsozialistische Verfolgung und der Vernichtung der Juden*, 303–14.

38. Dietrich Bonhoeffer, *Ethics*, edited by Eberhard Bethge, translated by Neville Horton Smith (New York: Macmillan, 1955), 26–27.

39. Bethge, "Dietrich Bonhoeffer and the Jews," 78. Pinchas Lapide sees in this passage a movement by Bonhoeffer toward reclaiming Judaism for the Christian church. See his "Bonhoeffer und das Judentum," in *Verspieltes Erbe: Dietrich Bonhoeffer und der deutsche Nachkriegsprotestantismus*, ed. E. Feil (Munich: Kaiser, 1979), quoted in Bethge, "Dietrich Bonhoeffer and the Jews," 50–51.

40. Bonhoeffer, *Ethics*, 208–9, 307.

41. Ibid., 48, 50.

42. Ibid., 116–22.

43. Bonhoeffer sat in prison as the Final Solution progressed. It is uncertain how much he knew about the death camps in the last two years of the war. For a highly speculative discussion of Bonhoeffer's theology of nonreligious Christianity and its relationship to Jews, see Peck, "From Cain to the Death Camps," 168–73. Peck sees Bonhoeffer's rejection of religion as a renunciation of Lutheran political philosophy and "teutonic religion"—a religious culture he had embraced as a young pastor and theologian that was both antisemitic and obedience-oriented.

Chapter 7: Guenter Lewy

1. Erhard Schlund, O.F.M., *Katholizismus und Vaterland*, Munich, 1925, 32–33.

2. Gustav Gundlach, S.J., "Antisemitismus," *Lexikon für Theologie und Kirche*, 2nd rev. ed., Freiburg, Br., 1930, I, 504. The new edition of this work, published after the downfall of Nazism, has replaced this article with one that condemns all types of antisemitism.

3. Michael Buchberger, *Gibt es noch eine Rettung?*, Regensburg, n.p. [1931], 97–98.

4. Franz Steffen, *Antisemitische und deutschvölkische Bewegung im Lichte des Katholizismus*, Berlin, 1925; Felix Langer, *Der "Judenspiegel" des Dr. Justus kritisch beleuchtet*, Leipzig, 1921.

5. Memorandum of unknown authorship, *Documents on German Foreign Policy*, Series C, Vol. I, Doc. 188, 347.

6. Article "*Rasse*" in Konrad Gröber, ed., *Handbuch der religiösen Gegenwartsfragen*, Freiburg, Br., 1937, 536.

7. Sermon of December 31, 1933, in Michael Faulhaber, *Judaism, Christianity and Germany*, trans. George D. Smith, London, 1934, 107.

8. Sermon of December 17, 1933, *ibid.*, 68–69.

9. *Amtsblatt für die Erzdiözese München und Freising*, November 15, 1934, supplement.

10. J. Scherm, "Der alttestamentliche Bibelunterricht: Planungen und Wegweisungen," *Klerusblatt*, XX, 1939, 225.

11. Pastoral letter of January 30, 1939, *Amtsblatt für die Erzdiözese Freiburg*, no. 3, February 8, 1939, 15.

12. Pastoral letter for Lent 1939, *Amtsblatt des Bistums Limburg*, no. 1, February 6, 1939, 1–8.

13. Article "Marxismus," Gröber, *Handbuch der religiösen Gegenwartsfragen*, 404.

14. Article "Bolschewismus," *ibid.*, 86.

15. *Ibid.*, 87.

16. Article "Kunst," *ibid.*, 372.

17. Karl Adam, "Deutsches Volkstum und Katholisches Christentum," *Theologische Quartalschrift*, CXIV, 1933, 60–62.

18. "Vor 17 Jahren: Marxismus über Deutschland," *Klerusblatt*, XVI, 1935, 785–88.

19. F. Schühlein, "Geschichte der Juden," *Lexikon für Theologie und Kirche*, 2nd ed., Freiburg, Br., 1933, V, 687.

20. Gustav Lehmacher, S.J., "Rassenwerte," *Stimmen der Zeit*, CXXVI, 1933, 81.

21. "Verdient die katholische Kirche den Namen 'Judenkirche'?," *Klerusblatt*, XVIII, 1937, 542.

22. Theodor Bogler, O.S.B., *Der Glaube von gestern und heute*, Cologne, 1939, 150.

23. Erwin Roderich Kienitz, *Christliche Ehe. Eine Darstellung des Eherechts und Ehemoral der katholischen Kirche für Seelsorger und Laien*, Munich, 1938, 47–54.

24. *Denkschrift über die Reform des Deutschen Strafrechtes*, mimeographed, 39 pp., copy in Diocesan Archives Passau.

25. Circular letter of the "*Kirchliche Informationsstelle der Bischöflichen Behörden Deutschlands,*" no. 341, September 16, 1935, Diocesan Archives Eichstätt.

26. This was the complaint of Alfred Richter, "Parteiprogramm der NSDAP und Reichskonkordat: Zum dritten Jahrestag der Unterzeichnung des Reichskonkordats (20 Juli 1933)," *Deutschlands Erneuerung*, XX, 1936, 468. The occurrence of such marriages was confirmed to me by the former Vicar General of Hildesheim, Dr. Wilhelm Offenstein, in an interview on February 5, 1962. The German Federal Republic subsequently legalized these illegal marriages.

27. *Deutsche Briefe*, no. 52, September 27, 1935, 6–7.

28. Regierungsrat Münster, "Die Regelung des Rassenproblems durch die Nürnberger Gesetze," *Klerusblatt*, XVII, 1936, 47.

29. Alois Hudal, *Die Grundlagen des Nationalsozialismus*, Leipzig, 1937, 75 and 88.

30. The Conference of the Bavarian Bishops in March 1934 decided to request permission from the Ministry of the Interior to charge a small sum so that priests would be able to hire additional research help. *Niederschrift der Konferenz der bayerischen Bischöfe in München am 21. März 1934*, 3.

31. J. Demleitner, "Volksgenealogie," *Klerusblatt*, XV, 1934, 503.

32. All of the diocesan archives preserved contain voluminous files of correspondence in connection with the certification of Aryan descent.

33. Bertram to Pacelli, September 2, 1933, copy in Diocesan Archives Passau.

34. *Protokoll der Verwaltungsratssitzung und der Hauptversammlung des St. Raphaelsvereins in Dortmund am Freitag, den 27 August 1937*, mimeo, 12 pp. Diocesan Archives Mainz, file "St. Raphaelsverein"; minutes of the Fulda Bishops' Conference of August 1939, Bundesarchiv (Koblenz), R43II/177a. The recent claim of a German Catholic paper, *Petrusblatt* (Berlin, April 16, 1966), that the St. Raphaelsverein helped 1,950 Jews to emigrate and supported 25,000 Jews has no foundation in fact—unless one still wants to use the concept "Jew" as a term of racial classification.

35. Bundesarchiv (Koblenz), R43II/174.

36. Von einem deutschen, römisch-katholischen Priester, "Die katholische Kirche und die Judenfrage," *Eine heilige Kirche*, XVI, 1934, 177.

37. Report of the Gestapo, Munich, January 1, 1937, *Bayerisches Geheimes Staatsarchiv* (Munich), MA1946/019.

38. Quoted in Alfons Erb, *Bernhard Lichtenberg*, Berlin, 1949, 43.

39. Quoted in Leon Poliakov, *Harvest of Hate*, London, 1956, 30.

40. Quoted in Raul Hilberg, *The Destruction of the European Jews*, Chicago, 1961, 262.

41. Several such letters can be found in Diocesan Archives Limburg, file "*Nichtarier*."

42. Bertram to the German bishops, September 17, 1941, Diocesan Archives Limburg, file "*Nichtarier*."

43. Berning to Bertram, October 27, 1941, copy in Diocesan Archives Limburg, file "*Nichtarier*."

44. Hilfrich to Wienken, October 27, 1941, Diocesan Archives Limburg, file "*Nichtarier*."

45. Wienken to Hilfrich, October 30, 1941, Diocesan Archives Limburg, file "*Nichtarier*."

46. *Niederschrift über die Konferenz der Bischöfe der Kölner- und Paderborner Kirchenprovinz am 24. und 25. November 1941 in Paderborn*, mimeo, 5.

47. Stewart W. Herman Jr., *It's Your Souls We Want*, New York, 1943, 234; Bernhard Lösener, "Das Reichsministerium des Inneren und die Judengesetzgebung: Aufzeichnungen," *Vierteljahresheft für Zeitgeschichte*, IX, 1961, 310.

48. Inge Scholl, *Die weisse Rose*, Frankfurt a.M., 1961, 126–28.

49. "Augenzeugenbericht zu den Massenvergasungen," *Vierteljahresheft für Zeitgeschichte*, I, 1953, 193. The opening scene of Hochhuth's play *Der Stellvertreter* is based on Gerstein's account, which is considered fully reliable by all students of the subject.

50. Interview with Dr. Gertrud Luckner, March 9, 1962. One such officer, Dr. Alfons Hildenbrand, took special leave from his unit stationed near Minsk in order to report about the massacres he had witnessed to Cardinal Faulhaber. Cf. Thomas Dehler, "Sie zuckten mit der Achsel," Fritz J. Raddatz, ed., *Summa inuria oder Durfte der Papst schweigen?* Reinbeck bei Hamburg, 1963, 231.

51. Interview with Dr. Joseph Müller, March 26, 1962.

52. Hilberg, *op. cit.*, 267.

53. Bertram to Thierack, November 11, 1942. Archives of the Ministry of Justice (Bonn), R 22 Gr. 5/XXII-2; copy in Diocesan Archives Aachen.

54. Ruth Andreas-Friedrich, *Berlin Underground 1938–1945*, trans. Barrows Mussey, New York, 1947, 92.

55. Bertram to Thierack, March 2, 1943. Archives of the Ministry of Justice (Bonn), R 22 Gr. 5/XXII-2; copy in Diocesan Archives Mainz, 1/1.

56. Preysing to the German bishops, April 16, 1943, Diocesan Archives Limburg, file "*Nichtarier*."

57. Memo on oral information from Preysing relayed to the Bishop of Limburg, etc., on June 26, 1943, by Father Odilo Braun, O.P., Diocesan Archives Limburg, file "*Nichtarier*."

58. Bertram to the Minister of the Interior and the RSHA, November 17, 1943, copy in Diocesan Archives Limburg, file "*Nichtarier*."

59. Archbishop Joseph Frings, Pastoral letter of December 12, 1942, in Wilhelm Corsten, ed., *Kölner Aktenstücke zur Lage der Katholischen Kirche in Deutschland 1933–1945*, Cologne, 1949, doc. 218, 269.

60. Joint pastoral letter of August 19, 1943, *ibid.*, doc. 227, 301–3.

61. Bertram to Thierack, January 29, 1944, *Bundesarchiv* (Koblenz), R 22 Or. 5/XXI, 1a.

62. From an internal report, National Archives, (Washington, D.C.), T-580, roll 42, file 245.

63. Erb, *op. cit.*, 46–65.

64. For the text of the protests, see W. W. Visser't Hooft, ed., *Holländische Kirchendokumente*, Zollikon-Zürich, 1944, 58–60.

65. Werner Warmbrunn, *The Dutch under German Occupation 1940-1945*, Stanford, 1963, 161.

66. Philip Friedman, *Their Brothers' Keepers*, New York, 1957, 70–71; C. Leclef, ed., *Le Cardinal von Roy et l'Occupation Allemande en Belgique: Actes et Documents*, Brussels, 1945, ch. 8.

67. Emile Maurice Guerry, *L'Eglise Catholique en France sous l'Occupation*, Paris, 1947, 33–65; Jules Geraud Saliege, *Fürchtet euch nicht: Hirtenbriefe und Ansprachen*, Offenburg, 1949, 150–51; Friedman, *op.cit.*, 49–51.

68. The case of a Jewish mother and her son, who were hidden in a monastery near Berlin, is described by Kurt R. Grossmann, *Die unbesungenen Helden*, Berlin, 1957, 153.

69. Grossmann, *op. cit.*, 113; Ernst Schnydrig, "Hilfe für die verfolgten Juden," *Zentralvorstand des Deutschen Caritasverband, An der Aufgabe gewachsen* [sixtieth anniversary *Festschrift*], Freiburg, Br., 1957, 74–77; interview with Dr. Gertrud Luckner, March 9, 1962.

70. Cf. Gertrud Ehrle, ed., *Licht über dem Abgrund*, Freiburg, Br., 1951, 118–24.

71. Heinrich Grüber, "Zu Rolf Hochhuth's 'Stellvertreter,'" Raddatz, *op. cit.*, 202.

72. "Thesen christlicher Lehrverkündigung im Hinblick auf umlaufende Irrtümer über das Gottesvolk des Alten Bundes" (Schwalbacher Thesen), *Freiburger Rundbrief*, II, 1949–1950, no. 8/9, 9.

73. Cf. Hilda Gräf, *Leben unter dem Kreuz. Eine Studie über Edith Stein*, Frankfurt a.M., 1954, 130.

74. Note of the Papal Secretariat of State to the German government, September 9, 1933, *Documents on German Foreign Policy*, C, I, doc. , 794.

75. *Civilta Cattolica*, no. 2024, quoted in Daniel Carpi, "The Catholic Church and Italian Jewry under the Fascists (to the death of Pius XI)," *Yad Vashem Studies*, IV, 1960, 51.

76. *Ibid.*, 51–52.

77. Cf. Yves M.- J. Congar, *Die Katholische Kirche und die Rassenfrage*, trans. W. Armbruster, Recklinghausen, 1961, 69.

78. The statement was first reported in *La Croix*, no. 17060, September 17, 1938. It is accepted as accurate by Luigi Sturzo, *Nationalism and Internationalism*, New York, 1946, 47.

79. Domenico Tardini, *Pius XII*, trans. Franz Johns, Freiburg, Br., 1961, 59.

80. Quoted in Poliakov, *op. cit.*, 300.

81. Abetz to Foreign Ministry, August 28, 1942, *Politisches Archiv des Auswärtigen Amtes* (Bonn), *Staatssekretär, Vatikan*, Bd. 4.

82. Tittmann to the Secretary of State, July 30, 1942, *U.S. Diplomatic Papers 1942*, III, 772.

83. Taylor to Maglione, September 26, 1942, *ibid.*, 776.

84. Tittmann's summary of Holy See statement of October 10, 1942, *ibid.*, 777.

85. Tittmann to the Department of State, December 22, 1942, Department of State Papers, 740.0016 European War 1939/689.

86. Corsten, *Kölner Aktenstücke*, doc. 220, 280. The message was mimeographed and distributed in Germany by the diocesan chanceries. I have seen a copy in Diocesan Archives Eichstätt.

87. Pius XII to the Cardinals, June 2, 1943, excerpts in *Amtsblatt für die Erzdiözese München und Freising*, August 12, 1943.

88. Memo of Wörmann, *Politisches Archiv des Auswärtigen Amtes* (Bonn), *Staatssekretär*, Bd. 4.

89. Weizsäcker to Wörmann etc., December 5, 1941, quoted in Hilberg, *op. cit.*, 441.

90. Hilberg, *op. cit.*, 427.

91. Gumbert (of the German Embassy at the Quirinal) to the Foreign Ministry, October 16, 1943, *Politisches Archiv des Auswärtigen Amtes* (Bonn), Inland II g, 192. Bishop Hudal had signed this letter at the urging of several anti-Nazi officials in the German legations at the Quirinal and Holy See, who had composed it. I have used the English translation of Hilberg, *op. cit.*, 429.

92. Weizsäcker to the Foreign Ministry, October 17, 1943, *Politisches Archiv des Auswärtigen Amtes* (Bonn), Inland II g, 192. The translation is that of Poliakov, *op. cit.*, 297–98, n. 16.

93. Cf. Robert Leiber, S.J., "Pius XII und die Juden in Rom 1943-1944," *Stimmen der Zeit,* CLXVII, 1960–61, 429–30.

94. Weizsäcker to the Foreign Ministry, October 28, 1943, *Politisches Archiv des Auswärtigen Amtes* (Bonn), Inland II g, 192. The English translation is that of Poliakov, *op. cit.,* 297–98, n. 16.

95. Cf. Hilberg, *op. cit.,* 539; Gerald Reitlinger, *The Final Solution,* New York, 1953, 431–32. The successful intervention of the Papal Nuncio in Rumania was attested to by the former Chief Rabbi of Rumania at the Eichmann trial (cf. *New York Times,* May 24, 1961, 12).

96. Statement of Dr. Senatro on March 11, 1963 at a public discussion in Berlin, Raddatz, *op. cit.,* 223.

97. Poliakov, *op. cit.,* 302.

98. Louis de Jong, "Jews and non-Jews in Nazi-Occupied Holland," Max Beloff, ed., *On the Track of Tyranny,* London, 1960, 148–49.

99. Tittmann to the Department of State, October 6, 1942, *U.S. Diplomatic Papers 1942,* III, 777; Tittmann dispatch of September 8, 1942, Department of State papers, 740.00116 European War 1939/573, 1/2.

100. Reported by Weizsäcker, September 23, 1943, *Politisches Archiv des Auswärtiges Amtes* (Bonn), *Staatssekretär, Vatikan,* Bd. 4.

101. Robert Leiber, S.J., "Der Papst und die Verfolgung der Juden," Raddatz, *op. cit.,* 104.

102. Pius XII to the German bishops, August 6, 1940, copy in Diocesan Archives Regensburg.

Chapter 8: Michael B. Lukens

1. This Fr. Mayer is not to be confused with the Munich Jesuit, Fr. Rupert Mayer, who was one of Nazism's most persistent opponents and later became the subject of a significant and widely reported controversy, centering on his arrest on 5 June 1937. Rupert Mayer's case became famous because Cardinal Michael Faulhaber of Munich changed his remarks to the convention of Catholic Men on 4 July 1937 to deal specifically and bluntly with Mayer's arrest as an attack on the Catholic Church and a violation of the 1933 Concordat between the Third Reich and the Vatican. For an English translation of Faulhaber's speech, see *The Persecution of the Catholic Church in the Third Reich* (London: Burns & Oates, 1940), appendix 3, 538–43.

2. Article 24 from the official program of the NSDAP reads as follows: "We insist upon freedom for all religious confessions in the state, providing they do not endanger its existence or offend the German race's sense of decency and morality. The Party as such stands for a positive Christianity, without binding itself denominationally to a particular confession. It fights against the Jewish-materialistic spirit at home and abroad and believes that any lasting recovery of our people must be based on the spiritual principle [that] the welfare of the community comes before that of the individual." Cited from *The Third Reich and the Christian Churches,* ed. Peter Matheson (Grand Rapids, Mich.: Eerdmans, 1981), 1.

3. The texts of the inquiry and the Mayer response are found in *Katholische Kirche und Nationalsozialismus: Dokumente 1930–35,* ed. Hans Müller (Munich, 1963), documents 1 and 2, pp. 13–15. Guenter Lewy cites this incident as an example of the growing sense of alarm about National Socialism within Germany's Catholic bishops as well as the difficulty of maintaining episcopal unity against the Nazi Party in the face of fears that left-wing social radicalism was threatening the Church. See G. Lewy, *The Catholic Church and Nazi Germany* (New York: McGraw-Hill, 1964), 8–15.

4. The key point of this change in position was the declaration of the German bishops on 28 March 1933, which lifted the prohibitions against the Nazi Party.

5. See Lewy, *The Catholic Church and Nazi Germany;* Klaus Scholder, *Die Kirchen und das Dritte Reich,* vol. 1, *Vorgeschichte und Zeit der Illusionen, 1918–1934* (Frankfurt am Main: Verlag Ullstein, 1977, 2nd ed., 1986). Scholder's work was translated into English by John Bowden and published as *The Churches and the Third Reich* in two volumes: vol. 1, *Prelimi-*

nary History and the Time of Illusions, 1918–1934 and vol. 2, *The Year of Disillusionment, 1934* (Philadelphia: Fortress Press, 1988); Heinz Hürten, *Deutsche Katholiken 1918–1945* (Paderborn: Ferdinand Schöningh, 1992). Ludwig Volk has done extensive work in this area. See especially *Katholische Kirche und Nationalsozialismus: Ausgewählte Aufsätze von Ludwig Volk*, ed. Dieter Albrecht (Mainz: Matthias-Grunewald Verlag, 1987). See also John Conway, *The Nazi Persecution of the Churches 1933–45* (New York: Basic Books, 1968); and Ernst C. Helmreich, *The German Churches under Hitler: Background, Struggle, and Epilogue* (Detroit: Wayne State University Press, 1979).

6. After the war the Allies set up tribunals to investigate the background of persons who wished to assume or continue in positions of public service, including all levels of teaching. This was part of a policy to remove Nazi beliefs from places of influence in German society and culture. In the process of trying to pass through "denazification," one gathered letters of testimony to one's good character, as often as not from fellow former Nazis. Germans, most of whom quickly learned to disrespect and elude the process, still sardonically refer to the paper declarations associated with denazification as *"Persilscheine,"* Persil being the trade name for a common brand of German detergent. In English one might translate this as "Tide certificates," or perhaps as "soap certificates."

7. Joseph Lortz, *Geschichte der Kirche in ideengeschichtlicher Betrachtung: Eine Sinndeutung der christlichen Vergangenheit in Grundzügen* (Münster: Aschendorff Verlag, 1932). Lortz was revising this text for its second edition in the early part of 1933. In 1965 the 23rd edition of this text was published! It was first translated into English by Edwin G. Kaiser and published in 1938 under the title: *History of the Church* (Milwaukee: Bruce Co., 1938).

8. Lortz, *History of the Church*, v.

9. Ibid., 390 [emphasis in the original text].

10. Ibid., 550. The importance of this statement, made in 1932, becomes even more decisive when we turn to the supplement Lortz added to the second edition of his *History of the Church* in 1933. This supplement, titled "National Socialism and the Church," appeared again in the third edition and then in a revised and expanded form in the fourth (1936). However, it suddenly disappeared from the fifth edition in 1937, with no replacement or explanation.

11. Lortz, "Nationalsozialismus und Kirche," in *Geschichte der Kirche, Nachtrag*, [a "Nachtrag" is an appendix to the text], 3.

12. Ibid., 4.

13. Joseph Lortz, "Katholischer Zugang zur Nationalsozialismus," *Reich und Kirche* 2 (Munster i.W., Aschendorff, 1933), 5ff. Translation by the author.

14. Ibid., 7.

15. Ibid., 10.

16. "National Socialism understands life basically as task and obligation, not as pleasure. It recognizes as fundamental the *God-given arrangement* of human society and rejects the egalitarianism which destroys genuine living as a disastrous and fundamental mistake. On the other hand, it proclaims straight out the right of craftsmen and farmers to a dignified existence and so remains true to the authentic Christian content of true socialism. It recognizes the unnatural and untraditional nature of modern urban areas and industrial cities as centers of disease, which threaten the life of humanity, physical as well as spiritual, and it draws out of this recognition fundamental conclusions for the formation of the whole nation. So, while National Socialism strives to bring people's lives once again to health, by leading us back to a natural basis, it serves the re-formation of a humanity restored to full and healthy substance. In this way, however, National Socialism (assuming the realization of its program and the liberating effect of its outgrowth) produces the inescapable condition of all religious life, regulated according to a fundamental theological proposition, namely, that grace operates in accordance with the realities of nature. A sound, mature generation which lives with a restrained simplicity and an acknowledgment of positive Christianity presents the truths of basic Christianity, namely, that grace offers entirely other for-

mative possibilities than liberalism, whose outcome is alienated from nature and rooted in a hostility to religion. The natural person is the Catholic person." Lortz, "Katholischer Zugang zur Nationalsozialismus," 10–11.

17. Ibid., 13ff.

18. Ibid., 14. The full passage reads as follows: "It is unfortunately not the case that the various disciplines of Catholic thinking have remained free of a bloodless, merely abstract and consequently spiritless intellectualism. But if this is true, it is certain that in this way they have diverged far from the creative masters of Catholic thought. The aversion of National Socialism to intellectualism, its demand for a spiritual life which arises out of the concrete, out of the particular and distinctive dimensions of reality, which fills the whole person with this intellectual-spiritual-physical essence—this demand again wonderfully coincides with the principles of classical Catholic thinking. So, after several decades, Catholicism again struggles vigorously for clarity. And even such an affinity—to the very great amazement of many!—acts according to a typically Catholic kind of spirituality, which knows nothing of prayer that is one-sided, merely inner-directed, pale, and so easily extraneous to life. Rather, Catholic spirituality concerns the concrete and the whole of being human and even the whole of nature. Such a spirituality summons the Catholic to share in God's own prayer and glory."

19. Lortz, "Katholischer Zugang zur Nationalsozialismus," 26.

20. Ibid., 3.

21. Ibid., 3–4.

22. Ibid., 5.

23. Ibid., 19–20.

24. Ibid., 20–21. The full passage reads as follows: "In the Middle Ages, the preaching of the Church and the ecclesiastical abundance arising from the very ground of Germanic cultural and communal life shaped not only the life of the Church, but rather life in its entire scope. The history of the Church shows further that nature does not just represent a merely external contact point for grace, beyond which this divine reality, 'the wholly Other,' hovers in some kind of disconnected fashion. This history has repeatedly confirmed the fact that in the Kingdom of God the ordering of an inner correlation [*Aufeinanderbezogensein*] of nature and grace belongs to the nature of reality. It shows, therefore, '*in concreto*,' the banal truth which is so seldom taken seriously that the Church can develop in no other way than through the cooperation and reciprocity of concrete individual persons, including distinctive ethnic groups, in our case these peoples and races, and thus the particular strengths of a people under the effect of grace."

25. Lortz, "Katholischer Zugang zur Nationalsozialismus," 18.

Chapter 9: Micha Brumlik

1. Only one title from each author is mentioned here, although all, particularly Pinchas Lapide, have published substantially more. A complete list would require another work, namely a description of the confrontation between Jewish postwar theologians in Germany—mostly marginalized—and Christianity. Robert Raphael Geiss, *Es ist ein Weinen in der Welt*; Bernd Günter Ginzel, *Die Bergpredigt* (Heidelberg: Lambert Schneider, 1985); Pinchas Lapide, *Und er predige in ihren Synagogen* (Gütersloh: Verlaghaus Mohn, 1980); Schalom Ben Chorin, *Bruder Jesus* (Munich: List, 1967); Ernst Ludwig Ehrlich and Franz Kardinal König, *Juden und Christen haben eine Zukunft* (Zurich: Pendo Verlag, 1988); Peter Levinson, *Der Messias* (Neukirchen: Neukirchener Verlag, 1994); Pnina Nave Levinson, *Einführing in die Rabbinische Theologie* (Darmstadt: Wissenschaftliche Buchgesellschaft, 1982).

2. Wolfgang Gerlach, *Als die Zeugen schwiegen: Bekennende Kirche und die Juden*, (Berlin: Institut Kirche und Judentum, 1987).

3. Gerlach, *Als die Zeugen schwiegen*, 382. The editors wish to thank Victoria Barnett for her translation of this chapter. All additional quotations from German sources are hers as well, unless otherwise noted.

4. As printed in J. Beckmann, ed., *Kirchliches Jahrbuch für die Evangelische Kirche in Deutschland* (1950), (Gütersloh: C. Bertelsmann, 1951), 5ff.

5. Gerlach, *Als die Zeugen schwiegen*, 412.

6. "Nostra Aetate," printed in *Auschwitz als Herausforderung für Juden and Christen*, ed. G. B. Ginzel (Heidelberg: Lambert Schneider, 1980), 280.

7. As printed in Ginzel, *Auschwitz als Herausforderung*, 312–13.

8. *Christen und Juden: Eine Studie des Rates der Evangelischen Kirche in Deutschland*, commissioned by the Council of the Kirchenkanzlei der Evangelischen Kirche in Deutschland (Gütersloh: C. Bertelsmann, 1975). See also Rolf Rentdorff, ed., *Arbeitsbuch Christen und Juden: Zur Studie des Rates der Evangelischen Kirche in Deutschland, im Auftrag der Studienkommission "Kirche und Judentum"* (Gütersloh: C. Bertelsmann, 1979).

9. Ginzel, *Auschwitz als Herausforderung*, 369.

10. M. Brocke and H. Jochum, eds., *Wolkensäule und Feuerschein: Jüdische Theologie des Holocaust* (Munich: Christian Kaiser Verlag, 1982).

11. Ginzel, *Auschwitz als Herausforderung*, 375.

12. J. B. Metz, "Ökumene nach Auschwitz," in *Gott nach Auschwitz*, E. Kogon, et. al, eds. (Freiburg: Herder, 1979), 123.

13. Ibid., 138.

14. Martin Stöhr, ed., *Jüdische Existenz und die Erneuerung der christlichen Theologie. Versuch der Bilanz des christlich-jüdischen Dialogs für die systematische Theologie* (Munich: Chr. Kaiser Verlag, 1988); R. Rendtdorff and E. Stegemann, eds., *Auschwitz: Krise der christlichen Theologie* (Munich: Christian Kaiser Verlag, 1980).

15. Peter von der Osten-Sacken, *Die Heiligkeit der Tora: Studien zum Gesetz bei Paulus* (Munich: Christian Kaiser Verlag, 1989), 59.

16. F. W. Marquardt, *Die Gegenwart des Auferstandenen bei seinem Volk Israel* (Munich: Chr. Kaiser Verlag, 1972).

17. F. W. Marquardt, *Das christliche Bekenntnis zu Jesus, dem Juden*, vol. 1 (Munich: Chr. Kaiser Verlag, 1990), 139.

18. Peter von der Osten-Sacken, "Von der Notwendigkeit theologischen Besitzverzichts," in *Nächstenliebe und Brudermord* [originally *Faith and Fratricide*], ed. Rosemary Radford Ruether (Munich: Chr. Kaiser Verlag, 1978), 244.

19. Elie Wiesel, *A Beggar in Jerusalem* (New York: Schocken Books, 1989).

20. Rolf Rendtdorff, *Kanon und Theologie: Vorarbeiten zu einer Theologie des Alten Testaments* (Neukirchen: Neukirchen Verlag, 1991).

21. Bernd Klappert, "Die Juden in einer christlichen Theologie nach Auschwitz," in Ginzel, *Auschwitz als Herausforderung*, 504.

22. Ibid.

23. Ulrich Wilckens, *Der Brief an die Römer* (Neukirchen: Neukirchener Verlag, 1987); Ulrich Wilckens, "Das Neue Testament und die Juden: Antwort an D. Flusser," *Evangelische Theologie* 34 (1974): 611.

24. Franz Rosenzweig, *Die Schrift. Aufsätze, Übertragungen und Briefe* (Königstein: Jüdischer Verlag Athenäum, 1984), 217.

25. Micha Brumlik, "Fear of the Father Figure: Judeophobic Tendencies in New German Social Movements," *Patterns of Prejudice* (Winter 1987): 19–38.

26. Gerda Weiler, *Ich Verwerfe im Lande die Kriege* (Munich: Frauenoffensive, 1984). Later, after a debate with the Jewish feminist theologian Susannah Heschel, Weiler rewrote her book and published it under the title *Das Matriarchat im Alten Testament* (Stuttgart: W. Kohlhammer, 1989).

27. Christa Mulack, *Die Weiblichkeit Gottes* (Stuttgart: Kreuz Verlag, 1983).

28. Franz Alt, *Jesus: Der erste neue Mann* (Munich: Piper Verlag, 1989); Hanna Wolff, *Neuer Wein, Alte Schlauche* (Stuttgart: Radius Verlag, 1981). Cf. Micha Brumlik, *Der Anti-Alt* (Franfurt am Main: Eichborn, 1991).

29. Eugen Drewermann, *Das Matthäus Evangelium* (Olten: Walter Verlag, 1992), 115ff, 828.

30. Jörg Frey, *Eugen Drewermann und die Biblische Exegese: Eine Methodisch-kritische Analyse* (Tübingen : J. C. B. Mohr (P. Siebeck), 1995).

31. Elga Sorge, *Religion und Frau: Weibliche Spiritualität im Christentum* (Stuttgart: W. Kohlhammer, 1985), 149.

32. Marie Therese Wacker, ed., *Der Gott der Männer und die Frauen* (Düsseldorf: Patmos Verlag, 1987); Leonore Siegele-Wenschkewitz, ed., *Verdrängte Vergangenheit, die uns bedrängt: Feministische Theologie in der Verantwortung für die Geschichte* (Munich: Chr. Kaiser Verlag, 1988).

33. Edna Brocke, "Seit Auschwitz muss jeder wissen, das Schlimmeres als Krieg möglich ist," *Kirche und Israel* 1 (1991): 61–74; Jürgen Moltmann, "Das christlich-jüdische Verhältnis und der Zweite Golfkrieg," *Kirche und Israel* 1 (1991): 163–85. See also the correspondence between Brocke and Moltmann in *Kirche und Israel* 2 (1991): 163–85.

34. Moltmann, *Kirche und Israel* 2 (1991): 179–80.

35. *Christen und Juden II. Zur theologischen Neuorientierung im Verhältnis zum Judentum: Eine Studie der Evangelischen Kirche in Deutschland* (Gütersloh: Bertelsmann, 1991).

36. Franz Mussner, *Traktat über die Juden* (Munich: Kösel, 1979); Erich Zenger, *Das erste Testament: Die Jüdische Bibel und die Christen* (Düsseldorf: Patmos Verlag, 1994); Norbert Lohfink, *Der niemals gekündigte Bund: Exegetische Gedanken zum christlich-jüdischen Dialog* (Freiburg: Herder, 1989).

INDEX

CONTRIBUTORS

ROBERT P. ERICKSEN is Associate Professor of History at Pacific Lutheran University. He is the author of *Theologians under Hitler: Gerhard Kittel, Paul Althaus, and Emanuel Hirsch* (Yale University Press). He is also on the editorial board of *Kirchliche Zeitgeschichte*, and he is a Research Fellow of the Alexander von Humboldt Foundation.

SUSANNAH HESCHEL is the Eli Black Professor of Jewish Studies at Dartmouth College. She is the author of *Abraham Geiger and the Jewish Jesus* (University of Chicago Press) and co-editor of *Insider/Outsider: American Jews and Multiculturalism* (University of California Press).

SHELLEY BARANOWSKI is Professor of History at the University of Akron. She is author of *The Confessing Church, Conservative Elites, and the Nazi State* (Edwin Mellon Press) and also *The Sanctity of Rural Life: Nobility, Protestantism, and Nazism in Weimar Prussia* (Oxford University Press).

KENNETH C. BARNES is Associate Professor of History at the University of Central Arkansas. He is the author of *Nazism, Liberalism, and Christianity: Protestant Social Thought in Germany and Great Britain 1925-1937* (University Press of Kentucky).

DORIS L. BERGEN is Associate Professor of History at Notre Dame University. She is the author of *Twisted Cross: The German Christian Movement in the Third Reich* (University of North Carolina Press).

MICHA BRUMLIK is Professor of Education at the University of Heidelberg. He is the author of *Der Anti-Alt* (Eichborn Verlag).

GUENTER LEWY is Professor Emeritus of Religion at Smith College. He is the author of *The Catholic Church and Nazi Germany* (McGraw Hill).

MICHAEL B. LUKENS is Professor of Religious Studies at St. Norbert College. He is Director of the Killeen Chair of Theology and Philosophy and he is a Research Fellow at the Institut für Europäische Geschichte in Mainz.